Submission for Best Hardcover Book
MBA Awards

Contact
 Hugh McTavish   (MJPA member)
 804 N.E. 2nd St. #10
 Corvallis, OR 97330

 503-754-7311

Ending War in Our Lifetime

Ending War in Our Lifetime

A Concrete, Realistic Plan

Hugh McTavish

West Fork Press
Dixon, Kentucky

To order this book, call **1-800-517-7377**.
MasterCard and Visa accepted.

Or send check or money order for $17.95 per copy paperback, $24.95 per copy hardcover, plus $3.00 shipping and handling for the first copy, $1.50 for each additional copy, to:

West Fork Press
2564 State Route 132W
Dixon, KY 42409

Quantity discounts are available

If you have any questions or comments about this book, the author would be pleased to hear from you.
He can be contacted at the address above.

Copyright ©1994 by Hugh McTavish
All rights reserved, including the right of reproduction in whole or in part in any form.
Published by
West Fork Press
2564 State Route 132W
Dixon, Kentucky 42409
Manufactured in the United States of America

Printed on acid-free recycled paper

Publisher's Cataloging in Publication

McTavish, Hugh E.
    Ending war in our lifetime : a concrete, realistic plan / Hugh McTavish.
    p. cm.
    Includes bibliographical references and index.
    ISBN 0-9636865-0-X (hard.)
    ISBN 0-9636865-1-8 (paper.)

    1. Peace. 2. International organization. I. Title

JX1953.M38 1993   327.172
                                       QBI93-912

This book is dedicated to all those who have suffered jail or worse for doing what they believed to be right. Individual courage such as theirs is now and always shall be the world's only hope.

Contents

Chapter 1.	The Federalist Papers	1
Chapter 2.	The Parable of the Tribes	5
Chapter 3.	Designing a Supranational Organization	37
Chapter 4.	The First Goal of the Federation of Nations: To End War Between Member Nations	43
Chapter 5.	Maximizing the Membership of the Federation of Nations: Democracy and Free Speech	54
Chapter 6.	Ending Civil Wars in Member Nations: Human Rights and the Use of the Federation of Nations Military	62
Chapter 7.	Might Makes Right: Increasing the Power and Security of Every Member Nation	72
Chapter 8.	Money Makes the World Go 'Round	87
	Appendix 8-A. Why Nations Should Restrict International Trade	112
	Appendix 8-B. An Alternative System for Raising Soldiers	119
Chapter 9.	The Eleventh Commandment: Overpopulation and the Environment	122
	Appendix 9-A. The Absurd Arguments in Favor of Continued Population Growth	152
	Appendix 9-B. An Alternative Basis for Representation in the House of Representatives That Avoids Providing Any Incentive to Increase Population	160
Chapter 10.	Summary of the Goals and Powers of the Federation of Nations	162
Chapter 11.	The Federation of Nations Government	168
Chapter 12.	Culture and Ethics in the Federation of Nations	208
Chapter 13.	A Possible Danger?	241
Chapter 14.	How the Federation of Nations Will Happen	245

Chapter 15.	Nuclear War	256
Chapter 16.	Two Truths	264
Chapter 17.	The Third Era	266
Afterword.	Today's International Organizations	277
Appendix A.	The Proposed Constitution for the Federation of Nations	283
Appendix B.	Additional Commentary on Some Provisions of the Constitution	310
Bibliography		324
Acknowledgements		331
Index		332

Chapter 1
The Federalist Papers

The Federalist Papers were a series of newspaper editorials, later collected in book form, written in 1787 and 1788 by Alexander Hamilton, James Madison, and John Jay under the pen name of Publius. The papers explain and defend what was in their day a revolutionary charter—the Constitution of the United States of America. They were written to argue that that revolutionary charter, which at the time was only a proposal, should be approved by the separate states, and that those states should unite under one federal government.

In this book I write with a similar purpose. Like the authors of the *Federalist Papers,* I will argue for the uniting of separate states under a new federation. Like them, I will propose and defend a new constitution. And like them, I will propose ideas that may at first seem revolutionary, but ideas whose time has come.

The primary goal of the work described in this book is to end war. You are laughing no doubt, but I am serious. We have lived for so long with war that we have come to believe it is an inevitable part of the human condition. But it is not. There was a long period of time in human history when war did not exist, and there will come a time again in human history when war ceases to exist. In fact, the message of this book is that that time is about to arrive.

This book operates on two levels. On the first level, it describes a plan to achieve world peace. It presents in very specific terms what we have to do to get there. But on a more important level, what it describes is not just one individual's plan, but rather the social forces that almost guarantee that that plan, or any similar plan, will work, and almost guarantee that we will achieve world peace.

To soften the shock of that last paragraph, I should explain what I mean by world peace. I do not mean that angry words will never be spoken or that no one will die violently. I do not even mean that small armed groups will never rise up in violent rebellion. I do mean, however, that what we know as war—the clash of armies of nations and armies of large revolutionary groups—will no longer exist and need never exist again. If that is our definition of world peace, then this book describes a totally realistic and quite concrete way whereby we can create that state. Furthermore, I believe that this state of world peace—permanent world peace even—can and will be achieved in the lifetimes of many of us now living.

Those are bold statements, and they have on occasion been made before, so I should explain why this time it is different. The difference between this plan and all previous plans to achieve world peace is that this one does not require one iota of change in human behavior. All previous plans to achieve world peace were based on perfecting human beings. They all required that all of us, as individuals and nations, always be nonaggressive, generous, and kind—in essence, be saints. The plan in this book requires no such change in human behavior. This plan acknowledges openly that people, societies, and nations pursue their own self-interests and are very willing to be aggressive and even violent in pursuit of those self-interests. That will never change, and I will not propose here that we attempt to change it.

This plan also acknowledges openly that power triumphs. When two groups or nations clash, the more powerful one gets its way. That fact of life too is not likely to change, and again I will not propose here that we attempt to change it.

Another reason that the plan for achieving permanent world peace described in this book will succeed where all previous plans have failed is that this one in many respects is not a plan at all. This book just describes the direction that societal evolution is naturally taking us. Moving in that direction will require very little effort on our part. So this book really does not describe a *plan* to create world peace as much as it describes a *process* whereby world peace will be created. That process will unfold, and is unfolding, naturally, and for the most part we do not need to make it happen but only steer it in the right direction.

The forces of societal evolution, in other words, are taking us, almost inevitably, toward world peace.

What are these forces of societal evolution that we will be able to thank for bringing about this glorious new era? Brace yourself for this. They are precisely those unpleasant facts of life that I just mentioned: the tendency for individuals, groups, and nations to pursue their self-interests, and the tendency for power to triumph, that is, the tendency when two groups or nations clash for the more powerful to get its way.

All previous efforts at creating peace have, of course, been stopped by those very facts of life, the triumph of self-interest and power. This one, though, is not stopped but aided by those facts. And that is why this effort will succeed where all previous efforts have failed.

Yes, the claims made so far in this introductory chapter are correct. We can, and I believe will, soon create permanent world peace. In fact, we can create more than that. The incredibly brazen claims made so far in this chapter may actually be too understated. What I will propose in this book will achieve several other wonderful things besides permanent world peace, and some of those things may be even greater accomplishments. What I propose in this book will guarantee human rights in every, or almost every, nation on earth, will decrease the total cost of government and decrease your total tax bill, and will go a long way toward solving our pressing global environmental problems.

But most important, it will create a world situation in which the human population, for the first time in history, will tend to decrease. And since, as I will detail, overpopulation is the most serious problem we face and is behind virtually every other problem in the world, especially all our environmental problems, when population begins to decrease that will go a long way toward solving, almost literally, every problem in the world.

What I describe here is not a day far off in the distant future. It is coming very soon. There is no doubt in my mind that we can create it in the lifetimes of many of us now living.

We living today can see within our lifetimes the dawn of the era that all mankind has always dreamed about but generally believed could never happen. I am here to tell you that it is about to happen.

Chapter 2

The Parable of the Tribes

Biological life on this beautiful planet, we now know, has changed, or evolved, over time. Many species alive millions or thousands of years ago are now extinct, and many species alive today have changed so considerably from their ancestors of millions or thousands of years ago that we classify their ancestors as different species. Charles Darwin and Alfred Wallace independently made one of the most significant intellectual advances in mankind's history by explaining the mechanism governing this evolution of life forms—the mechanism Darwin termed natural selection. They observed that offspring of all species tended to have the characteristics of their parents, and further observed that for most species, the overwhelming majority of the individuals of the species do not survive long enough to reproduce. So by surviving and reproducing, an organism insured that its characteristics would be present in the next generation, while an organism that died before being able to reproduce would not pass on its physical characteristics. Therefore, when nature selected those organisms that survived and succeeded at reproduction, nature was selecting the direction for the evolution of life—thus the term natural selection.

The subject of this book is another type of evolution: cultural evolution. This book will deal with questions of where our societies are going and where we should try to direct them. In other words, it will deal with societal, or cultural, evolution. The first thing to do, then, and the task of this chapter, is to get a handle on this concept of evolution, to determine how and why societies evolve. With that knowledge we may be able to predict some aspects of the future, and we can better decide which of our attempts at changing society are likely to be successful.

To understand cultural evolution we must look at the whole sweep of human history. While human biology has not changed appreciably in the last 30,000 years, our ways of life, our cultures, have changed revolutionarily. We have gone from hunter-gatherer societies of 40 individuals to agricultural-industrial societies of hundreds of millions of individuals.

Thirty-thousand years ago all human societies acquired their food by hunting and gathering rather than agriculture; all used stone tools; all were nomadic; and all were made up of travelling bands of about 40 individuals as the fundamental unit of society. Today, though, things have changed a bit. Today we are not nomadic; almost all of our food, whether animal or plant, is cultivated; and—defining the fundamental unit of society as the smallest division that is completely sovereign over its own affairs and has no higher level of organization restricting its actions—the smallest fundamental unit of the society in which I live is the United States itself, a unit of 250 million people.

Is there a selective force, akin to natural selection for biological evolution, that can explain this massive evolution of culture? Andrew Bard Schmookler has addressed that question in his magnificent book *The Parable of the Tribes.* What Schmookler calls the common sense theory of cultural evolution is that people have chosen the course of that evolution. As new innovations were developed, people simply chose those that improved their lives and rejected those that would make life worse or that they had no use for. Indeed, I think a first glance at many of the changes of culture we have witnessed tends to support this hypothesis. The growth of television, the use of graphite tennis rackets to replace wooden ones, and the use of word processors to replace typewriters, for instance, are all changes in culture that have occurred because of the cumulative free choices of a large number of individuals.

But those examples are all rather trivial ornaments on our culture. The question to be addressed is, has free choice selected the directions of the *major* trends in cultural evolution—trends in fields like government, structure of the military, division of labor, stratification of society, and methods of food acquisition? If it has, we would expect our cultural and political arrangements to have steadily created a more satisfying life for people over the course of history. Indeed, many claim that life *has* steadily improved over the course of history—generally basing that claim on a comparison of today's Western societies with the European societies of a few hundred years ago, and pointing out that there is now greater social equality, a higher general level of education, and a lower burden of backbreaking manual labor than there was in feudal Europe. But this general improvement of life would not have been quite so apparent a century-and-a-half ago if you were a black slave, or a century ago if you were working 100 hour weeks in the West Virginia coal mines or the London sweatshops, or a half-century ago if you were a Jew being gassed by the Nazis. Moreover, to examine the sweep of cultural evolution, we should not just look at the relatively short period of 600 years or so and only look at one part of the world. A more proper comparison is to compare many of the societies of the past few hundred years with the hunter-gatherer societies we all left behind.

If we made a survey of all societies present on earth over the past few hundred years, we would find that broad social equality has been rare if not nonexistent, that brutal coercion of large segments of society has been common, and that widespread famines have devastated societies many times.

In contrast, despite what you may have been taught in grade school, anthropologists have shown that today's hunter-gatherer societies (and by inference, our hunter-gatherer ancestors) lead a quite humane existence. Hunter-gatherer societies, without exception, spend less time working (that is acquiring food, building shelter, making tools and clothing, etc.) than any modern society, leaving more time for play, music, socializing, and storytelling than any modern society enjoys. The Bushmen, for instance, or !Kung San (! designates a click sound in the San language), a tribe of hunter-gatherers living in the Kalahari desert in South Africa, despite their harsh desert habitat, spend less than three hours per day per adult acquiring food. It is reported that in one day a woman can gather enough food to feed her family for three days. The rest of her time is spent "resting, entertaining visitors, doing embroidery, or visiting other camps. For each day at home, domestic routines, such as cooking, nut cracking, collecting firewood, and fetching water, occupy one to three hours of her time" (Richard Lee, reported in Harris, 1977). And again, the !Kung San, like essentially all surviving hunter-gatherer societies, live in a very harsh habitat. Our hunter-gatherer ancestors living in more bountiful areas undoubtedly worked even less than this.

Hunter-gatherer politics, like their work schedules, also appears, on unbiased examination, to be superior to ours. Hunter-gatherer politics is relatively free of coercion and inequality. Decisions are not made by one or a few people, or even simply by the majority and forced on the minority, but are made by consensus. The idea of a "chief" is completely foreign to them. All persons contribute to every important decision, something that obviously cannot be accommodated in societies whose populations number in the millions.

As for the social structure of hunter-gatherer societies, this also is clearly superior to that of modern societies. Societies of recent centuries have always been characterized by unequal and unfair class systems, and generally these class systems have been quite rigid and have made it very difficult for those trapped in the lower classes to escape. But hunter-gatherer societies have no inequality in wealth and very little inequality in status. To the extent that there is even any unequal status, surprisingly, it is not granted for such things as being a good hunter, but instead is granted for being generous.

Many will now say, "Perhaps all that is true, but agriculture and civilization were necessary to solve the basic problems of food acquisition and survival. The Stone Age people were always on the brink of starvation." Well, I'm sorry to dispel such a cherished myth, but that is completely false. All evidence indicates that starvation essentially never existed in hunter-gatherer societies, while unfortunately it has always plagued modern societies and is even worsening now. The reason for this is that hunter-gatherers are resistant or entirely immune to both of the major causes of famine: crop diseases and drought.

Hunter-gatherers are immune to crop diseases because, of course, they have no crops. They eat a large variety of naturally occurring species, and naturally occurring species, by definition, are at ecological equilibrium with their environment, meaning they have adapted to any diseases that may affect them in that environment. They are, therefore, very unlikely to be wiped out by disease. Moreover, in the unlikely event that one or two major food sources for a hunter-gatherer group were wiped out, the group would always be able to simply switch to other species for their food. The variety of the hunter-gatherer diet and the fact that their food sources are at ecological equilibrium with the environment makes hunter-gatherers, unlike us, completely immune to famine through diseases of plants and nonhuman animals.

The other major cause of famine in modern societies is drought. When we agricultural societies plant our crops, we assume it will rain. When it doesn't, and sometimes it doesn't, we are often in a lot of trouble. But when it doesn't rain on a hunter-gatherer society, they suffer little more than an inconvenience. Drought in a natural environment doesn't mean that everything dies; it just means that plant species that need a lot of rain die back, while those that do not need a lot of rain prosper and take their place. In a drought, hunter-gatherers just switch their diet from drought-sensitive species to drought-resistant ones. They don't have to worry about planting drought-resistant crops because nature already had the foresight to do it for them.

Moreover, not only was the hunter-gatherer diet more reliable than that of modern societies, but it also appears to have been of superior nutritional quality. Two pieces of evidence show that quality of diet generally declined over time for cultures after leaving the hunter-gatherer state. J. Lawrence Angel found that the average height of 30,000 year-old skeletons unearthed from Europe and Africa was 5' 11" (177 cm) for males and 5' 6" (165 cm) for females. Twenty-thousand years later the averages were 5' 6" (165 cm) for males, 5' 0" (153 cm) for females. Only in the last

100 years or so, and only in a few nations, has average height begun to approach the stone age levels again. Tooth loss shows a similar trend. In 30,000 B.C. adults died with an average of 2.2 teeth missing; in 6500 B.C., with 3.5 missing; during Roman times, with 6.6 missing (reported in Harris, 1977). Since the quality of diet is a strong determinant of both physical stature and the condition of teeth and gums, this is evidence that the nutritional quality of our ancestors' diets worsened after they left the hunter gatherer state. It also offers further evidence that hunter-gatherers rarely if ever suffered starvation, since if any significant portion of these people had ever suffered even brief starvation during their childhoods, their height would have been decreased.

Finally, although this point cannot be quantified and proven, in the opinion of virtually every anthropologist who has studied hunter-gatherer groups, their societal arrangements and ways of life are more emotionally and psychologically satisfying and nurturing than those of any modern society. The longing for fame and recognition would not exist in hunter-gatherer society since, in fact, each person already is famous: Every person he encounters knows him. The feelings of loneliness, of anonymity, and of being uncared for, feelings that are endemic in industrialized societies, are rarely observed by anthropologists in primitive cultures, and logically should be greatly reduced in a small society such as the hunter-gatherer, where every person is known and recognized and where each person's contributions are important to the whole group. Also, the jobs in hunter-gatherer societies—hunting, gathering, sewing, fire-building, and constructing shelters and tools—are generally free of both the mind-numbing repetition and the high stress that characterize many, if not most, jobs in an industrialized society. Finally, hunter-gatherers spend every day of their lives surrounded by scenes considerably more pleasant and pastoral than the traffic jams, concrete, and smog that most of us in "affluent" societies have to endure. After looking at the evidence, it is difficult to dispute the conclusion of anthropologist Leslie White that hunter-gatherer society "was unquestionably the most satisfying kind of social environment man has ever lived in."

I have spent so much time on hunter-gatherer societies because those societies are the starting point of human cultural evolution, and it is essential to understand hunter-gatherer society to understand cultural evolution. Leaving hunter-gatherer society and adopting agriculture was the most important transition in human history.

The other reason I have spent so much time describing the many advantages hunter-gatherers had over most modern societies is because it dispels the ridiculous story many of us have been taught that the march of history and of societal evolution is the march of continual improvement in human life. In order to understand societal evolution, we must first get rid of that absurd notion.

We have a very strong bias that in our "civilized" state our lives are greatly superior in every respect to those of our "savage" ancestors. But any remotely impartial look at the evidence flies in the face of that ethnocentric position. Rather, the evidence strongly argues that for most people in most societies on earth over the past few hundred years, life was distinctly worse than it had been for their hunter-gatherer ancestors twenty-thousand years ago. (In fact, I believe it is quite debatable whether even in today's richest Western democracies life is as satisfying for most people as it was for hunter-gatherers.) After twenty-thousand years of continuous cultural evolution, of enormous change in human life, there was, for most people over the past few centuries, nothing to show for it. If anything, life had only gotten worse.

Therefore, if the common sense theory that the free choices of individual human beings have been the major driving force for cultural evolution is true, then people have done a pretty lousy job of making choices. The teachings of many religions try to make this explanation for the lack of clear improvement in human life plausible: Man is basically a mess, they say, and we shouldn't have expected him to do any better than he's done. But that explanation does not stand up to scrutiny. It is true that we all make many mistakes, but to explain the lack of improvement in the human condition over the past 20,000 years, while still claiming that free human choice of the majority is the major driving force for cultural evolution, it is necessary to posit not merely that we make many mistakes but also that we never learn from those mistakes. It is necessary to assert that we somehow failed to notice it when a cultural change made life worse. That doesn't seem likely.

Selection for Power

Schmookler offers a different proposal for the major force directing cultural evolution. He says it wasn't that we failed to choose wisely but that choices were taken away from us. This has happened because an *impersonal, automatic selection for power has directed cultural evolution and taken from us our freedom to choose,* power being defined here as the capacity to achieve one's will against the will of another.

Why a selection for power would have to operate in a closed system of autonomous societies is explained by the parable of the tribes.

> Imagine a group of tribes living within reach of one another. If all choose the way of peace, then all may live in peace. But what if all but one choose peace, and that one is ambitious for expansion and conquest? What can happen to the others when confronted by an ambitious and potent neighbor? Perhaps one tribe is attacked and defeated, its people destroyed and its lands seized for the use of the victors. Another is defeated, but this one is not exterminated; rather, it is subjugated and transformed to serve the conqueror. A third seeking to avoid such disaster flees from the area into some inaccessible (and undesirable) place, and its former homeland becomes part of the growing empire of the power-seeking tribe. Let us suppose that others observing these developments decide to defend themselves in order to preserve themselves and their autonomy. But the irony is that successful defense against a power-maximizing aggressor requires a society to become more like the society that threatens it. Power can be stopped only by power, and if the threatening society has discovered ways to magnify its power through innovations in organization or technology (or whatever), the defensive society will have to transform itself into something more like its foe in order to resist the external force.
>
> I have just outlined four possible outcomes for the threatened tribes: destruction, absorption and transformation, withdrawal, and imitation. *In every one of these outcomes the ways of power are spread throughout the system.* This is the parable of the tribes. (Reprinted by permission from *The Parable*

of the Tribes (1984), Andrew Bard Schmookler, University of California Press, copyright the Regents of the University of California.)

It is important to emphasize here that this selection for power we are speaking of is not a matter of *some people* selecting that power should prevail, or even selecting which types of power should prevail. Rather, like natural selection and its selection of the "fittest" that directs biological evolution, the selection for power that directs cultural evolution is an impersonal, automatic force operating from outside of the system.

The Evidence

Schmookler's logic in his parable of the tribes is impeccable in its prediction that there has to be an automatic selection for power operating within a system of autonomous societies. Whenever one society chooses the way of power, chooses to try to force its will on its neighbor, power will spread because choices are taken away from its neighbor. That neighbor can no longer choose peace. It can no longer choose to just go on living the way it had been living. It must either be defeated or adopt some means of power to repel the aggressor. By either outcome, the ways of power spread.

Compelling logic notwithstanding, however, we should still look for empirical evidence that a selection for power has in fact operated over the course of the evolution of our societies. The evidence is not hard to find. First, let's look at the earliest and most important steps in the evolution of human society—those characterizing the transformation from what we call primitive societies to civilized ones. These are the transformations from a hunter-gatherer lifestyle to agriculture, from a nomadic lifestyle to living in permanent settlements and ultimately forming cities, and from loose and informal forms of social organization to more formal ones. We have a historical record of this process over the past few hundred years. As the "civilized" societies have encountered the "primitive" societies, most of the primitive societies have adopted civilization (if they weren't simply exterminated). So we can ask how this came about. Did they adopt civilization voluntarily? No, not a one of them. Despite the assiduous efforts of missionaries and others to "bear the white man's burden" and educate the savages about the virtues of civilization, there is no record of *any* primitive society *ever* going to civilization voluntarily. Primitive societies were interested in acquiring some of the tools of civilization when these could help them do their jobs more easily. They were interested for instance in acquiring guns, horses, iron pots, and even snowmobiles. But none have ever been interested in trading in the hunter-gatherer way of life for agriculture, nomadism for permanent settlements, or their loose social arrangements for a more structured government. Without exception, these transformations have only been made at the point of a gun.

The record becomes a bit murkier when we look at the transformations of culture made by larger, more civilized societies in recent times. In those cases it is not always so obvious whether a transformation was made by free choice or was forced on a society somehow by the selection for power. The free choice mechanism and selection for power mechanism are not always easy to distinguish in these cases basically because the selection for power operates by giving us a choice. We can choose to increase our society's power or we can choose to be defeated by another society. Much like the man accosted by a robber who demands, "Your money or your life," we are being given a choice. It is not exactly a free choice, but it is a choice.

The selection for power operates just like that robber. It limits our choices. But we aren't very good at recognizing that. When a robber demands, "Your money or your life," we immediately recognize that these are limited options. But when the selection for power demands of us, "Increase your societal power, or else," we don't even notice it. After 10,000 years of facing this demand continuously, we've tuned it out. All we ever do is increase our societal power. It is such an ingrained habit that we are not consciously aware there are other options. We could, theoretically, choose to *decrease* our societal power, but we have forgotten that. We could, theoretically, choose to throw away our nuclear weapons, go back to plowing our fields with horse-drawn plows, or even abandon agriculture and go back to hunting and gathering. Some of those changes might even make us happier. After all, no one likes nuclear weapons, horses are cuter than tractors, and anthropologists tell us that hunter-gatherers are generally happier than we are. So how come we don't even consider those options? Because, of course, they aren't realistic options. They would all decrease the power of our society, and if we chose very often to decrease the power of our society, we would soon be overrun, either culturally or militarily, by a more powerful society. We would, in essence, cease to exist as a society.

Thus, the demands of the selection for power have become completely ingrained. We are like an animal born in a zoo. We don't know what free choice is because we've never experienced it.

Maybe that explains why the reluctance of primitive societies to be civilized has so puzzled us. We go to them and say, "Settle down in one place, plant crops, choose a chief, increase your gross national product." What we are giving them truly is a great recipe for increasing their societal power. So we think it's wonderful. We think we're doing them a big favor. After all, that's all we've ever wanted—more societal power. Thus, when they respond to our generous offer by saying, "No thanks. We're not interested in power. We'd rather be happy," we are flabbergasted. It is such an alien response that we feel we have no choice but to kill them.

We are so good at choosing to increase our society's power that we don't notice this is not a free choice. We don't notice that this is a choice which has been forced on us by the reality of a world of competing societies, forced on us by the selection for power. Keeping that in mind will allow us to be more objective in looking at which major changes of modern societies came about because of free choice and which changes were due to choices that were coerced or at least encouraged by the need for greater societal power.

Seen in this light, to select one example, the Japanese history of emulating foreign powers and adopting their technology and economic systems does not appear to have been driven by free choice. For over 200 years Japanese society changed little, as the country lived peacefully under the military rule of a series of shoguns. The economy remained based on feudalism, subsistence farming, artisan guilds, and only minimal trade. Throughout this period, the shoguns forbade trade and contact with the outside world. Then, in 1853 Commodore Perry arrived from the United States with steam-powered warships. He soon forced the

Japanese to accept a consulate and a commercial treaty with the U.S. European powers quickly secured similar treaties. Having been humiliated by outside powers, the Japanese soon overthrew the shogun and remade their society. Upper class students were sent to school in Europe and the United States. Education in Japan was reformed with Western methods and extended to include students from all economic classes. Feudalism was revoked, land became transferable, industrial machinery was imported from the West, and a market-based economy was developed in the space of a few decades.

Then, after being defeated militarily in World War II, the Japanese remade their society again, accepting democracy and redoubling their efforts to adopt and adapt Western technologies and Western economic systems.

These decisions by the Japanese to remake their society would generally be considered to have been free choices. But were they really? The Japanese could have transformed their society before the American and European gunboats arrived in the 1850's and 60's, or before World War II, but they didn't. Both waves of change came only after they were defeated militarily, and both represented attempts to make themselves more like the enemies who had defeated them. It appears that these changes were not things that the Japanese exactly wanted, but rather things they were forced to accept because of the need to compete for power. They may be happy now about the changes in their society, but at the time they only made them because they had been defeated in war, made them in order to compete for power.

Other major decisions about the directions to take our societies also have not been freely chosen but rather have been forced on us by the demands of the competition for power. The decision to develop nuclear weapons is an obvious example. No sane person would choose for the world to live on the brink of annihilation, but in developing nuclear weapons our societies felt that they had no other options. The U.S. government believed that Hitler was developing an atom bomb and knew that if that was true we had better beat him to it. There was no other choice. Then, once the U.S. had the bomb, the Soviet Union felt that they had to have it also in order to guarantee their security. With both the U.S. and U.S.S.R. possessing nuclear devices, France and Britain felt that, in order to be great powers and in order to insure their defense, they also needed to develop them. And so it went through the other members of the nuclear club. Developing nuclear weapons wasn't really a *free* choice for anyone. For the U.S. and Soviet Union one could argue that it wasn't a choice at all. They felt that they simply had to have the bomb or they would be at the mercy of their enemy.

It doesn't take the fear of nuclear weapons, though, to get us to pursue power. We do it continuously. Even some of the accomplishments we are most proud of were achieved, not for their own sake, but only as an outgrowth of our pursuit of power. Putting a man on the moon is one example. During the cold war, although America feared and loathed the Russians, we imitated them at every turn because we were so terrified of falling behind them. One of the outgrowths of that was our sending men to the moon. Although that is now one of our proudest accomplishments, it was not something we freely chose to do for its own sake. We adopted that as a goal only because the Russians were ahead of us in the space race.

The selection for power directs the evolution of our societies. It takes choices away from us all the time and forces us to do things we otherwise wouldn't choose to do.

National Power

In biology, the fundamental units acted on by evolution, that is, the units selected amongst by natural selection, are individuals. Analogously, in the parable of the tribes, it is autonomous societies that are the units selected amongst by the selection for power—an autonomous society being defined as the smallest unit of human organization that is completely sovereign over its own affairs, is not under the control of any higher authority. Today, the unit fitting that definition is the nation-state.

Knowing that a selection for power has given us the cultures we have today, we would be well-advised to ask where it is going to take us tomorrow. To do that, since nations are the units being selected amongst, we need to examine national power. Let's begin that examination by asking what qualities determine national power. Hans Morgenthau, in his classic book *Politics Among Nations,* lists the following:

1. *Geography.* For instance, the location of the United States, isolated by two oceans from the other major powers, has always given the U.S. an advantage. The huge land area of Russia or the Commonwealth of Independent States likewise grants a power advantage in that it makes it very difficult to conquer, as Hitler and Napoleon should have known.

2. *Control of Natural Resources.* This encompasses, of course, control of petroleum, coal, uranium, and other strategic minerals. But it also covers control of the most important natural resource—food. It is vitally important to a nation's power that it be able to feed its own people without imports, and that it can continue to do so even while diverting labor to a war effort.

3. *Military Preparedness.* This means having the most advanced military technology, having soldiers trained and ready, and, preferably, having weapons stockpiled, or at least having the capacity to quickly produce them.

4. *Industrial Capacity.* This is closely intertwined with military preparedness in as much as it is industrial capacity that allows a nation to quickly produce weapons and other supplies for war. Likewise, industrial capacity is also tied to natural resources in production of power. Having natural resources in some respects does not itself confer power on a nation but only confers the potential for power. It is industrial capacity that transforms that potential into reality.

Military industrial capacity is of course the most important type for national power, but nonmilitary industries are vital too. Morgenthau writes that "victory in modern war depends on the number and quality of highways, railroads, trucks, ships, airplanes, tanks, and equipment and weapons of all kinds, from mosquito nets and automatic rifles to oxygen masks and guided missiles." Note that not all the items on that list are thought of primarily as military products. Many products whose primary use is not military often turn the tide in a war, and in some cases those vital products cannot be predicted in advance. For instance, the availability of railroads to transport troops was crucial in the victory of the North over the South in the U.S. Civil War, but the railroads were not built with that purpose in mind.

Nonmilitary industrial capacity contributes to national power in several other ways too. In war, it can often be converted to military production; in both war and peace it keeps the economy healthy enough to pay for the military industries; and, lest we forget, nations don't necessarily have to fight wars, or even threaten to, to exercise power—simply by producing and selling items to other nations, or for that matter by buying items from them, a nation exerts influence and gains a certain power over others.

5. *Population.* It has always been a rule that large populations confer power.

Now we enter three aspects of national power that are less concrete and amenable to quantification than the preceding five but no less real because of that.

6. *National Character.* Without stereotyping, it is clear that differences exist in the character of the peoples of different nations and that national character affects a nation's power—although it is not always easy to predict what type of character is best for maximizing power. To cite one example, the sense of honor seems to be unusually strong in the Japanese people, which probably helped allow the military to "volunteer" kamikazee pilots in World War II. A man would rather accept the suicide assignment than tarnish his honor and bring disgrace to his family by refusing it. Another example of national character and how it may affect national power would be the seemingly well-developed ability of the Russian people to endure hardship—a trait that may have helped them to persevere and triumph in World War II.

7. *National Morale.* This is defined in this context as the dedication with which a people will back their government's policies, particularly in the international arena.

8. *The Wisdom and Quality of Government and Diplomacy.*

Now, using this analysis of national power, I would like to discuss, with an eye toward history, how the countries of the world today, particularly the major powers, might improve their power in each of these areas.

Before I begin, however, I will tell you where I'm headed. I am going to argue that in almost all these aspects of national power, events or trends of the past century have suddenly made it considerably more difficult for any one nation to gain a significant power advantage over its neighbors.

1. *Geography.* The only way a nation can alter the geographic component of its power is to conquer territory, and that has never been easy. But even so, it seems that it has become considerably more difficult in the past few decades. There appear to be two reasons for that. The first is that the world has become so densely populated that conquering even tiny bits of territory often means conquering huge numbers of people. Even when those people are essentially unarmed, as in Israel's occupied Arab territories, their sheer numbers can make life very difficult for the conquerors.

The second reason it has become more difficult to conquer territory is the greatly increased speed of transportation and communication, which now allows the other nations of the world to more easily intervene and prevent a nation from conquering its neighbors. The principle that has to be remembered here is that any time a nation has a chance to increase its power, most of the other nations of the world have an interest in preventing that; so any time a nation has a chance to decisively alter the geographic component of its power by taking territory, many other nations have an interest in preventing that by rushing to the aid of the threatened land. In the past, though, this was difficult because it took so long to communicate news and to transport troops. But now, with the use of satellites to improve intelligence gathering, with improvements in the speed of communication, and with improvements in the speed of transport of troops and weapons, it is much easier than in the past, even the past as recent as 40 or 50 years ago, for the other nations of the world to aid the threatened territory and prevent this alteration in the conqueror's power. This, in fact, is exactly what we have recently witnessed in Iraq and Kuwait—the improved transport of troops and weapons allowing the other nations of the world to rush to the aid of a threatened land and prevent an aggressor, in this case Iraq, from conquering territory and increasing its power. So in geography, as in the other aspects of power I will discuss, it appears to have become considerably more difficult in recent times for any nation to dramatically increase its power.

2. *Control of Natural Resources.* Competition for control of natural resources has been very intense in recent centuries, and it has been quite easy for nations, especially the great powers, to increase their power in this field. They increased their power by improving their access to natural resources both outside and inside their borders. Outside their borders, the great powers improved their access to natural resources through colonialism and imperialism. Inside their borders, they did it through improving their mining technology and increasing their mining activities. All of those options, though, have now largely closed, and it has suddenly become considerably more difficult in this century for a nation to dramatically improve its access to natural resources. First, the era of European colonialism ended, as the colonies acquired the power to throw off their colonial masters—a case, I should point out, of the ways of power spreading, as dictated by the parable of the tribes. And now even the slightly more subtle examples of colonialism are ending—as exemplified by Iran's overthrow of the Shah and rejection of U.S. imperialism. It seems clear that emerging nationalism and power in the less developed countries will make it ever more difficult for any nation to so completely control another that it can truly guarantee access to its natural resources.

If nations want to dramatically improve their access to natural resources, therefore, they will have to look within their borders. But here also options have dwindled in the 20th century. As our populations have grown and we have increased our mining of domestic resources, we have discovered that we are depleting those resources and that there are limits to how much more mining we can do. Thus, both within their borders and outside their borders, nations in recent times have suddenly found it to be dramatically more difficult to use access to natural resources to increase their power.

3. *Military Preparedness.* I'll skip this for now and discuss it last.

4. *Industrial Capacity.* The factor here that has made it

dramatically more difficult than in earlier times for nations to gain a power advantage is that, for the major powers at least, the process of industrialization has now been completed. In the past, nations could gain a very large power advantage over their neighbors simply by becoming industrialized or by accelerating the pace of their industrialization. But now, in the world's wealthier nations, the process of industrialization is complete. Practically every product is produced on a large scale by a mechanized process and is produced about as efficiently as current techniques permit. To increase its industrial capacity relative to other nations, then, an industrialized nation has to develop new ways to organize labor or new technologies of production. But advantages gained in those ways tend to be fairly small and tend to be temporary, as they are quickly copied by the other nations. Thus, it has now become very difficult for the fully industrialized nations to significantly alter their industrial capacity relative to one another, and very difficult to significantly alter their power in this area.

5. *Population.* For the past few centuries we have witnessed a staggering growth in human population, which has been driven in part by the need of nations to compete for power. But now, in the 20th century, we have reached the end of the line. The populations of virtually all nations are at or over their environmental carrying capacities. It just will not be possible for most nations to further increase their populations without destroying their environments, further impoverishing their people, depleting their resources, and risking an inability to feed their people without imports. For virtually every nation on earth, any further significant increase of population will decrease, not increase, the nation's power.

6. *National Character.* This is the only aspect of national power in which it has not become dramatically more difficult in the 20th century for nations to gain a significant power advantage over their neighbors. But then again, this aspect of national power has never been an arena for intense competition anyway, at least not at the level of conscious policy. While cultures and national characteristics have certainly changed over history, and while a selection for national power has clearly played a major

role in governing the direction of that process, making the national character more conducive to developing a powerful society has rarely been a field of conscious competition at the national policy level. The people of different nations are justly proud of their distinctive national cultures and characters, and they aren't likely to change even if they could be convinced that changing their national character would increase the nation's power. In addition, even if they wished to change, they could not change their character overnight. National character is basically a given, and we needn't worry about a rapid competition for a power advantage in this area.

7 and 8. *National Morale* and *Quality of Government and Diplomacy.* Improving national morale, that is, increasing the support for the government's policies, seems to be a fairly unpredictable business, so it is difficult for governments to try to improve their power in this area with any hope for consistent success. Propaganda and controlling the flow of information is one way governments have approached the problem. Sometimes propaganda works and sometimes it doesn't; the success seems to depend mostly on whether the economy is healthy and people are well fed—in other words, on whether the government is doing a good job. And that's the other radical approach occasionally taken to generating support for governmental policy—generating governmental policies that are worthy of support.

In this regard, there are some things that could be done. For one, nations could convert to democracy, which, although it isn't perfect, seems to be clearly the best form of government anyone's developed for societies that are much larger than the hunter-gatherer band. And indeed, nations are currently converting to democracy in droves. The reason for this trend, it should be pointed out, is not so much that the governments involved were suddenly touched by an altruistic desire to renounce control and respect human rights, but rather that a conversion to democracy was necessary to continue competing in the international race for power. In other words, the trend to democracy, like all important long-term trends in societal evolution, is driven by the selection for power. This occurs because democracies have two important advantages in the competition for power. First, almost by definition, they have greater public support for the government than nondemocracies, since in a democracy, by definition, a majority supports the government. Second, by observation, democracies have better quality of government, that is, democratic governments tend to make better decisions than totalitarian ones.

In the past, nations have been able to dramatically improve their power in the areas of national morale and quality of government by converting to democracy. But now that nearly all of the most powerful nations, and close to a majority of all nations, have converted to democracy (at least have outwardly converted to democracy, although certainly all of them, including the United States, could be more truly democratic), further improvements in these aspects of national power will be smaller and more difficult to achieve.

This is not to say, though, that further improvements in national morale and quality of government will be impossible. Reforming election laws and improving education, for instance, should lead to better government by helping people to make more intelligent choices of officials. But then again, the amount of education churned out in the United States has certainly increased since 1776; yet few would claim that today's elected officials are as far-sighted as those that founded this nation. Further improvements in democratic governments are obviously possible, but they are not likely to come suddenly or dramatically, and they are not likely to be as large as the improvement in governance that a nation can achieve by simply converting to a democratic form of government.

To reiterate, then, the dramatic step that has occurred over the past two centuries or so to make gaining a power advantage in the areas of national morale and quality of government more difficult is the conversion of most nations to democracy. Converting to democracy confers on a nation a significant power advantage over the nondemocracies in the areas of national morale and quality of government; but after most of the world's nations have taken that step, as they now have or soon will have, achieving any further significant advantage in those areas of power will be more difficult.

Finally, let's return to #3, *Military Preparedness.* This has been by far the most intense arena of competition for power in the twentieth century. The two world wars were largely caused by arms races and by competition to build up peacetime armies. Then, after World War II, the two major victorious powers, the U.S. and U.S.S.R., again went on a breakneck arms race that lasted for 45 years. But even in this aspect of power, there are clear limits to how much more can be gained. In fact, the superpowers finally recognized that when they slowed the arms race over the past few years. They did that, I think, not primarily for the sake of their material comfort, nor even primarily because of the democratic reforms in the former Soviet Union, but rather because continuing to stockpile arms was not contributing to either nation's power. It was not contributing to national power because the arms race was damaging their economies and thus, on the whole, was decreasing rather than increasing national power.

Damaging its economy decreases a nation's power in many of the aspects of power I have discussed. The strength of the economy, of course, is a basic determinant of industrial capacity. But it also determines how much can be spent on basic research in science and technology and on education. This basic research in turn will yield further dividends in industrial capacity as well as in technology of weapons and thus military preparedness. Furthermore, the spending on education should (at least in a democracy, where the populace selects its government) yield benefits in future quality of government, which should then also benefit national morale.

In damaging their economies, the superpowers were truly damaging their national power. Moreover, and this obvious point never did seem to hit home, after a certain level, stockpiling nuclear weapons has no effect on national power. All that is necessary is enough weapons to survive a first strike and launch a devastating retaliation; and both superpowers were way beyond that point years ago. Once you've turned every structure in Russia to dust, there's not a lot of point to blowing them up again. Once you've started nuclear winter, conceivably causing the extinction of our species, there is nothing left that you can threaten to do.

Which brings us to another aspect of how stockpiling nuclear weapons has little effect on national power: It is simply irrational to use them. Any use, at least any use against another nuclear power, is suicide because it will bring retaliation. In fact, the theory of nuclear winter dictates that using nuclear weapons may be suicide even if it does not bring retaliation. There is still disagreement about this theory in the scientific community, but it is possible that even a small first strike would trigger climate changes severe enough to destroy our societies.

In several ways, then, at least as far as nuclear weapons are concerned, the arms race has reached the point where it is doing nothing to add to national power.

What about improvements in "conventional" military preparedness? Obviously wars are still being fought, and the same factors that have always decided them are still deciding them: quality of military leadership and strategy, number of troops, and technology of weapons and accessory equipment. Has anything changed in these areas of the competition for national power?

I think nothing has happened in recent times to lessen or increase the importance of military strategy, nor to make it more or less difficult for nations to gain an advantage here, but it is becoming more difficult for nations to increase the number of soldiers. Ecology on a finite planet dictates that population cannot increase much more, so for more troops, countries will need to recruit larger percentages of their populations. But that is rapidly becoming impossible. In Israel, for instance, every able-bodied man is already either a full-time soldier or in the reserves. While it is true that most other nations in peace-time could still conscript more men into military service (or could begin conscripting women), doing so would have costs in terms of economic productivity, industrial capacity, science, education, and national morale that would probably more than offset any potential increases in the military component of national power. Furthermore, in war-time in this century, it has very often not been possible for nations to increase the number of their military personnel, at least not the number of their male military personnel. Several nations, during the World Wars and other wars, have conscripted almost every able-bodied man into the military. There is very little opportunity left for nations to increase their power by adding more soldiers.

Note also that this phenomenon of total war, of using almost every available man for the military, rather than using small armies of mercenaries, is essentially a 20th century phenomenon. Although it has its roots with the law of 1793 of the French Republic, which made military service compulsory for all men between the ages of 18 and 25, it has reached its full, hideous, worldwide development only in this century.

What about competition for advantage in the technology of conventional weapons and accessories? Has anything changed here? In view of the fact that nonnuclear wars are being fought throughout the world and that the relative merits of the weapons of the two sides often decide those wars, it would be absurd to claim that competition in the technology of nonnuclear weapons is irrelevant to national power. So I will claim nothing of the sort. But ... but, several things about the race for advantage in conventional weapons have changed in this century that make it more difficult than in earlier times to gain a decisive advantage over one's neighbor in this component of national power:

a. The evolution of weapons seems to be giving defensive weapons the advantage over offensive weapons. This is a general rule of sports, that as the players get better and tactics improve, the defense gains the advantage over the offense (almost all of the rule changes that have had to be instituted in professional baseball, basketball, and football in the U.S. have been to favor the offense, to allow the offense to keep up with the defense as the game changed). Likewise, with the exception of nuclear weapons, against which no defense has been developed, the same trend of defensive advantage appears to be the case in war. Surface-to-air missiles, for example, which are basically defensive weapons against the offensive weapon of the airplane, have a tremendous record of success in modern war. Soviet anti-aircraft missiles in the hands of the Arabs were devastating against Israeli planes in the 1973 Arab-Israeli war, and surface-to-air missiles also greatly helped the Vietnamese and the Afghans in their wars against the U.S. and Soviet Union. The Vietnam and Afghanistan examples are particularly instructive in that the United States and Soviet Union had overwhelming advantages in those wars in the number and technology of their weapons, and yet those advantages were largely neutralized by the inherent advantages that defense has in war and by the effectiveness of defensive weapons.

In war on land and at sea the advantage of the defensive weapons is also apparent. The most important type of offensive weapon for ground forces is still mobile heavily armored artillery—tanks. But some military thinkers go so far as to say that antitank guided missiles have made the tank useless. While that is probably an overstatement, it is true that for just $5,000 you can buy an antitank missile that has a better than 50% chance of destroying a one million dollar tank.

At sea, the offensive weapons system the U.S. navy is almost entirely built around is the aircraft carrier. But to give you an idea of how susceptible the aircraft carrier is to defensive weapons, consider the fact that, except for the nuclear-armed submarines, *the entire remainder of the U.S. navy, for all practical purposes, exists solely to protect the carriers.* The threats to the carriers are airplanes, air-and surface-launched missiles, other ships, and submarines; to which threats the carrier must respond by employing long-range patrol aircraft for intercepting incoming planes and missiles, escort ships (destroyers and frigates), and antimissile defenses. And all that is just to defend against the planes, missiles, and ships; we haven't even talked about defending against the most effective threat to the carrier—the submarines.

Despite all that, it is still possible that carriers will be able to protect themselves and maintain their effectiveness. But even if they can, the cost in accessory weapons required to give the offensive weapon, the carrier, the advantage over the defenses against it is enormous. The trend still seems clear that the defense is gaining on the offense.

Of course, it could be argued that perhaps examples of other weapons systems (aside from the obvious one of nuclear weapons) could be found where the offense appears to have the edge. But the statistics clearly suggest that the trend toward defensive advantage is real. Despite the advances in weapons that give them greater potential lethality, that is, greater potential to cause deaths than earlier weapons if used against soldiers in the same formations with the same defenses as before, the actual lethality of battle (the percentage of troops in active combat killed per day of combat) has steadily declined over history, as shown in Figure 1 (the only figure in this book).

b. The cost of the weapons to destroy things may be getting to be greater than the value of the targets destroyed. This was alluded to already with the cost of all the accessory weapons used to keep an aircraft carrier in operation. Some of those weapons and others are included below in a partial list of some expensive nonnuclear weapons from the 1985 U.S. budget. (List adapted from Luttwak, 1985.)

Cost in Millions of Dollars for One Weapon	
B1-B Bomber	226
226 F-16 Falcon Lightweight Fighter Aircraft, considered to be a relatively "low-tech" plane	27
CG-47 Cruiser, a ship used to protect carriers from missiles with its own surface-to-air missiles	1,066
SSN-688 Attack Submarine, defends carriers against other subs.	750
F/A-18 Fighter-Bomber, a "low-cost" fighter	32
F-15 Fighter Jet	46
M-1 Tank	2.5
AV-8B Harrier Vertical Takeoff Fighter-Bomber	26

Because of advances in the countermeasures against weapons, the weapons themselves have had to, and will inevitably continue to, become bigger (or smaller), better, more technically advanced, and, as a consequence, more expensive, while the value of defending our nation or of imposing our nation's will upon another, whatever that value may be, is a constant. Therefore, logic dictates that as the weapons continue to get more expensive, at some point the weapons have got to cost more than the targets they destroy are worth.

This is not to say that when that intersection point is reached,

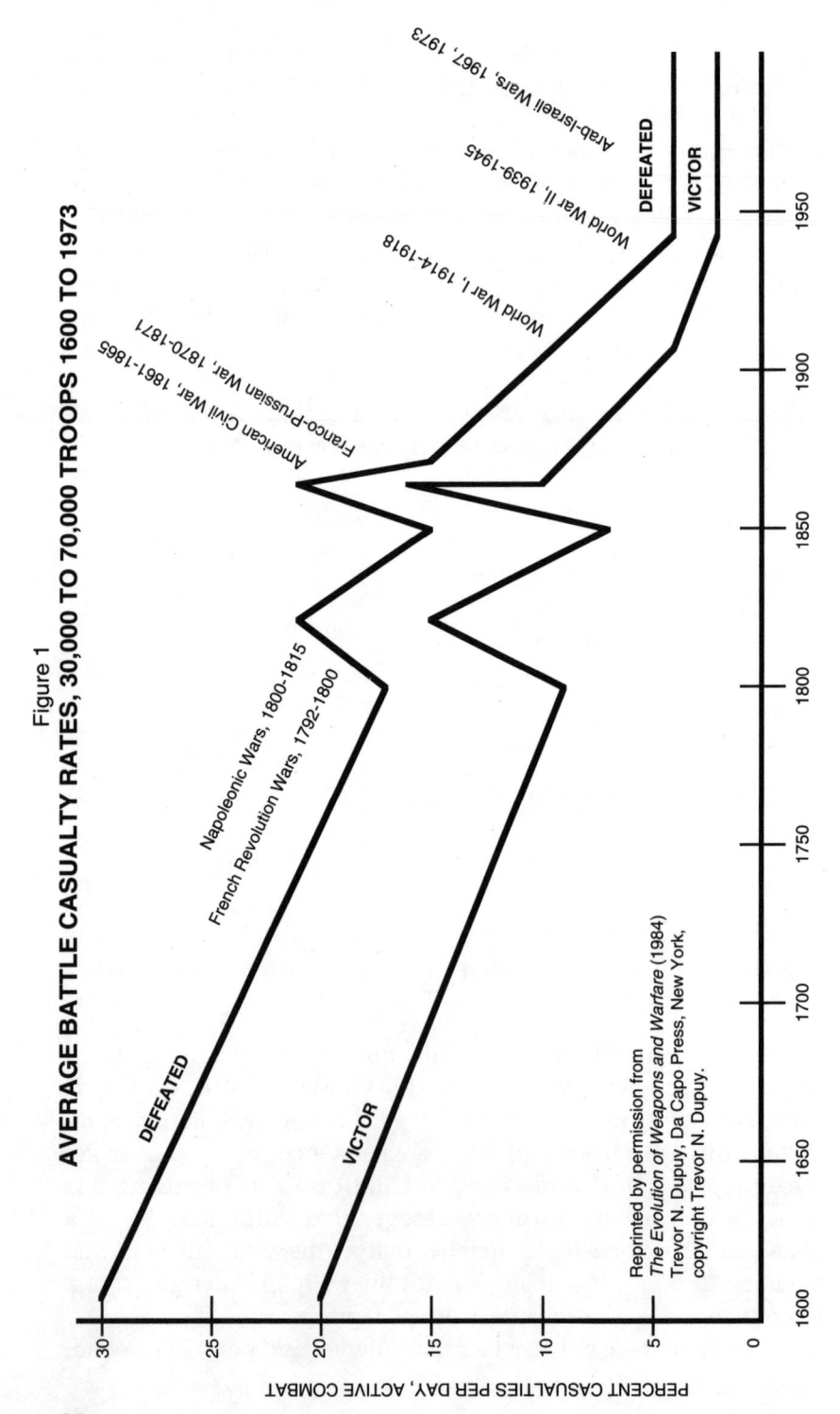

Figure 1
AVERAGE BATTLE CASUALTY RATES, 30,000 TO 70,000 TROOPS 1600 TO 1973

nations will stop building those particular weapons. In many case they won't, for one reason because it isn't really possible to calculate in dollars how much it is "worth" to be able to use a certain weapon. But that does not change the fact that a nation which cannot recognize when a weapon costs more than it is worth will not be increasing but actually *decreasing* its power by building that weapon.

c. The Uncertainty Factor. There are so many weapons systems and advances occur so quickly in all of them that it is almost impossible to say who has the advantage in any one area and even closer to impossible to say which of the possible advantages in different areas might prove decisive. But making that analysis accurately is exactly what a government must do if it is considering waging war. Compounding the difficulty, comparing the weapons themselves is not the only analysis to be made, because for the theoretical capabilities of weapons to be realized, they have to be incorporated into a military doctrine; and more often than not it has taken a little trial and error before the best way to use a weapon is found.

To assess a balance of power in conventional military strength between two comparable nations, then, not only must you gauge the relative merits of a bewildering array of technically advanced weapons on both sides, but you must guess at how each side intends to use each weapon and at whether that is the best use for it. All that makes it much more difficult than in earlier times to make an intelligent comparison of conventional military strength between two roughly technologically equal nations. In other words, a country can rarely feel very certain that it has an advantage in nonnuclear weapons over a potential enemy. And I submit that not being able to *know* whether you are stronger than your neighbor is almost the same thing as not being able to *be* stronger than your neighbor.

d. The Factor of Nuclear Weapons. The most fundamental difference between today's competition for supremacy in conventional weapons development and the competition in all previous eras is that today we are competing to develop weapons that are not our most powerful. That makes it a very odd competition, and it may very well be that the competition doesn't matter much. In previous times, the very existence of the nation depended largely on whether that nation's weapons were better than its neighbors'. Today, for the first time in history, at least for the nuclear powers, that really isn't true. In World War II, if Great Britain's conventional forces could not have withstood the German aerial bombardment, Britain would have ceased to exist as an independent nation, just as so many nations on the continent already had. But today, if Britain's conventional forces failed to repel a Russian or German invasion, the British would still have a choice: They could choose between losing their sovereignty and launching a nuclear attack. Viewing the situation from the standpoint of a potential aggressor, I would certainly never want to force any government to make that choice.

We should keep in mind what is and is not at stake in the race to develop better conventional weapons. At stake is whether Britain can control a few almost uninhabited islands off the coast of Argentina, whether the U.S. can prop up a friendly government in South Vietnam, or whether the Soviet Union can prop up a friendly government in Afghanistan. At stake is not, at least not for the nuclear powers, national sovereignty.

I have argued that it is more difficult today than in the fairly recent past to gain an advantage in power, particularly to gain a decisive advantage, in the fields of geography (conquering territory), control of natural resources, industrial capacity, population, and military preparedness. In addition, with the conversion of most nations to democracies, further large improvements in national morale or in the quality of government will not come easily. In fact, the only aspect of national power in which dramatic changes have not occurred to make it more difficult to gain a power advantage is national character, an aspect that has never been a particularly intense arena of competition for power, anyway. In two of the most important aspects of national power, population and the nuclear weapons component of military preparedness, two areas where the competition has been most intense and escalated most rapidly (although the exponential growth of most nations' populations may not have been fueled by any conscious governmental policies), it is now essentially impossible to gain further power or to gain a significant power advantage. And in every one of these aspects of power listed—

national morale, quality of government, geography, natural resources, industrial capacity, population, and both nuclear and conventional military preparedness—the changes that have made it more difficult for a nation to gain a power advantage have occurred most dramatically in the past 100 years or so.

Under the present system of nation-states as the fundamental units in this system of competing societies, gaining an advantage in the selection for power is, and will continue to be, very difficult. One might hope and expect then that nations would slow down their competitive efforts, knowing that it will be difficult for others to gain a large advantage over them. But it is obvious that just the opposite has happened: As exemplified by the nuclear arms race, competition has become even more frenetic. It seems that no matter how small (or even nonexistent) the potential gains may be, nations cannot slow their drive for more power.

The Logical Next Evolutionary Step

There is a way off this treadmill, a simple way any group of nations could choose to decisively improve their power in virtually all these areas: They could band together. I am speaking of forming a supranational government, or at least a supranational defense organization. The crucial characteristic of the organization that would be required to increase the power of this group of nations is that the militaries of the member nations function as one unit under one commander-in-chief. The nations would have to give up individual control of their militaries to the supranational organization.

In every one of these aspects of power in which an increase of power is difficult or impossible for any nation to achieve today, forming a supranational defense organization from several nations would instantly and dramatically increase power for every member nation.

A huge geographical advantage would be gained. The land area that must be conquered to conquer the nation would suddenly become not just that country itself but all the countries in the organization. In addition, particular desirable features of geography or strategic locations could be gained. For instance, by joining a group including nations with warm-water ports, Russia could have its long-dreamt of warm-water port.

A nation would make a quantum leap in its access to natural

resources by joining such an organization. At least as far as its military needs are concerned, it would have guaranteed access to the resources of all other member states.

The industrial capacity would become that of all the member nations, not just one, dramatically increasing the diversity and size of industrial capacity a nation has access to, and also creating a cumulative industrial capacity much less vulnerable to swings in the economy than that of any one nation.

As for population's contribution to power, the population to be considered in an analysis of power would become that of the entire organization instead of just one nation. And this increase of population would be accomplished without any increased depletion of food or other natural resources.

In the nuclear half of the military component of power, a nonnuclear nation would effectively join the nuclear club if it joined an organization with a nuclear power.

In conventional military might, joining a federation could speed the pace of technical development of a nation's weapons. The U.S., for instance, would improve the technology of its weapons were it to join with Japan in a federation and thus gain full use of the considerable skills of Japanese scientists. Equally important for military power, a supranational organization, with its larger population, would of course be able to field more soldiers than any one member nation.

Any group of nations that formed such an organization would have an enormous power advantage over the nations that remained independent. Therefore, the parable of the tribes says that were such an organization to be formed, it would be selected for. It would outcompete all other societies. Other nations would probably either have to join or have to form rival supranational organizations. However, the parable of the tribes does not dictate that the development of forming the first supranational military organization* must occur any more than the biological theory of

---

*No true supranational military organization has yet been formed. NATO, the North Atlantic Treaty Organization, for instance, is, as its name states, just a treaty organization. The militaries of the nations in NATO are entirely separate from each other and entirely under the control of the separate nations.

natural selection dictates that a certain potentially beneficial mutation must occur. Both theories only state how selection will operate once the variant forms of life—or of culture—are present. But, whereas biological variation is created purely randomly by mutation, the cultural variation that is the raw material for power selection is not randomly created, but comes about by the choices and innovations of human beings. And the speed of cultural evolution in the direction of power strongly suggests that, consciously or subconsciously, people and societies have been aware of the selection for power and have tried to create cultural innovations conducive to power. So if there is an obvious innovation like this that could be made to increase power, I think we would be stupid to believe that it won't be made

It is my thesis, then, that we ought to start planning. Whether we like it or not, I believe some type of supranational government is inevitable. In this book I will examine how we can make this innovation conducive to human needs and to the enrichment of human life. Unfortunately, however, those worthy goals are not the only ones that must be addressed in designing such a federation. The parable of the tribes tells us that if we are going to form a supranational government, we need to do everything possible to maximize its competitive power with other societies in the world. If we don't, someone else will, and our organization will be outcompeted and selected against—whether it betters our lives or not. Happily, I find that maximizing the power of such an organization and designing it to improve our lives are not at all contradictory goals.

Summary of Chapter 2

- An automatic selection for power has directed human cultural evolution in much the same way that a selection for the "fittest" has directed biological evolution.

- This selection for power has given us all the most important characteristics of our societies, including our organization into large nations as the fundamental unit of society.

- Since nations are the fundamental unit of society, that is, are the smallest subdivisions of society that are totally sovereign over their own affairs, it is nations that are the units evolving and selected amongst by the selection for power. So an analysis of national power and the history of competition for national power will help us predict where the selection for power will take our cultures and societies in the future. That analysis clearly shows, for virtually every component of national power, that in the 20th century it has suddenly become dramatically more difficult than ever before for any one nation to gain a significant power advantage over other nations.

- One simple step, however, will allow nations to suddenly break out of this dead end in the growth of power. That step is for any group of nations to give up individual control of their militaries and instead band their militaries together under the control of one supranational organization.

- Since this step will dramatically increase the power of every participating nation, it will be strongly selected for by the selection for power. It is, therefore, inevitable, and we had better start planning for it.

Chapter 3

Designing a Supranational Organization

Whatever type of supranational organization we choose to form, it necessarily involves giving up some control of our own behavior. That's the minus side. The plus side is that it also involves gaining some control over the behavior of others.

Any government, any functional society, involves this tradeoff. The state in which people have failed to accept some loss of control over their behavior is called anarchy. It is correctly viewed as unacceptable at the local and national levels, and it ought to be viewed as unacceptable at the international level.

At the local and national levels, somewhere along the line each society has assembled and decided what powers to grant to the government and what rights to retain for the individual or for lower levels of government. In the United States this process occurred most notably in 1787 with the constitutional convention. At that time, for instance, the writers of the Constitution agreed to grant to the federal government and prohibit from lower governments the power to coin money, and agreed to prohibit all levels of government from passing *ex post facto* laws (laws that apply retroactively and allow punishment for actions that were not illegal when they were committed).

Likewise, if we design a supranational government or military organization—or just a treaty organization, free trade group, or economic cartel—we will have to decide what powers to grant it and what powers not to. When we do that we will of course be making trade-offs. Any granting of powers to an organization involves a trade-off: We give up some power to do as we wish in some area of behavior, but as members of the organization we gain some power to control the behavior of others in that area. For instance, in nearly every society on earth, people have given up the power to murder their fellow citizens at will, but have gained assurances that their fellow citizens will not be able to murder them, or at least will be deterred from doing so because of the severe consequences that will follow. For most of us, that is clearly a good trade. On the other hand, in the United States we have chosen not to give up our right to speak our minds on issues of the day in exchange for controlling the free speech of others. We have specifically prohibited the government and our fellow citizens from infringing on our right of free speech. So we agree that in the area of controlling murder it is good to grant powers to a higher organization, while in the area of controlling speech it is not.

In designing a supranational organization, it is those types of decisions that have to be made. We have to decide in which areas it is good to trade our rights for powers, and in which areas it is not. The traditional position on that issue up to now has been that no nation should ever trade away any right in the international society. But that position is, of course, at least as ludicrous, probably more so, as the idea that no individual should ever trade away any right, that none of us should ever accept the slightest infringement on our individual right to do absolutely anything we wish to any other person.

On what logical basis does the traditional defense of absolute national sovereignty rest? None. It only rests on tradition. On what basis should a nation have the right to attack its neighbors? We don't grant that right to individuals; we don't grant it to cities; we don't grant it to provinces. Why are nations different? On what basis should a nation have the right to violate basic human rights? We don't allow parents to violate the basic rights of their children; we don't allow city police departments and prosecutors to violate basic rights; we don't allow state or provincial governments to violate rights unchecked. Yet when it comes to nations, we say that they may do whatever they want and no international organization may force them to do otherwise. Why? Or how about pollution. We don't allow families to dump their garbage on their neighbors' lawns; we don't allow corporations to pollute unchecked; we don't allow cities to dump their sewage unchecked. But when it comes to nations, we say they can do whatever they want. Why?

The idea of absolute national sovereignty is completely without rational foundation. The position that anarchy should exist at the international level is every bit as absurd as the position that it should exist at the national or local levels.

Tossing away that ludicrous traditional position then, let's look rationally at what powers a supranational organization should have. The first thing we have to decide is what goals we want the organization to achieve. That will determine what rights we will have to trade away for powers. For instance, if your goal is to secure your property, then that determines that you should trade away your right to commit robbery for the power to punish others who might commit robbery. A few possible goals for a supranational organization are listed below.

1. To keep the peace between member nations.

2. To maintain domestic tranquility within each member nation.

3. To provide for the common defense and to strengthen the effective military defense of each member nation over that which it would have as an independent nation. To maximize the power of the organization over nonmember nations or other organizations.

4. To reduce the cost of government, especially to reduce the cost of military defense.

5. To reduce the number and severity of wars a member nation could expect to be involved in (or, ideally, to eliminate war).

6. To guarantee a list of basic human rights for citizens of all

member nations, or at least to promote the observation of those rights.

7. To guarantee a democratic form of government at all levels for every member nation.

8. To limit human population. To protect the environment. To protect member nations against pollution and environmental disruption caused by other member nations. To protect the rights of other species.

9. To reduce or eliminate the danger of nuclear war.

10. To control trade among member nations and between member nations and nonmember nations so as to maximize the economic health of the organization.

11. To improve the effectiveness of nonmilitary means of exerting power, such as economic boycotts and embargoes.

12. To guarantee a certain minimum standard of living and to provide basic health care for all citizens of all member nations.

In the ensuing chapters I will consider at one point or another how each of those goals could be achieved. I will argue, though, that not all of those goals should be the responsibility of a supranational organization. In part, that is because attempting to achieve those goals would prevent the supranational organization from achieving certain more important goals. And in part it is because my bias will be to leave all powers to national and local governments whenever possible. But for other goals, to achieve them we will need to cede certain powers to a supranational organization. What those goals are and what those powers are will be the subject of the rest of this book.

Before we go on though, one point should be settled. Let's dispense with this clumsy terminology of a "supranational organization" and decide on a name for this thing. The discussion in this chapter has hinted at what that name should be. I have said that several separate nations should band together and give up some powers, where appropriate, to the supranational organization, while forbidding other powers from that organization or retaining them for themselves. The word for that type of organization is a federation. In a federation, separate states or entities have banded together and agreed to subordinate their power to the central authority in matters of common interest, while retaining their separate powers in matters that are not of common interest. So I will call this the Federation of Nations.

Summary of Chapter 3

- All societies in their evolution have agreed to trade away certain individual rights for certain collective powers. For instance, they have all traded away the right of the individual to commit murder for the power of the society to punish those who would commit murder.

- This agreement has never been reached between nations. Nations to this day continue to insist that they must have total "sovereignty," that they and their people may behave any way they wish in the international arena, and no higher authority may have any right to control their behavior. This situation is called anarchy. It is correctly viewed as unacceptable at the national and local levels, and it is time we faced the obvious fact that it is unacceptable at the international level as well.

- It is time we designed a federation of nations to end this state of anarchy. The question to be faced in designing this federation of nations is the same question societies have faced in designing their national and local governments: In which areas is it wise to trade away the right to behave as we wish for the power to control the behavior of others, and in which areas is that not wise? Answering that question will be the task of the rest of this book.

Chapter 4

The First Goal of the Federation of Nations: To End War Between Member Nations

"Power corrupts, and absolute power corrupts absolutely." I am very aware and fearful of the truth of that adage. My strong bias in designing this supranational government, if indeed we determine that we need a government and not just some looser and weaker organization, is to grant the government itself, and also any individuals in that government, as few powers as possible. But that was the bias also of the designers of the League of Nations and the United Nations, and those experiments in world federalism failed. The reason those experiments failed was foreseen and avoided by the framers of the United States Constitution, which was another, more successful, effort to join autonomous states or nations into an overarching federation.

The framers of the United States Constitution understood that *any organization given responsibilities or aims must also be given the powers it will need to carry out those responsibilities or aims, or else it is doomed to fail.* That point is one of the major themes of *The Federalist Papers,* repeated over and over again by its authors, Hamilton, Madison, and Jay. Now, you may ask, "Why would Hamilton, Madison, and Jay have repeated over and over again such an obvious point?" They emphasized it so much because they had just seen the disregard for that point cause the failure of the first attempt at a constitution for the federal government of the United States—the Articles of Confederation. And just as in their century the disregard for that point caused the failure of the Articles of Confederation, so in our century it has caused the failure of the League of Nations and United Nations. In each of those three cases, the framers of the organization were so fearful of the dangers of granting too much power to their proposed organization (or the states or nations were too jealous of their own power to surrender any) that the organizations simply did not have the minimal powers required to carry out the responsibilities they were entrusted with.

There are two traps to avoid in designing a federation of nations: granting it too much power or not enough power. History indicates we will be more than sufficiently aware of the dangers of granting the federation too much power, so there is almost no risk from that front. The trap much more likely to ensnare us is not granting the federation enough power, dooming it to failure by not granting it the minimal powers necessary to execute its responsibilities.

With those lessons in mind, then, let us begin.

The first responsibility of the Federation of Nations, the overriding goal in designing the organization, has got to be to keep the internal peace, to eliminate war between member nations. *The only way that can be done is to take control of the military away from the national governments and give it to the Federation of Nations government* (Art. I, Sec. 6, Provs. 1 and 9 of the proposed constitution in Appendix A). If the member nations have the *ability* to wage war against each other, they *will* wage war against each other.

I'll repeat that for emphasis.

The most important responsibility of the Federation of Nations, or F.O.N. for short, must be to keep the peace between its member nations. And the only way that can be done is for all member nations to surrender to the F.O.N. the control of their militaries.

The approach of the U.N. and the League of Nations to stopping war was based on the idea that war occurs because nations have no peaceful forum for settling their disputes. So the U.N. and League of Nations provided that forum with the naive hope (I say hope rather than belief because I imagine few people actually believed it would work) that when an "impartial" organization judged their dispute, both sides would accept the nonbinding judgment and not resort to war. The plan is naive on several levels: No organization can really be impartial; even if it were impartial, both sides of the dispute would never perceive it that way; and in any remotely important dispute, no nation will let a nonbinding judgment stop it from using every tool at its disposal to get its way, including using military power. But the most important way it is naive is in the assumption that war is caused by "disputes." Though the pretense for initiating a war is often some supposed injustice, the real reasons for waging war are so numerous we could hardly catalog them, let alone make an effort to remove all of them. There's religious fanaticism—the desire to impose the one true religion on some uncooperative savages. There's the modern stepchild of religious fanaticism, political fanaticism—the desire to impose the one true system of governance on some uncooperative savages. There's the potential for national economic gain, the potential for economic gain by one influential subgroup of the nation, some leader's drive for political gain, a national need for vengeance, overpopulation and the consequent national need for additional resources, a national need to let off steam. The list goes on.

Eliminating the causes of war can never be done. But eliminating the ability to wage war can. The only way to stop power is with power. If we don't want a member nation to wage war against another, the F.O.N. had better have a bigger army than that nation does. If we *really* don't want any member nation attacking another, in the same way that we rest assured Missouri won't attack Kansas, the member nations should control no significant military at all compared to the size of the military controlled by the F.O.N.

It's very simple. If we don't want member nations waging war against each other, in other words, if we don't want any member nation waging war without the permission of the F.O.N., the F.O.N. needs a bigger stick than its member nations. But having a slightly bigger stick won't be good enough. The F.O.N. military would constantly be fighting wars against the militaries of its member nations trying to keep them in line. The difference in size of the militaries has to be overwhelming, has to be such that the member nations can never even consider a military action on their own. This means the member nations should control virtually no military at all. (Of course they will, however, need to control police or some national guard to enforce their laws and keep their own internal peace).

It is this overwhelming difference in military strength between the federal and state governments in the U.S. that is responsible for the last 125 years of peace between the states. The peace has not been because the states do not control any military power. They do. They control the state police and their national guard units. But those units will never do anything the president and the federal military oppose. A recent example vividly demonstrates this. In 1957, three years after the 1954 Brown vs. Board of Education Supreme Court school desegregation ruling, the school system of Little Rock, Arkansas, finally, after federal court orders, was to be integrated. Nine courageous black children were to begin attending the previously all-white Little Rock Central High School. On the day that school began, however, there was a surprise. The governor of Arkansas ordered the Arkansas National Guard to surround the school and prevent the entrance of any negro children. This confrontational defiance of court orders and federal rule forced President Eisenhower reluctantly to intervene. After two weeks of negotiation and delay, during which time the national guard remained stationed around the school, Eisenhower finally sent in the army and federalized the Arkansas National Guard, ordering them to turn their guns around and, rather than block the entrance of the negro children, escort them to class and see that no one interfered with them. Now, why did that national guard unit, down to the last man, obey the new order and turn their guns around? Is it because they were all closet civil rights activists who were really on the side of the black children all along? I think not. Is it because they all understood the court decisions surrounding the constitutional question of whether a president can override a governor's authority in controlling the national guard? I doubt it. It's because they knew if they didn't, the president could turn the army against them and they'd all wind up killed or court-martialed.

Likewise, the peace between the states has not been because the states have had nothing to fight about. Ill feeling by states toward the federal government, such as occurred during the civil rights era, is not at all uncommon; and even with most powers belonging to the federal government, specific grievances of one state against another still develop. Were it not for the fact the states cannot wage war, it is not impossible to imagine war developing. After all, it did develop once.

The fundamental reason, then, for the peace we have enjoyed between the states is only the enormous difference in military power between the federal and state governments.

There are two approaches that could be taken to ending war: eliminating the causes of war or eliminating the ability to wage war. (I am speaking here only of ending war between a group of nations that have agreed to band together, rather than between all the nations on earth. I will later discuss, though, how we could extend the ending of war to all, or nearly all, the nations on earth.) The potential causes of war are almost endless and perhaps could never all be foreseen, so trying to take preemptive measures against their ever arising is, I believe, a hopeless task. Tending to confirm this, the two organizations that were formed to try to eliminate or reduce war by taking this approach, the United Nations and the League of Nations, not only have not eliminated war, but have had no perceptible effect on reducing it at all. But it is easy to see how the other approach, eliminating or reducing war by eliminating the ability to wage it, can be successfully accomplished: Simply reduce the military power of the nations or states whose wars you are trying to eliminate and create a much greater military power above them to keep them in line. The relative internal peace created by the most notable experiment of this type in modern times, the uniting of the United States of America, confirms the great potential of this approach.

The one time the peace between the states broke down in the U.S. illustrates again that both of the factors mentioned here, neither of which was present in the U.S. before the American Civil War, are necessary for keeping the peace between the states or nations in a federation. The first factor is that the states or nations in a federation should control essentially no military of their own. This was not the case in the U.S. before the Civil War. The bulk of U.S. military forces, both before and during the Civil War, were state militias and state-organized volunteer units. When you read a history of the Civil War, you will notice that all the army units have names like the 6th Massachusetts Regiment or the 57th Illinois. All of the men in those units came from, respectively, Massachusetts or Illinois. Is it any wonder we had a war between the states? We didn't have a federal army; we had a collection of state armies. When the southern states withdrew from the union, they already had in their state militias a military force that was roughly the equal of anything the federal government possessed. This historical lesson, then, indicates that the F.O.N. army should *not* be organized into divisions by nation. Although the language barriers will make it difficult, as much as possible we should intermingle the soldiers from different nations. This must be one F.O.N. military, not just an aggregation of national militaries.

The second factor necessary for keeping the peace between the states in a federation is that the federation's military should be large enough to immediately crush any attempts at waging war or at raising an army that the states or nations might make. This requirement was not met in the U.S. before the Civil War because the U.S. had a strong historical prejudice against a large standing army in peacetime, considering it an instrument of oppression. The U.S. army at the outbreak of the Civil War consisted of just 13,000 men scattered over 3 million square miles of territory. After the Confederate states withdrew, it was six months before the Union could raise enough troops to begin the war against the Confederacy.

Since the Civil War, though, both requirements for keeping the peace between the states have been met in the U.S., and we have never come close to another war between the states.

Therefore, if nations band together into a supranational federation, one simple, though politically difficult, action will guarantee peace between the member nations. The nations simply have to give up control of their militaries to the federation. The nations would still control police to enforce their laws and perhaps enough national guard to keep their own internal peace, but the transfer of the military to the federation would guarantee both conditions for peace between the member nations—that the nations control essentially no military and that the federation have sufficient power to quickly crush any act of war by a member nation.

You are no doubt already objecting that no nation would ever willingly give up control of its military, that it is politically impossible. I think it is not, though, and the basic reason it is not was stated at the end of Chapter 2: Fusing their militaries together will increase the power of any group of nations. But the more elaborate discussion of why it is not politically unrealistic to expect nations to surrender their militaries to a supranational organization will be deferred until later. For now, let me just remind you of the need to grant powers commensurate with responsibilities. If we charge the F.O.N. with keeping the peace between member nations, we must turn over all military power to the federation. There are no two ways about it. If you find that unacceptable, fine, but you must give up the pretense that you want peace, for there is no other way to have it.

The next objection I am raising with myself, and perhaps you are raising, is that eliminating the ability to wage war does not eliminate the desire to. But if we look at the evidence, I think it indicates that, surprisingly enough, eliminating the ability to wage war usually *does* also eliminate the desire—or at least eliminates some of the desire. The modern nation-states were not always this large. Most of them within the past few hundred years consisted of several smaller states within what is now the geographical area of one nation—with some examples being Germany, Italy, the U.S., and formerly the U.S.S.R. Looking at the example of Germany, we see that since its unification in 1871, although it has been in a lot of wars, they have not been civil wars. There is not much evidence that the people of the formerly separate states harbor a great desire to attack each other if only they could. In general it never crosses anyone's mind.*

---

*Another example of a modern nation that formerly consisted of several smaller states—Yugoslavia—appears to support the opposite contention. But I'm not certain it does. Many interpret the current war there to mean that for the past half-century, since the formation of Yugoslavia, the Serbs, Croats, and Muslims have been just aching to start killing each other. I doubt that, though. I'm sure they disliked each other (cont.)

So it is possible to entirely eliminate the ability of member nations in a federation of nations to wage war against each other, and the historical record indicates that this will also largely eliminate any desire the nations may have to wage war against each other. However, believe it or not, this still will not completely end war within the F.O.N. People can be unarmed, but if the hostility is deep enough it will still be war. They will use rocks, gasoline, their bare hands, anything at all, and, as Israel is finding with the Palestinians, you've got a war on your hands, and a war that cannot be won. For that reason, one other constitutional provision is necessary to keep the internal peace in an F.O.N.: Nations have to be allowed to withdraw. We can only keep peace among nations that want to be members.

(It should also be mentioned here that allowing nations to withdraw not only makes sense for promoting a peaceful organization, but also for promoting a powerful one. Perennially subduing a chronic internal enemy will only weaken the organization and make it susceptible to attack by external enemies.)

The principle involved here is that it is in the F.O.N.'s interest to have as members only those nations that really want to be members. This principle applies as much in dictating procedures for allowing nations to join the F.O.N. as procedures for allowing them to withdraw. Therefore, both to allow a nation to join the F.O.N. and to allow it to leave, we should insist on a mandate from the people of the nation that that is what they desire. And this mandate should be the only thing we insist on. Whether the government of the nation wants to join or leave the F.O.N. is unimportant; it is the will of the people that should concern us most.

---

*(cont.) and had prejudices against each other. But that's different from wanting to start a war. More likely, the desire to start a war only began when the central government responsible for keeping the peace weakened—a process that began with the death of Marshal Tito in 1980. As the central government weakened, the different peoples in Yugoslavia began to have valid reasons to fear each other because there was no overarching force capable of restraining the other groups. Eventually it became a rational course of action for them to start arming themselves. In other words, the desire of each group to make war on the other groups arose only when it became possible for those other groups to make war on them.

To go into the details of these procedures, then, the required procedure for joining should be a national referendum on the issue, with a simple majority required for passage (Art. V, Sec. 4, Prov. 1). After this referendum passes (and after the nation's joining is ratified by the F.O.N. legislature, as specified in Article V, Section 4, Provision 1 of my proposed F.O.N. constitution in Appendix A, and as discussed in Appendix B) the nation's membership in the F.O.N. should be considered to be effective immediately and the F.O.N. should immediately begin integrating the nation's military into the F.O.N. Since the nation's national government will have permitted the referendum to be held, it can be presumed that the government will abide by the referendum's results. We want therefore, to begin integrating the military immediately after the referendum, before a new national government comes to power that might try to block that integration.

On the issue of withdrawing from the F.O.N., as I mentioned, we should also require only a national referendum (Art. V, Sec. 4, Prov. 3). The other nations of the F.O.N. should have no say at all in the issue, only the people of the nation concerned. The requirement for passage of the referendum, however, should be not a simple majority, but a 55% vote in favor of withdrawing. The reason for this is that, naturally, we would like nations to remain members. So rather than letting them leave at the drop of a hat, we should require a clear consensus that the people truly want to leave the F.O.N. before we let them withdraw. Furthermore, after passage of this referendum, there should be a delay before a nation is permitted to withdraw—the delay I propose being five years (Art. V, Sec. 4, Prov. 3). The purpose of this delay is two-fold. First, it is to give the F.O.N. time to adjust to the loss of that nation's military forces, and second, it is to discourage nations from joining the F.O.N. for short-term gain. We do not want nations joining the F.O.N. every time they feel threatened militarily and then withdrawing as soon as the threat passes. Requiring a five year delay before a nation withdraws should discourage that abuse and should establish that both joining the F.O.N. and withdrawing from it are long-term commitments.

That's it. Those few simple provisions guarantee that the

F.O.N. will never be plagued by a serious war between its member nations. It is not a prescription for world peace ... yet—only for peace among the group of nations that freely choose to join the F.O.N. But if someday that group would include nearly every nation in the world, then, indeed, these provisions would serve as a prescription for world peace.

The next subject to discuss, then, a subject that will be a major theme for the rest of this book, is how to maximize the number of nations that will join the F.O.N.

Summary of Chapter 4

- In designing any organization or government, the organization must be granted the powers necessary to carry out whatever responsibilities it is entrusted with, or else it is doomed to fail.
- The first responsibility or goal of the F.O.N. must be to prevent war between the member nations.
- There is only one way to achieve this goal, and that is to surrender the national militaries to the control of the F.O.N.
- However, even with that, it will be possible to keep the peace only among nations that wish to be members. So nations must be allowed to withdraw from the F.O.N. whenever a national referendum on the issue certifies that is what the people want.

Chapter 5

Maximizing the Membership of the Federation of Nations: Democracy and Free Speech

In order to extend the spread of peace, and to ultimately achieve world peace, the next question we must address is, How do we maximize the number of nations in the Federation of Nations? How do we induce as many nations as possible to join? The answer to that question may seem odd, since it will apparently limit the F.O.N.'s membership to democracies, but the answer is to make the F.O.N. a democracy. The F.O.N.'s representatives must be democratically elected (Art. I, Sec. 2, Prov. 1; Art I, Sec. 3, Prov. 1).

Requiring that F.O.N. representatives be democratically elected is essential. The reason it is essential centers on the necessity, as discussed in the last chapter, of surrendering the military to the F.O.N. The first purpose of this organization has got to be to keep the peace between its member nations. If we are not going to make that the central goal, then I don't see much point in forming the organization at all. And to achieve that goal, the member nations simply must surrender their military power to the F.O.N. There is no other way about it. But the only way any democracy, any nation, any sensible person, would ever willingly surrender military power to such an organization is if all representatives in the F.O.N. are democratically elected.

Consider the alternative. What if we take the position that in order for the F.O.N. to grow, it must avoid offending any potential member nations. So it must be nonjudgmental about the types of political systems they may have and must recognize the representatives they choose to send to the F.O.N., regardless of how those representatives are chosen. Then you have the spectacle of representatives chosen by whites-only elections in South Africa, appointed by corrupt and brutal dictators in Latin America, and appointed by genocidal party chairmen in China. What nation would ever be crazy enough to surrender military power to that cast of characters?

Although at first glance it might appear to limit the membership of the F.O.N., the representatives must be democratically chosen in direct, secret ballot elections by the people. Any nation that refuses to accept that simply will not be a member—and good riddance. Is this a Catch-22, though? I just pointed out that if we do not require democratic selection of representatives, we guarantee that the organization will never grow; but if we do require democratic selection of representatives, do we also guarantee that not enough nations will join? No. Obviously the organization will not begin with 150 member nations. It will probably begin with two or three. But, as Chapter 2 argued, those two or three countries, by banding together, if the organization is properly designed, will have become stronger. A few other democratic nations will see that they too can increase their power, their security, and their influence on what happens outside their borders by joining, and so they too will join. If properly designed, as Chapter 2 explained, the organization will have an evolutionary advantage over the independent nations and will be selected for by the irresistible selection for power. So it will continue to grow. In the early stages of the growth, this clause of the constitution that would tend to limit potential members to only the democratic nations will be no limitation on growth since about half the nations on earth are democracies. And since democracy is clearly on the rise in the world today—with fledgling democracies beginning in the former Soviet Union, the Philippines, South Korea, Argentina, Pakistan, Chile, throughout Eastern Europe, and hopefully about to begin in South Africa—it may be that the clause requiring democratic election of representatives will never limit the F.O.N.'s membership. Even if it does begin to limit its membership, it will not do so until the F.O.N. includes most of the world's democratic nations—includes about half or more of the world's countries—and at that point the Federation of Nations will be by far the most powerful society on earth and will be attracting new members not just with a carrot, but also with a big stick. The nonmember nations will feel their power slipping away, and many will be likely to want to join the F.O.N. badly enough to be willing to accept democratic elections.

Requiring democratic elections will not be a hindrance to the F.O.N.'s growth; it will in fact be essential to its growth.

Relations With National Governments

Making the F.O.N. a democracy creates other benefits besides just aiding the F.O.N.'s growth. Making the F.O.N. a democracy, that is, requiring direct election of F.O.N. representatives and requiring, as discussed in the last chapter, popular referendums in order for a nation to join or leave the F.O.N., also creates the distinction that the F.O.N.'s power and its right to make decisions and laws comes directly from the people, rather than from its member nations' governments. That is a crucial distinction, and it gives rise to two very important consequences. The first consequence is that it greatly strengthens the F.O.N.'s position when it must deal with the member nations' national governments. If the F.O.N. were to derive its power from the national governments, when it came time for it to try to control one of those governments, the national government would say: "We made you and we can destroy you. You are not in a position to give us orders." But by deriving its power directly from the people, the F.O.N. will have the legitimacy and strength needed to deal with national governments as an equal.

To explain this idea, consider what would happen if the F.O.N. needed to arrest the president of a member nation for some crime—let's say for ordering an assassination attempt on the head of state of some other member nation. If this president and his national government could withdraw from the F.O.N. on their own, without submitting that question to a referendum, it is almost certain that that is exactly what they would do. Surely this person would rather be president of a nonmember nation than in jail in a member nation. Because of that situation, it would be impossible for the F.O.N. to ever do anything that seriously offended a national government. Whenever it threatened to do something that a national government strongly opposed, that government would just withdraw from the organization.

The other factor involved here is how F.O.N. representatives are chosen. If the representatives are chosen by national governments, those representatives will never criticize their national governments and will never support measures that their own governments oppose. But if the representatives are democratically elected, they can afford to be their own men and women. They can take independent stances.

The second important consequence of the F.O.N.'s deriving its power from the people rather than from the national governments is that, although deriving its power directly from the people will give the F.O.N. a stronger position in dealing with the national governments, paradoxically it will also diminish the need for the F.O.N. to worry about those governments and meddle in their affairs. If the F.O.N. were to derive its power from the national governments, it would have to devote most of its time to either controlling those governments or keeping them happy. But if it derives its power from the people it can largely ignore the national governments.

The issues involved here are again whether the national governments could withdraw from the F.O.N. without submitting the question to a referendum and how representatives will be chosen—by national governments or by direct election. If the national governments could withdraw from the F.O.N. on their own, then the F.O.N. would have a clear interest in controlling them to prevent them from doing that. It would have an interest in installing, if it could, national government officials who would favor F.O.N. policy. Likewise, if the national governments were to appoint F.O.N. representatives, the F.O.N. again would have a clear interest in controlling those governments so it could control who would get appointed to the F.O.N. On the other hand, if the

F.O.N. could not succeed in controlling the national governments under those circumstances, it would, as we have seen be little more than their puppet—unable to ever do anything they opposed. Thus, if the F.O.N. were to derive its power from the national governments it would have to either control them or be controlled by them. There would be almost no middle ground. If it derives its power directly from the people, though, it can largely ignore the national governments. It need not control them and it will not be controlled by them.

For both the reasons discussed in this chapter—in order to grow and in order to have effective relations with the national governments—the F.O.N. must be a democracy.

Democratic National and Local Governments?

In the spirit of this paean to the virtues of democracy, you probably next expect I will argue that the F.O.N. should also guarantee a democratic form of government at the national and local levels for all member nations. I won't. The U.S. Constitution has a clause guaranteeing a republican form of government for the states, but the F.O.N. constitution should have no such clause. That type of clause could be used by the F.O.N. as an excuse for intervening in a nation's legitimate internal affairs and even overthrowing its government—*even if the government already was democratic.*

Chapter 4 began with the warning that we must grant an organization sufficient powers to carry out its responsibilities. But we must grant it no more. The power to determine what form a member nation's government should take is not a power the F.O.N. needs or should be allowed to have. Some constraints on the behavior of member nations, their governments, and their government officials are necessary, and the F.O.N. needs the power to enforce those constraints and prosecute their violation (some of those constraints will be discussed later in this chapter and in the next). But a vague power to dictate the form of government a member nation must have is not a power the F.O.N. should be trusted with.

This failure to impose democratic national governments on member nations will be attacked by some as a compromise with totalitarian regimes, but it is nothing of the sort. First, if you really believe democracy is the best form of government, then you should believe that giving people a taste of democracy in the F.O.N. will induce them to demand a democratic government at home soon enough without it being imposed from above. And second, at the core of a belief in democracy, I think, is a belief in the virtue and beauty of diversity. But if we set up the F.O.N. as judge of what is and is not an acceptable form of government, we will have a single, narrow form of government in all member nations—hardly the epitome of diversity. Moreover, while representative democracy is probably the best type of government for large societies we have yet developed, it is not perfect, and I would like to see member nations tinkering with different forms of democracy to try to improve it. The best form for one nation will not be the best form for another. Maybe even some experiments with forms that some would not consider democracy could yield improvements. As Thoreau said, "The world is wider than our view of it."

Free Speech

This subject of democracy next leads us into human rights, because for voters to make good decisions, they have to be informed about what is happening and be able to freely discuss issues—and, unfortunately, some governments do not allow that. As a rule, the F.O.N. should meddle in its member nations' internal affairs as little as possible, but F.O.N. officials must be elected democratically, and for that to work, the candidates and voters must be informed and be free to say whatever they want without fear of reprisals.

Thus, the F.O.N. constitution must echo the beautiful words of Article 1 of the Amendments to the United States Constitution:

> Congress shall make no law respecting an establishment of religion, or prohibiting the free exercise thereof; or abridging the freedom of speech, or of the press; or the right of the people peaceably to assemble and to petition the Government for a redress of grievances.

I propose that the F.O.N. version should read:

Article IV, Section 1.
 Provision 1. The Federation of Nations shall neither make

nor enforce any law respecting an establishment of religion. Neither shall the Federation of Nations or any national or local government within the Federation of Nations make or enforce any law prohibiting the free exercise of religion; or abridging the freedom of speech, or of the press; or the right of the people peaceably to assemble, and to petition the Federation of Nations or any other level of government for a redress of grievances.*

Only by guaranteeing these magnificent principles of freedom of speech, freedom of the press, freedom of assembly, and freedom of religion will the F.O.N. make itself a true democracy. And only if the F.O.N. is a true democracy will it grow and will the reign of peace spread throughout the world.

---

*I have prohibited only the F.O.N. from establishing a state religion, not nations or lower levels of government. Some nations, of course, now have official religions, and I think that is acceptable as long as those with differing beliefs are not restrained from practicing their own religions.

Summary of Chapter 5

- Repeating from Chapter 4, the most important goal of the F.O.N. must be to ensure peace between its member nations. And the only way that can be achieved is for all member nations to surrender control of their militaries to the F.O.N. *But the only way any nation would ever consider surrendering its military to the F.O.N. is if all F.O.N. representatives are democratically elected.* Thus, F.O.N. representatives must be democratically elected.

- Because of the requirement for democratic elections, nondemocratic nations obviously are not likely to join the F.O.N. This, however, will not limit the F.O.N. membership because there is more than a sufficient number of democracies to form a core group of F.O.N. members, and once the organization is formed, the selection for power will guarantee that the organization will continue to grow and grow. Eventually, nonmember nations, whether they are democracies or not, will have little choice but to join the F.O.N. and accept democratic elections.

- Making the F.O.N. a democracy is also essential for effective relations between the F.O.N. and the national governments. Making the F.O.N. a democracy establishes that its power comes directly from the people, rather than from the national governments. This gives the F.O.N. a legitimacy equal to the national governments and puts it in a position of strength when it must deal with those governments. Paradoxically, though, since the F.O.N.'s power would not derive from the national governments, the need of the F.O.N. to concern itself with those governments and attempt to control them or meddle in legitimate national affairs would be minimized.

- The F.O.N. does not need and should not be trusted with a vague power to guarantee a democratic form of government at the national and local levels in its member nations.

- In order to be a democracy, the F.O.N. must guarantee in all its member nations the cherished principles of freedom of speech, freedom of the press, freedom of assembly, and freedom of religion.

Chapter 6

Ending Civil Wars in Member Nations: Human Rights and the Use of the Federation of Nations Military

So far, in talking about keeping the peace in the Federation of Nations, I have talked only about preventing wars between member nations. I have ignored the problem of wars within member nations, civil wars. If I could, I would continue to ignore that problem. It is essentially an internal affair of the nation concerned, and if the F.O.N. is to grow, if it is to attract nations to join, it should meddle in a nation's internal affairs as little as possible. But unfortunately, since we took control of the military away from the national governments, we have to make the F.O.N. partially responsible for keeping the internal peace of each nation, because a national government without a military may sometimes find that, on its own, it cannot maintain its nation's internal peace.

Since the F.O.N. must have this responsibility, how can it carry it out? The responsibility can be broken down into two parts: to prevent civil wars from happening, and failing that, to stop them when they do happen. The first question is, How can the F.O.N. prevent civil wars from happening? The answer is to enforce a bill of rights and remove from national and local governmental office (and F.O.N. office) anyone who violates those rights. This will prevent civil wars by preventing the injustices and oppression that create those wars.

Some of the most important provisions of the F.O.N. bill of rights were just mentioned in the last chapter—the guarantees of freedom of speech, freedom of the press, freedom of assembly, and freedom of religion. The remaining provisions of the bill of rights will be discussed in detail in Chapter 11, but I will list some of the highlights here also:

Article IV, Section 2
   Provision 1. No person may be detained or arrested without being immediately told the reason, and no person may be jailed for more than 24 hours without being charged with a crime.
   Provision 2. No person may be deprived of life, liberty, or property without due process of law.
   Provision 5. Excessive bail shall not be required, nor cruel and unusual punishment inflicted.
   Provision 6. No person may be held to answer for a crime without reasonable basis for the charge, nor may any person be detained or jailed unless for reasonable cause.

The legislature of the F.O.N., as in any constitutional government, will have the duty to pass laws that will protect and carry out this constitution. With that duty in mind, the bill of rights section of the constitution dictates that, among other things, murder, torture, kidnapping, and theft will all be illegal under F.O.N. law, as will be any interference with the exercise of free speech, or any interference with a free press or with peaceful political demonstrations. Those laws and rights, therefore, mean that most acts of violent rebellion and most acts that provoke violent rebellion will be illegal in the F.O.N.

"Big deal," you say. "Those acts are already illegal in almost every nation, but that hasn't stopped certain governments from violating the laws and oppressing their people." Yes, I reply, and that is exactly why the F.O.N. will be different. Governments and government officials, particularly national governments and national government officials, have been able to violate their laws with impunity up to now because they control the police and the courts. In essence they are the police and the courts. But under the F.O.N. they will have to answer to an independent level of government—with police and courts that they do not control. Thus, under the F.O.N. even national and local government officials will be subject to the law. No guilty person will be able to avoid punishment just because of his position. (Of course there is some danger that F.O.N. government officials could attempt to put themselves above the F.O.N. law, but Chapter 11 will discuss ways to prevent this from happening.) With its rights, laws, and courts, the F.O.N. will be able to reduce violence, rebellion, and civil war because it will be able to reduce the crimes and injustices that cause violence, rebellion, and civil war.

An example may better illustrate how this will work. Today, in a nation like Guatemala, the government routinely sends out military death squads to torture, intimidate, or kill its political opponents—actions that, of course, eventually only create rebellion, civil war, and more bloodshed. Guatemalan government officials can get away with those crimes because they control the police, the military, and the courts. They have no fear of repercussions. But if Guatemala were a member of the F.O.N. and those abuses continued, the friends of the victims could come to the F.O.N., and the F.O.N. would have the organization and the power to investigate, prosecute, and punish the individual policemen or national guardsmen and government officials responsible. Then these killings would largely stop. The craven murderers would slither back under their rocks. The need for rebellion would be over. The cycle of violence would be broken.

As the example of Guatemala suggests, though, enforcing human rights will do more than just prevent civil wars. It will also give the F.O.N. a magical tool to guarantee legitimate and just national and local governments for its member nations—and to guarantee that without in any way interfering with the right of a nation to determine its own government.

The key to this process is the following clause in the F.O.N. constitution:

Article I, Section 6
Provision 30. Any person convicted of violating a felony

statute of Federation of Nations, national, or local laws may, at the Federation of Nations president's discretion or as specified by Federation of Nations law, be removed from, and permanently barred from holding, office in the Federation of Nations government or military forces, or in the national or local governments of member nations, or in national guard or police forces of member nations. Felony statutes for the purposes of this provision and other provisions of this constitution shall be defined by the legislature, but may be any statutes of the Federation of Nations government or of national or local governments.

Using this clause in conjunction with the bill of rights will allow the F.O.N. to overthrow a dictator without spilling a drop of blood and without ever assuming responsibility for governing the nation. To overthrow a dictator, all the F.O.N. will have to do is prosecute him in F.O.N. courts for his crimes. Upon conviction, he will be removed from office. That's it. The dictatorship will be over. It wouldn't even matter how the new government is selected. The dictator could even be allowed to appoint his own successor, because if the new leader or new government he appointed were no improvement, the F.O.N. could and would just continue to prosecute people until a government formed that would obey the law.

This technique of simply prosecuting criminals and removing them from office will end or prevent the vast majority of all cases of civil war and violent rebellion. It will be both the best way to prevent civil wars from occurring and the best way to end them when they do occur. Equally important, it will allow the F.O.N., without ever taking a political position or interfering with a nation's right to self-determination, to guarantee that all member nations' governments respect human rights.

A Government of the People

Implicit in the previous discussion is the idea that F.O.N. laws apply to individuals and that the F.O.N. has the right to try and to punish individuals for violating its laws. That may seem like an obvious necessity—after all, that's the way every government works—but there is an alternative way for an international government to work that is likely to be suggested:

Its laws and powers could apply to national governments instead of to individuals. That is essentially the way the United Nations works. To the extent that the U.N. has any powers at all, those powers are over governments rather than over individuals.

If all F.O.N. laws applied to governments instead of to individuals, how would they be enforced? What would happen when a government violated the laws? Obviously it would have to be punished, but how do you punish a government? You can't throw it in jail. You can only throw people in jail. Of course, I suppose you could indiscriminately jail every government official, but that would obviously mean punishing the innocent along with the guilty, and such an injustice would probably do more harm than good. It would also amount to violating the human rights we are supposedly trying to protect. Moreover, it would leave the nation without a government.

(At this point some might suggest that you could selectively punish only those specific government officials who are responsible for violating the F.O.N. law. To which I reply, yes, that is exactly what I am arguing for, because if you do that, you are applying the law to individuals rather than to governments. But if you are going to apply the law to individuals, you should apply it to all individuals, not just to government officials. Private citizens can commit crimes, too. Moreover, government officials should not be able to escape prosecution just by leaving office.)

Since prison will not be a feasible punishment against entire governments, the other logical punishment to consider is fines. But as a punishment for governments rather than individuals, fines turn out to be just as ineffective and counterproductive as prison. Any fine against a government would only be passed on to its citizens in higher taxes.

Neither of the two standard means of criminal punishment, jail and fines, can work when laws apply to governments instead of individuals. Only one punishment can work in that situation. The F.O.N. would have to overthrow the government. But that would almost certainly require a military action, meaning it would cause the deaths of many F.O.N. soldiers and other innocent persons. Then it would require the F.O.N. to assume the burden of governing the nation until a new government could be selected—at least temporarily denying the nation its right to self-determination. All of which adds up to a fine formula for creating resentment: Kill innocent people and then dictate to the survivors what government they should have.

In other words, applying F.O.N. laws to governments rather than to individuals would be an unmitigated disaster. Just as we determined in the last chapter that the F.O.N. must *derive* its power from the people rather than from governments, it also must *apply* its power to people rather than to governments. It must be a government of the people, not a government of governments.

Use of the Military

We have now accomplished the first goal to be discussed in this chapter, which is to minimize the incidence of civil war and minimize the need of the F.O.N. to use military force in its member nations. But violence in member nations will still occur, and sometimes it may still be necessary to use the F.O.N. military to quell that violence. That is a very dangerous scenario. Though there may sometimes be legitimate reasons to use the F.O.N. military in member nations, when we allow the military to be used in member nations, we open up the possibility that it will be used unjustly. It could be used to crush a legitimate rebellion against oppression, or it could be used to overthrow a legitimate national government and install a puppet government in its place. No one in his right mind is going to vote for his country to join the F.O.N. unless we can insure that neither of those unjust military actions can occur.

The way to insure that is very simple. Just require approval from the democratically elected representatives of a member nation before the F.O.N. military can be used in that particular member nation. The wishes of the F.O.N. president and F.O.N. delegates from all other nations should not matter. The F.O.N. representatives from a particular nation must have veto power over any use of the F.O.N. military in their own nation.

By this simple provision, since democratically elected representatives will reasonably reflect the wishes of their countrymen, we guarantee that the F.O.N. military could never be used either to crush a legitimate popular rebellion or to overthrow a legitimate government.

Now, before I present the section of the constitution giving the F.O.N. representatives from a particular nation this power to veto military actions in their own nation, I should explain two other provisions included in that section. These two provisions represent a balance between two competing concerns. First, while a nation's representatives must have veto power over the use of the military in their own nation, in general the F.O.N. military must function as a single unit and must be controlled by the full F.O.N., not divided up into pieces, with each piece to be controlled by a particular member nation's representatives. Otherwise the F.O.N. would be a crippled giant, moving in a thousand directions at once and thus no direction at all. But on the other hand, if we require every military action to be approved by the full F.O.N. legislature, we leave open the danger that the F.O.N. will refuse to act when it should be required to act, will default on its duty to help a member nation maintain its internal peace. (I remind you again that the member nations will be without their own militaries and thus will sometimes depend on the F.O.N. military for their internal peace.)

The compromise I have chosen between these two concerns is to allow two paths for dictating a military action in a member nation: approval by a majority of all F.O.N. delegates and a simple majority of the delegates from the nation concerned, or just approval by three-quarters of the delegates from the nation concerned, regardless of voting by delegates from other nations.

Article II, Section 4

Provision 4. Except in pursuance of a legally declared war against a nonmember nation, and except for use of the military in law enforcement under Provision 8, and except for military actions authorized under Provision 5, use of the Federation of Nations military in a particular member nation for anything other than routine training shall require the approval in a recorded vote in both legislative houses of a majority of the legislators from that particular nation and a majority of all legislators present in that house. Provisions enacted in this manner may be vetoed by the president, whose veto can then be overridden by a two-thirds vote of all the legislators present in each legislative house and, again, a simple majority of the legislators in each legislative house from the nation concerned.

Provision 5. Alternatively, a military action in a member

nation may be dictated simply by a three-quarters vote in both legislative houses of all legislators from that particular member nation, regardless of voting by legislators from other nations. Provisions enacted in this manner may not be vetoed by the president and must be faithfully executed by the president and the military with all reasonable force available to them.

Finally, we have to turn our attention to simple law enforcement, because allowing F.O.N. representatives from a particular nation to veto all military actions in their own nation could interfere with law enforcement.

The easiest way to imagine this interfering with law enforcement is to imagine what could happen if the F.O.N. needs to arrest the president of a member nation for violations of F.O.N. laws. A president is likely to have a fairly large police force or national guard at his disposal, so if he chooses to resist arrest it may take more than just a few officers with guns to apprehend him; it may take the F.O.N. military. But if this president happens to be popular with his countrymen, the F.O.N. representatives from his nation would probably refuse to authorize the military action needed to arrest him. Under the constitutional provisions just discussed, giving the representatives from a particular nation the right to veto military actions in their own nation, that would be the end of the matter. The military action would be blocked and this president would go free. Obviously that cannot be allowed. No person, whether popular or not, can be above the law. So I have put the following provision in my proposed F.O.N. constitution:

> Article II, Section 4
> Provision 8. The president and his executive branch officers may use any force available to them, including the Federation of Nations military, for the limited purpose of apprehending specific persons, named in advance in legally obtained warrants, for questioning or arrest in connection with accused Federation of Nations crimes or in connection with extradition orders issued by a Federation of Nations court.

Notice that by no means is this a blank check for the executive branch to launch indiscriminate attacks whenever it pleases. The only military action it authorizes is a very narrow one—capturing specific persons, named in advance, who are reasonably suspected of committing crimes or of having information about crimes. It does not interfere with the other limitations on military actions discussed in this book. In particular, it does not interfere with the right of a nation's representatives to control peace-keeping missions and any other ordinary military missions in their own country. It only states that the F.O.N. will not be intimidated by mere physical force. It only states that the F.O.N. is prepared to enforce its laws.*

---

*Other constitutional provisions that pertain to keeping the peace within the member nations but that are not discussed in this chapter are the provisions of Article V, Section 5, printed in Appendix A and discussed in Appendix B.

and good governance isn't enough; we need to show that it will increase power and security—both for the F.O.N. as a whole and for each and every member nation.

That the F.O.N. will be more powerful than any one member nation could be independently was discussed somewhat in Chapter 2, where it was pointed out that the F.O.N. would have a larger population, more natural resources, a larger industrial capacity and one more stable to swings in the economy, and a larger pool of scientific and technical talent than any of its member nations could have independently. In other words, the F.O.N. will be bigger than any one member nation and so will be more powerful than any one member nation. But the F.O.N.'s increased power is caused by more than just its bigness. An equally important contributor to the F.O.N.'s increased power is the factor of cooperation. Not only will the F.O.N. have a larger pool of scientists, but those scientists from different nations will, in the F.O.N., be able to cooperate rather than compete in developing weapons and technologies. The nuclear deterrent of the F.O.N. will need to be no larger than that for just one independent nation, yet the cost can be shared among all member nations, thus freeing resources that will increase the society's power in other ways. Likewise, the F.O.N. will need fewer soldiers than its member nations would cumulatively need if they were independent, thus freeing for society not only the resources that would otherwise have been needed to pay and support those soldiers, but also the talents of those soldiers who are no longer needed. Finally, the cooperation involved in fusing the national militaries will create an internal peace that will enormously increase the organization's external power—having fused their militaries, the member nations will no longer be wasting their military power directing it against each other. So not only will the F.O.N.'s power be larger than the power of any one member nation, but because of the effects of this cooperation, it will be significantly larger than even the sum of the power held by all its member nations independently.

It is not enough, however, for the F.O.N. as a whole to be more powerful than any individual member nation could be. Every member nation must feel that it, individually, is more powerful and more secure as a member of the F.O.N. than as an independent nation. That will be the litmus test nations will use in deciding whether to join or not.

Fortunately, the F.O.N. will indeed increase the power and security of every member nation. First, as we just saw, because of the effects of cooperation, the total power of a group of nations will increase upon their banding together to form the F.O.N. This means that, in theory at least, the proportionate share of power held by each nation individually also will increase upon its joining the F.O.N. But that is just one way that joining the F.O.N. will increase a nation's power and security—and probably the least important way. Basically, that analysis covers just one component of power—offensive power, and specifically just offensive military power. Where the F.O.N. will really improve a member nation's position is in defensive power—national security, that is—and in nonmilitary means of exerting offensive power.

National Security

Joining the F.O.N. will increase a nation's security in at least three ways. The first way is that it will eliminate the F.O.N. and its member nations as potential attackers. Like any other independent society in the world, the F.O.N. will reserve the right to use military force to accomplish its goals. As a nonmember nation, therefore, you do run a certain risk of being attacked by the F.O.N. When you join the F.O.N., though, you eliminate that risk. After having joined the F.O.N., you no longer have any risk that the other F.O.N. member nations could attack you because, like you, they have surrendered their militaries to be integrated into the single F.O.N. military, and thus no longer control any military forces with which to attack anyone. And after having joined the F.O.N., you no longer have any risk that the F.O.N. itself will attack you, because the F.O.N. would have no reason to attack one of its members. After all, in essence the F.O.N. would already militarily occupy its member nations, just as the United States militarily occupies its states, and would be able to control their behavior, in matters of international interest, with its laws. Furthermore, as the last chapter discussed, the representatives from a particular nation will have veto power over military actions in their own nation and would be able to block any type of an F.O.N. "attack" against their nation and any type of military oppression.

The next way that joining the F.O.N. will increase a nation's security is that it will make nonmember nations much less likely to attack that nation. After a nation joins the F.O.N., when nonmember nations consider whether to attack that nation, they will face the prospect of fighting a war against the entire F.O.N. military force, rather than against just the military force of that one nation. It stands to reason, therefore, that they are not going to be as eager to initiate a war.

However, I must point out that for this type of deterrence to work, for nonmember nations to be deterred from attacking F.O.N. member nations, it must be quite clear to those nonmember nations that all of the F.O.N.'s great cumulative military power will be used to defend each and every member nation. That is a very important point, and I think it is a potential problem. It is easy to imagine that if the F.O.N. contained several of the most powerful nations and several tiny Third World nations, it might use some of its smaller members as bargaining chips, or might choose not to make a "major diplomatic incident" of an attack on a less powerful member.

For any nation to be expected to voluntarily join the F.O.N. and give up control of its military, it must have absolute assurance that if it is attacked, the F.O.N. will use all available resources and wage an all-out war to defend the country, just as the nation itself would do if it still controlled its military.

We need to put a clause in the constitution guaranteeing that, and we need to give it teeth. Nations must be assured that if for some reason the F.O.N. does not immediately move to defend a threatened member, then the F.O.N. representatives of that nation will be able to force it to. To fulfill that requirement, I have chosen to use the constitutional provision discussed in the last chapter whereby three-quarters of the legislators from a particular nation could force the F.O.N. to carry out a military action in their own nation. In that way, if a nation is attacked or if its legislators believe it is about to be attacked, those legislators will be able to order the F.O.N. military to defend it. The nation would not depend on the F.O.N. president or on legislators from foreign countries.

> Article II, Section 4
> Provision 5. ...a military action in a member nation may be dictated simply by a three-quarters vote in both legislative

houses of all legislators from that particular member nation, regardless of voting by legislators from other nations. Provisions enacted in this manner may not be vetoed by the president and must be faithfully executed by the president and the military with all reasonable force available to them.

But to really make sure this constitutional provision is obeyed and that any ordered military actions are faithfully carried out, I have added another provision to the constitution.

Article II, Section 4

Provision 6. If, 48 hours or more following a vote dictating a military action in a member nation under Provision 5, three-quarters of the senators from the nation concerned and three-quarters of the representatives from the nation concerned believe that that directive has not been fully carried out under the requirements of Provision 5 by the president, his executive branch officers, and the military forces, those legislators shall receive an immediate hearing before the Supreme Court, at which hearing the Court shall expeditiously decide whether the requirements of Provision 5 have been fully carried out by the executive branch and the military forces. If the Court finds that they have not been fully carried out, the group of legislators petitioning the Court shall have the right at that time to replace any and every official in the executive branch and the military who they feel bears responsibility for the failure to carry out the requirements of Provision 5, including, if they wish, the president. The executive branch and military officials appointed in this manner shall hold office for one year, after which time the positions shall again be subject to normal selection procedures.

It is very important that we be able to guarantee to any member nation that it absolutely will be defended against any attack. This provision guarantees that. It puts teeth into the guarantees of provision 5 that the legislators of a particular nation will be able to order military actions in their own nation.

Notice that in Provision 6 there is no burden of proof to "convict" specific executive branch and military officials before they can be replaced. The only thing that must be demonstrated to the court is that the ordered military action was not faithfully carried out. After that, nothing matters except that the situation be corrected *immediately*. If doing that means sacrificing the careers of a few honest officials, so be it. The political careers of a few individuals are of no consequence in comparison to the existence and security of a member nation.

Another important point to notice about these provisions is that they only give the legislators from a particular nation the right to order a military action *within the borders of their own nation.* The legislators cannot order the F.O.N. to attack a nonmember nation. All they can do is order the F.O.N. to defend their own nation.

Notice also the use of the word "reasonable" in Provision 5. That is to indicate that while the F.O.N. must defend its members, that doesn't mean it has to launch Armageddon. Choosing to surrender a member nation's territory rather than use nuclear weapons would not be a violation of this clause if all reasonable military effort had been made to defend or recapture the territory. Likewise, the wording of the clause is meant to recognize and allow for the idea that the F.O.N. may simultaneously be under attack elsewhere or may somehow be strategically limited in its ability to defend the member nation. If F.O.N. troops are already in combat defending another threatened F.O.N. territory, I would not expect the F.O.N. to be required to move all of those troops.

But, I should add, if F.O.N. troops are engaged in war *outside* of F.O.N. territory, especially in a war of F.O.N. aggression, that would be no excuse for not redeploying those troops to defend a threatened member nation.

I should also add parenthetically here that I do not expect Provision 5 to ever be used. Merely its presence in the constitution, and the threat of its being used, should be enough to induce office holders to perform their duty of defending member nations.

Thus, this basis for national security—that countries which wish to attack you will be deterred by your evident capacity to resist—will also be strengthened by joining the F.O.N. It will certainly be evident that F.O.N. power is greater than the power the nation could have mustered independently. And these clauses of the constitution should make it evident to any enemy that all of the F.O.N.'s power will be used to defend every member nation.

Finally, the last and most obvious way that joining the F.O.N. will improve a nation's security is that if for some reason that nation has to fight a war, it will be a lot more likely to win the war if it has fighting for it the enormous military power of the Federation of Nations—comprising the cumulative military force of all member nations—than if it has to fight the war with just its own national military.

In at least three ways, joining the F.O.N. will very significantly increase any nation's security. First, it will eliminate any danger of war with the F.O.N. and its member nations. Second, it will deter other nations from attacking because those nations will see that attacking will mean a war with the entire F.O.N. military force rather than with just one nation's military force. And third, if despite those first two factors it is still attacked, it will be much more likely to win the war when it has the entire F.O.N. military force on its side.

Boycotts and Embargoes

Up to this point, the only tool I have talked about for exerting power is military force. Although I have discussed several other contributors to national power, such as education and the economy, these are not, for the most part, tools for exerting power in themselves. They are important in this context primarily because they support and create military power. This book, in other words, has revolved around military power. The reason for that is that until now military power has been the primary way nations have exerted power over other nations. But this era of military might being the primary way to exert power is about to end. The Federation of Nations will have a new, bloodless, yet very effective tool for exerting its power over other societies. And, basically, that tool will be available only to the F.O.N. and not to independent nations. That tool is economic coercion—boycotts and embargoes (Art. I, Sec. 6, Prov. 15).

My assertion here that economic coercion will be an effective way to exercise power may surprise some people, because economic coercion has had a few well-publicized failures lately and has begun to get a bad reputation as a way to pursue policy goals. The U.S. grain embargo of the Soviet Union, for instance, used as retribution for invading Afghanistan, barely even inconvenienced the Soviets, who just bought from other nations, but was a major economic hardship on some American farmers. U.S. economic sanctions against Panama in 1988 and 1989 also appeared to fail in that, while they succeeded in destroying Panama's economy, they did not succeed in ousting its dictator, Manuel Noriega. Likewise, the various half-hearted international sanctions against South Africa failed for years to end apartheid. And because the U.S. has not gotten full European cooperation for embargoes against Iran and Libya for terrorism (and because the U.S. has not even obeyed its own embargo policies in those cases), those embargoes also have failed—in fact, they have had no perceptible effect at all.

But economic sanctions can work. The basic causes of the failures listed above are either a failure to fully carry out the embargo or a lack of cooperation among enough nations. Obviously, if you have something another nation truly needs and you withhold it from them, they have to deal with you. That doesn't mean they will come crawling on their knees, begging for mercy—pride dictates that they will not—but they will be in a more cooperative mood for negotiations. For instance, in response to U.S. sanctions, Manuel Noriega did offer to relinquish power and leave Panama. But he asked that charges of drug dealing against him in U.S. courts be dropped, and the U.S. refused. Perhaps that refusal was justified, but my point is that sanctions did bring Noriega to the negotiating table and would have worked to achieve the major policy goal of removing Noriega from office if the U.S. had chosen to negotiate.

For another case of successful economic sanctions, we could consider South Africa's sanctions against the West. That's right, South Africa's sanctions. South Africa is the major supplier of several strategic metals for the Western democracies, and it is because the Western democracies were afraid of losing that supply that they never imposed much more than token sanctions on South Africa. By the threat of an embargo, South Africa has successfully controlled our policy.

Economic sanctions can work. The problem is that they usually require complete cooperation of several nations, and that can virtually never be achieved among independent nations. The F.O.N., though, can legislate it. If a majority of member nations would like to stop all trade with South Africa, they could force the remaining member nations to go along with them. With an F.O.N., you wouldn't need to get the cooperation of every party in an economic boycott; you would only need the agreement of a majority of F.O.N. representatives. For the F.O.N., economic boycotts would be a viable tool for exerting power—and virtually an entirely new tool, available only to the F.O.N. and not to independent nations.

Initially, when the F.O.N. is first formed and has relatively few members, economic coercion would not be an especially powerful weapon—not much more powerful than it is for most independent nations. Since F.O.N. members could legislate the cooperation of other members with their boycotts, boycotts would still be a more powerful tool for them as members than if they were nonmembers. But since an F.O.N. of only a few members would probably lack a monopoly of any of the natural resources it might like to withhold from its enemies, and since it would lack the overwhelming economic power needed to make most boycotts effective, it would be limited in its ability to use economic coercion on its own. It would usually need to get some nonmember nations to join its boycotts also.

However, when the F.O.N. grows and has maybe a third or more of the world's nations as members, economic coercion would become a devastating weapon for it. With that kind of economic power, merely by refusing to buy the major export of some nonmember nation, it could bring that nation to economic ruin. And when the F.O.N. comes to contain a majority of the world's nations, population, and economic power, *it would perhaps never again need to use military aggression*. It could always accomplish its foreign policy goals very easily and efficiently with boycotts, embargoes, and economic coercion.

The advantages of economic coercion as a means of exerting power, it should be pointed out, go well beyond the fact that it saves lives. It also saves money, and it also will be a far more effective way to exercise power than war will be. The reason it will save money, despite the fact that a boycott or embargo does have some economic cost, is that it's a lot cheaper to pay the few law enforcement officials needed to enforce a boycott or embargo than to pay the thousands or millions of soldiers needed to accomplish the same foreign policy goal by military aggression.

And badges for those few law enforcement officials cost a lot less than aircraft carriers and B1 bombers. Plus, after the boycott is over, you save money by not having to pay all those grave diggers that you need after a war.

The reason economic coercion will be a more effective way to exert power than war is basically that economic coercion can be used much more freely and often. Even if we ignore the moral problems of military aggression, we cannot ignore the many practical problems. Military aggression will nearly always condemn us in the court of world opinion; it will solidify our enemy's resolve; it will probably cause political problems at home, especially if casualties are heavy or a military draft is required; and most important, military aggression in this era will always run the terrible risk that it could lead to nuclear retaliation. Boycotts and embargoes, though, suffer much less from those problems. In particular, they will rarely be condemned as immoral, certainly much less often than war will be, and they will run almost no risk of inducing a nuclear retaliation.

Safeguards for Boycotts and Embargoes

Boycotts and embargoes will be tremendous tools for the F.O.N. But there are some potential problems with their use, and safeguards are needed. First, obviously, any boycotts or embargoes must apply to all F.O.N. members (as must all F.O.N. laws). You cannot have the rest of the F.O.N. members pass a law saying, "The United States is forbidden to sell wheat to Iran." It would have to say, "All F.O.N. member nations are forbidden to sell wheat to Iran."

Even embargoes and boycotts that apply uniformly to all F.O.N. nations, though, could unfairly burden particular members. Take, for example, if the F.O.N. refused to sell tin to some nonmember nation. Well, there are very few countries in the world that export significant amounts of tin (Bolivia and Malaysia together produce more than 50% of the world supply), and for those few countries, tin is their major source of revenue. So, while the law banning the export of tin would apply uniformly to all F.O.N. members, it would only affect a handful of them, and for that handful the embargo could be economically devastating. Therefore, the constitution needs a clause to guard against the burden of an embargo or boycott falling unfairly on only one or a few members.

I propose:

Article I, Section 6
   Provision 21. A majority of the Federation of Nations senators or representatives of any member nation may file a lawsuit in Federation of Nations courts that legislation for an economic boycott or embargo unfairly burdens their nation relative to other Federation of Nations member nations without adequate compensation. If the court finds this to be true, it shall strike down the legislation.

I would hope that under this clause the tin embargo discussed above, for example, would be declared unconstitutional. But I have included the words "without adequate compensation" so the F.O.N. will not be unduly restrained from using embargoes and boycotts. Thus, the F.O.N. could use a tin embargo if it made payments to the tin-producing member nations so that the economic burden of the embargo fell about equally on all member nations (Art. I, Sec. 6, Prov. 20).

Next arises the question of whether the F.O.N. should be allowed to use embargoes and boycotts against member nations as well as nonmembers.

One of the principles that needs to be observed in designing the Federation of Nations is that member nations must have special advantages and privileges over nonmembers. Nations should always see a clear advantage to joining the F.O.N. (or not withdrawing from it), regardless of their circumstances or the politics of their governments.

That means, at the least, it must be more difficult to use economic coercion against members than against nonmembers. One option, then, would be just to constitutionally ban economic coercion used against a member nation. The F.O.N. could survive without this tool because it could ensure tolerable behavior from the national governments of its members just by enforcing F.O.N. laws on the individuals in those governments.

But I tend to favor, with one strict limitation, allowing the F.O.N. to use embargoes and boycotts against its members. The one strict limitation is that the embargo or boycott would have to be approved by a majority of the F.O.N. representatives of the nation to be victimized (Art. I, Sec. 6, Prov. 19). That would appear to be an adequate safeguard. It means that for an embargo or boycott to be approved against a member nation's government, that government would have to be opposed by almost all its citizens. Also, that safeguard, in that it grants a veto power to members that is not available to nonmembers, provides the clear advantage for members over nonmembers that we need.

Power Over Other Member Nations

National power has been defined here as the ability of a nation to influence or control the behavior of other nations. And I have said that the F.O.N. will increase the power of its member nations in that it will improve their ability to influence or control nonmember nations. You may be realizing, though, that this ability only encompasses part of the definition of power. An F.O.N. member nation would like to influence not just nonmember nations, but also other member nations.

Well, obviously we cannot promise, and would not want to promise, member nations the right to completely control other member nations. What we can promise, though, is that as members of the F.O.N., they can participate in controlling or restraining *certain aspects* of the behavior of their fellow member nations. In exchange for this, they will give up some control over those aspects of their own behavior. As was explained in chapter 3, that is the trade-off of government, the exchange that is made when we leave the state of anarchy.

In this way, a member nation has a certain power over other member nations. And obviously, only by joining the F.O.N. is a nation allowed to participate in this type of power over the other F.O.N. member nations. Thus, joining the F.O.N. not only increases a nation's power and influence over nonmember nations, but also over member nations.

Now, since this power over other member nations is limited to only some aspects of their behavior, we should review what those aspects are. In what aspects should a nation give up some control over its own behavior in exchange for some control over the behavior of others? We have so far specified three. The first is the right to attack other nations. Just as when individuals initially join together in a government of some sort, the first right they give up is the right to freely murder each other, so when nations initially join together in the Federation of Nations the first right they will give up is the right to freely attack each other. This means that nations will give up control of their militaries to the F.O.N. They will thus lose the ability to attack other F.O.N. nations but will gain the ability to prevent those nations from attacking them.

The second aspect of behavior in which I have advocated that member nations should accept some loss of sovereignty over their own behavior in exchange for gaining some power over the behavior of others is in the area of human rights. The F.O.N. should guarantee certain human rights. Thus, the member nations will lose the sovereignty they currently have that allows them to violate human rights at will, but will gain the power to prevent other member nations from violating human rights.

The third place where I am advocating that nations should give up partial control of their own behavior in exchange for partial control over the behavior of others is in the enforcement of boycotts and embargoes. In making this trade-off, a nation will occasionally lose a few dollars by being forced to join a boycott that it would rather not, but it will gain a tremendous tool for exerting power in foreign policy and over the course of time will save thousands or millions of lives by using economic coercion rather than war to accomplish its goals. Seems like a good trade-off to me.

Summary of Chapter 7

- Power and security are the dominant concerns of every national government. The litmus test by which every nation will decide whether to join the F.O.N. is, Will the F.O.N. increase the power and security of our particular nation?

- Because of its larger population, greater natural resources, and larger industrial capacity, the F.O.N. as a whole will be more powerful than any one member nation could be independently. But more than that, because the member nations will be cooperating and sharing costs rather than competing, and will have fused their militaries rather than wastefully directing military power against each other, the F.O.N. will not only be more powerful than any one member nation, but will be more powerful than even the sum of its member nations independently. The cumulative power of member nations will thus increase upon their banding together to form the F.O.N. This means that the proportionate share of power held by each member nation will also increase. This additional power translates into greater influence and control over nonmember nations.

- As for a nation's influence and control over other member nations, this too will increase upon a nation's joining the F.O.N. In joining the F.O.N., a nation will gain the ability to participate in enacting F.O.N. laws and thus will gain the ability to control those aspects of the other member nations' behavior that are of international concern.

- The more important part of national power, though, is not the ability to control other nations, but rather the ability to prevent those other nations from controlling you, the ability to protect national security. Joining the F.O.N. will enormously increase a nation's security in that when a member nation is attacked, it will have the force of the entire F.O.N. to defend it, a force that is vastly more powerful than the force the nation could have mustered on its own as an independent nation.

- It is preferable, though, to avoid attack entirely. The best foundation for national security is that other nations either do not wish to attack you or are not able to attack you. Joining the F.O.N. will strengthen for a given nation this basis of national security because in joining the F.O.N. a nation will entirely eliminate the F.O.N. and the other member nations as potential attackers.

- The second best foundation for national security is that even if another nation wishes to attack you, it will be deterred by your evident capacity to resist. To strengthen for its member nations this basis of national security, not only must the great power of the F.O.N. be evident, which of course it will be, but it must also be evident to all potential enemies that all of that great power will be used to defend each and every member nation. To insure this, a clause in the constitution should specify that the executive branch and military must use all available power to defend each member nation against any type of attack or threat. And that clause must be very easily enforced.

- Perhaps the most important way in which the F.O.N. will increase the power of its member nations is by giving them a new and, I expect, very effective tool for exercising power that is essentially not available to independent nations. That tool is economic coercion—boycotts and embargoes.

- Boycotts and embargoes, though, can be effective tools for the F.O.N. only if compliance can be legislated and enforced over all member nations, including those that would not otherwise wish to participate. That entails, of course, a loss of sovereignty for member nations. They will occasionally be forced to join a boycott or embargo that they would prefer not to. But this is a small price to pay for the increased power over nonmember nations this tool will give them and for the enormous savings in money and lives they will receive from using economic coercion rather than war to achieve foreign policy goals.

- When the F.O.N. contains a majority of the world's nations, population, and economic power, economic coercion will have become such a powerful tool that the F.O.N. may never again need, or want, to use war to achieve its foreign policy goals.

Chapter 8

Money Makes the World Go 'Round

Most of the book so far has been devoted to arguing that the F.O.N. would satisfy a nation's desires for power and national security, desires that are the biggest determinants of the behavior of nations. But you may have noticed another factor that tends to motivate both nations and individuals: money. I turn my attention now to that.

The basic question posed by this chapter is, Can the F.O.N. improve the economic condition of its member nations? The answer is yes. As for HOW the F.O.N. can do this, the answer is that *it can do it best by simply saving money for its member nations and their taxpayers.* It should not do it by regulating the economy, nor by redistributing wealth between nations, nor by redistributing wealth between citizens, nor by promoting capitalism, nor by promoting socialism, nor by doing a lot of other things people might suggest it should do.

Let's examine some of those possible suggestions. First, some will surely say that the F.O.N. should redistribute wealth from the richer nations to the poorer ones. To address that, I must first reiterate that we need to induce nations to join the F.O.N. The F.O.N. will not exist at all if nations do not freely choose to join it and to remain members out of their own sense of self-interest. Moreover, for the F.O.N. to work best, to provide the greatest benefits to its member nations in bringing them peace, national power, national security, and the economic and environmental benefits to be discussed, it should have as many member nations as possible.

This means that we cannot ask the rich nations to make economic sacrifices to benefit the poor nations, because if we do, the rich nations will not join: It wouldn't be in their economic self-interest. The U.S. cannot be asked to bear the burden of Mexico's overpopulation and foreign debt.

We should distinguish what we are talking about when we say "redistributing wealth between nations." If we mean *really* redistributing wealth between nations, insuring that every nation has about the same standard of living, then it is immediately clear that the idea is completely impracticable. The rich nations would never consent to that and would never join an organization that had that as its goal. If we are talking about smaller amounts of investment from the rich nations just to supply capital and help prime the pump of economic development in the poor nations, then the idea seems more feasible. But it is not at all clear that this level of aid needs to be, or should be, coerced by an international government. The developed nations already provide aid to the poor nations. They do this for humanitarian reasons and because the economic development of the poor nations is actually in the interest of the richer nations. The poor nations must develop if they are to buy the rich nations' goods, and the rich nations want to sell their goods. Even without coercion by the F.O.N., then, the rich nations can be counted on to send some aid to the poorer nations. Nonetheless, it might seem desirable for the F.O.N. to increase the amount of this aid. But the moment we pass from voluntary aid to coerced aid, we make it less likely the rich nations will join. Coerced aid means we are forcing the rich nations to give more than they want to. They aren't going to like that and when that happens they will be less likely to join the F.O.N. That isn't in the interest of the F.O.N., and it really isn't in the interest of the poorer nations.

It is very much in the interest of poor nations to have as many rich nations as possible as members of the F.O.N. This is so, first, because the rich nations hold the power, so in order to have a strong military defense, the poor nations need rich nations to join them in the F.O.N. It is also so because, just in general, the larger the F.O.N. is, that is, the more member nations it has (be they rich or poor), the greater the benefits the F.O.N. will provide for those members. A larger organization means greater financial savings on military defense; it means more control over worldwide pollution; and it means a more powerful organization with greater control over nonmember nations. But from the standpoint of improving the welfare of poor nations, the most important benefit of attracting rich nations into the F.O.N. is that this means the rich nations will no longer control individual militaries and so will no longer be able to attack and exploit the poor nations.

There are three causes of the extreme disparity of wealth we see between the nations today: (1) the fact that different nations adopted industrialization and capitalism at different times, (2) the explosive population growth of the Third World nations, and (3) exploitive power relations between the nations. The first factor is a historical fact that should fade in importance as time goes by. That is, it *will* fade in importance as long as the other two factors are taken care of. But the other two factors must be taken care of first. The second factor, explosive population growth, is entirely under the control of the nations themselves. If the Third World nations choose not to get their populations under control, they have no one to blame but themselves. And the third factor, exploitive power relations, will be eliminated by the F.O.N. That is, it will be eliminated by the F.O.N. if the F.O.N. is able to attract a significant number of rich nations to join.

The most important factor in the economic development of Third World nations is that they reduce their populations— something that they have complete control over. The second most important factor is that they no longer be attacked and controlled by the rich nations. If Guatemala is ever to develop, the United States has to stop installing and supporting military dictatorships in Guatemala. Guatemala has to be allowed to develop a democratic and responsible government that will pursue the interests of Guatemala instead of the interests of the United States.

The most important contribution of the F.O.N. to Third World development, and the most important contribution that could be made to Third World development, is that it will end these exploitive power relations. The United States will no longer control an independent military with which to install governments in Guatemala. If the United States does somehow try to overthrow the Guatemalan government or intervene in Guatemala's affairs, Guatemala's government or citizens will be able to have the individuals responsible in the United States arrested and tried in F.O.N. courts. Furthermore, to the extent that tyrannical and corrupt governments in the Third World stand on their own, without the intervention of the rich nations, they will be brought down by the F.O.N.'s human rights laws.

This is the most important contribution to Third World development that could be made by outsiders, and the F.O.N. will make it. (The most important contribution that could be made by insiders is to reduce the Third World population.) While directly redistributing wealth from the rich nations to the poor would also help speed the equalization of wealth in the world, it is a much smaller factor than the first two factors discussed here—the ending of exploitive power relations between the nations and the reduction of population—and it will accomplish nothing until those first two factors are taken care of. Furthermore, direct redistribution of wealth will tend to reduce the number of rich nations that join the F.O.N. and will thus interfere with the F.O.N.'s achievement of the much more important goal of ending the exploitation of the poor nations by the rich.

Thus, in my proposed constitution, deliberate redistribution of wealth between nations will not be allowed.*

Next, some are likely to suggest that the F.O.N. should adopt

---

*The relevant constitutional clauses here are the provisions concerning taxes, which will be discussed later in this chapter, and Article I, Section 7, Provision 1, which says that "no payments shall be made to nations, organizations, or individuals that are not in exchange for goods or services rendered, except for compensatory payments to nations authorized under Article I, Section 6, Provision 20 [compensatory payments for bearing a disproportionate share of an F.O.N. embargo]..."

the powers of the welfare state and guarantee for all its citizens some minimal standard of living and perhaps some basic health care. But I think it is fairly clear that this would be a bad idea. For one thing, what is poor in one society is not necessarily poor in another, and so it would be impossible for the F.O.N. to apply the same minimal standard of living to all its member nations. An income in the United States that would consign you to abject poverty, unable to even afford food and shelter, would in many Third World nations almost allow you to live like a king. So different minimal standards would be necessary in different nations. Given that fact, doesn't it make sense that the nations themselves, being more familiar with their own economic realities and cultural norms, should be the ones to set those standards?

Of course, it might be true that some nations won't be able, on their own, to guarantee a decent minimal standard of living for all their citizens. Some nations have so little total wealth that even if they distributed it exactly evenly this might only mean that everyone would be unacceptably poor. For those nations it might seem that the F.O.N. should intervene. But in that case what we are talking about is not really redistributing wealth between citizens but rather between nations. And again, redistributing wealth between nations cannot be a purpose of the F.O.N., because if it is, the rich nations won't join.

The ultimate argument, though, against insuring a minimal standard of living for all citizens in the F.O.N. is just that, with almost six billion people, there isn't enough money or food in the world to do that. If we really attempted to do that, it would only result in impoverishing us all. The demands made on the wealthy nations would be so large that there is no chance any wealthy nation would join the organization.

Furthermore, if we were to grant the F.O.N. the power to redistribute wealth between nations and individuals, we would have to grant it certain other powers too—powers that the poor nations and poor individuals might not be so eager to grant it, and powers that in any case the F.O.N. should not have. If the F.O.N. is to be saddled with paying the bill for poverty, then it will certainly insist, and rightfully so, that it must have the powers necessary for reducing poverty. It must have first the power to regulate almost all types of economic activity. It will insist on the power to regulate the relations of labor and management, to fund economic development projects, to regulate economic competition, to regulate and subsidize agriculture, determining what crops farmers in different nations should grow, to abolish national tariffs, or perhaps even to enact national tariffs against the will of the nations in which they are enacted, and so on. Most important, though, the F.O.N. will have to have the power to legislate mandatory sterilization in Third World nations. If it is to pay the bill for poverty in the Third World, then it must have the power to put an end to the one factor that is overwhelmingly responsible for that poverty—overpopulation. I don't notice people in the Third World clamoring for mandatory sterilization by their own governments. I don't think they'd be too happy about foreigners slapping that on them.

In short, if we charge the F.O.N. with responsibility for alleviating poverty in the world, it will open the floodgates. We would then have to grant it almost all the traditional powers of government, and maybe a few more. After 10,000 years of international anarchy, we would suddenly have to surrender all powers of government to an international government. I don't think that's too likely, and even if it were likely, I would still argue against it because it's not a good idea.

We should grant the F.O.N. only those powers that it needs, and the power to guarantee a minimal standard of living is not one that it needs.

The next potential economic powers for the F.O.N. that I want to argue against are two that were alluded to above: a power to spend money for "economic development" and a broad power to tax or regulate trade and the economy for "maximum economic benefit for all."

There are several reasons why it would be a bad idea to grant these powers to the F.O.N. First, even if one believes that the world is in urgent need of further economic development, which I certainly do not believe, there are ample organizations and individuals devoted to that cause already. How to make more money appears to be the cause that obsesses the large majority of the world's people. Yet another organization devoted to it is not what the world needs. Furthermore, a glance at experience shows that gargantuan organizations such as the F.O.N. would be, organizations like the United States government or the Soviet government or the World Bank, have done a pretty miserable job of spending or loaning money for development, both in the Third World and in the industrialized world. Smaller organizations closer to the local interests, being more familiar with the local natural environment and with locally established ways of life, can do a much better job of it.

The corruption that inevitably infects the awarding of economic grants by governments also weighs against giving the F.O.N. this power.

Another reason to leave these decisions to the nations and to local organizations is that financial matters would be a huge and unnecessary cause of political fighting within the F.O.N. F.O.N. delegates would spend most of their time fighting to maximize their nation's share of the F.O.N.'s grants, loans, and development projects. It would not be at all conducive to union within the F.O.N., and the bickering would almost certainly limit membership by driving away nations that felt shortchanged.

Even if the F.O.N. confined itself to regulating the economy, rather than offering loans and grants for economic development, the same problems would arise. Trying to pursue the greatest economic good for any group as a whole inevitably means making trade-offs. Any move benefits one subgroup and hurts another subgroup. When the U.S. invokes protectionism for the steel industry, it may help the steel industry, but it hurts the auto industry because it drives up the price of steel. Likewise, if the F.O.N. tries to manipulate the F.O.N. economy, any action will inevitably benefit some nations and hurt others. That will only lead to disagreement and tear the organization apart. It will also be unfair to the smaller and less powerful member nations, who are bound to end up on the losing side of most trade-offs.

The best argument, though, for not giving the F.O.N. power to regulate the economy is just that we should leave as many powers as possible to the national governments. Again, I remind you that we want as many nations as possible to join. Given that, we should not infringe on the nations' rights and powers unless we have a compelling reason to do so. In this case there is no compelling reason. Although it might be true that by regulating the global economy the F.O.N. could increase the total amount of money in the world (just what the world needs), this would not justify denying nations their right to economic self-determination and their right to regulate their economies.

On what basis are we to deny nations the right to regulate their economies? If a nation wants to protest another nation's human rights abuses by enacting a boycott or embargo or tariffs against that nation, why shouldn't it be able to? If one nation raises its cattle on grain laced with antibiotics, thus creating bacteria that are immune to the antibiotics and rendering them useless for medicine, shouldn't other nations be able to protest this by refusing to buy that nation's beef? If one nation cannot raise food as cheaply as its neighbors, but nonetheless wants to maintain a population of farmers and a healthy rural economy, shouldn't it be able to assess tariffs on farm imports? Does anyone seriously want to argue that because Japan cannot produce food as cheaply as some other nations, it should be forced to relinquish all agricultural price supports and tariffs, forced to import more food, and forced to put its farmers out of business?

The issue is not whether the F.O.N. could statistically enrich the world by regulating the international economy. The issue is whether that would justify denying the nations their right to economic self-determination.

For those reasons, the F.O.N. should be banned from spending money to promote economic development, either for a part or even the whole of the F.O.N., and should be banned from regulating trade between or within member nations.

> Article I, Section 6
> Provision 15. The Federation of Nations is forbidden to spend or loan funds for projects designed solely to economically aid or promote the economic development of a part or the whole of the Federation.
> Provision 16. The Federation of Nations is forbidden to regulate trade among or within member nations or between member and nonmember nations, except for the powers of enforcing boycotts and embargoes granted in Provisions 18 and 19 ...

Finally, one particular type of regulation of the international economy deserves special mention. That is the breaking down of tariffs and of trade barriers. This is of course the founding principle of the European Community, and many think it must be the cornerstone of international government.

Extolling the benefits of free trade between nations is currently a great fad among economists. They constantly tell us that allowing free trade increases the total wealth in the world. That is probably true. But then again, it is also probably true that unrestrained capitalism maximizes the total wealth within a nation—another point economists are fond of making. The fact that social welfare systems and environmental protection laws decrease the total money that can be made in a nation does not mean that they are not wise and perfectly legitimate governmental policies. Likewise, the fact that the European nations' tariffs on agricultural imports limit the amount of money the U.S. can make from food sales to Europe doesn't mean that tariffs are not a perfectly legitimate policy. Economists have a terrible time understanding this, but there is more to life than maximizing the total amount of money in the world.

There are several things nations should not have the right to do. Nations should not have the right to attack each other. They should not have the right to pollute each other beyond certain limits. And they should not have the right to violate human rights. But it is a perfectly legitimate right of nations to regulate what goods are produced and sold within their borders and to assess tariffs on imports. It is absurd to make the promotion of free trade—in other words, the denial of the nations' right to regulate their economies—the cornerstone of international government.

Once again, the issue is not whether entering free trade agreements is a wise policy or not. It probably is in most cases a wise policy.* But that does not mean it should be jammed down the throats of unwilling nations. It does not mean that nations should not have the right to control their economies.

What I have discussed so far means that the F.O.N. should have almost nothing to do with economics. It should not regulate trade or economic activity. It should not attempt to promote economic development. It should not redistribute wealth between nations. It should not redistribute wealth between citizens. All of those powers should be left to the nations.

---

*By no means, however, is it always a wise policy for nations to reduce tariffs and promote free international trade. This point is discussed in Appendix 8-A at the end of this chapter.

This near total lack of economic powers for the F.O.N. means that there will be very little constraint on a nation's trade and economic policy. One of the outgrowths of this fact, which may at first seem surprising, is that there is no reason a nation belonging to the F.O.N. couldn't simultaneously belong to another international cartel or economic group that included nonmember nations. There is no reason, for example, a nation couldn't simultaneously belong to the F.O.N. and the European Common Market, even if most Common Market nations were not F.O.N. members. Obviously if there was a conflict between F.O.N. law and Common Market policy, the F.O.N. law would reign supreme for its members. For instance, if the F.O.N. instituted an embargo against a European Common Market nation, of course all F.O.N. member nations would be required to obey the embargo, even though that might conflict with their being members of the Common Market. But since I am proposing that the F.O.N.'s power to regulate trade be quite limited, such conflicts between F.O.N. law and a member nation's trade agreements should be very rare and would usually not prevent an F.O.N. nation from continuing its membership in a cartel or economic community.

Likewise, although the F.O.N. will have the power to legislate embargoes and boycotts, in a case in which it does not legislate an embargo or boycott, member nations would still be free to carry one out on their own.

Paying the Bill

The next question is, How are we going to pay for all this? I have not detailed the structure of the F.O.N. government completely yet, but a number of things are clear. The F.O.N. will be in charge of the military, so it will have to raise the money to pay all those soldiers. The weapons and services for the military will also have to be bought, and the bureaucrats that run the purchasing of military supplies will have to be paid. I've indicated that there will be F.O.N. courts and F.O.N. legislative representatives—those people and their staffs will have to be paid. So, again, how do we pay for it?

I will break the expenses of the F.O.N. into two categories: paying soldiers, and everything else—and I will treat the funding of those two categories as separate issues.

Recruiting and Paying Soldiers (Art. I, Sec. 6, Prov. 1)

The F.O.N. legislative branch (composed of the elected representatives from all the F.O.N. member nations) will, in my proposed constitution, be in charge of determining the necessary size of the military, the number of soldiers. *Once that number is determined, quotas should be assigned to each member nation in direct proportion to its population.* In other words, every member nation should be required to raise the same percentage of its population as soldiers.

There are two reasons for this quota system. The first reason is that an imbalance of nationalities in the F.O.N. military could be dangerous. If the military were dominated by one nation (even if only the enlisted men and women were dominated by one nation and not the officers), it might begin to fight only for the interests of that nation and not for the whole F.O.N. It might even begin to tyrannize the other F.O.N. nations.

The second reason for the quota system of soldiers is to insure that every member nation bears an equal burden for the F.O.N. defense, not just in economic terms but in human terms. If an F.O.N. representative wants to start a war, I want him to know it will be his constituents doing the dying.

Next, having assigned a quota to each nation, we have to decide how to meet that quota, how to raise that number of soldiers. I propose that *each nation should independently decide how it will raise its quota of soldiers.* By "nation" though, I do not mean the national government, but rather the elected F.O.N. representatives from that particular nation. The group of F.O.N. delegates would know they need to induce, say, 100,000 of their citizens to volunteer to join the F.O.N. military. They would then be able to decide, independently of the rest of the F.O.N., exactly how to induce that number of people to join—what salary and other perquisites such as college scholarships to offer to volunteers.

One outgrowth of this system is that different countries will naturally offer different salaries to soldiers. Presumably you need to offer more money in the United States to get volunteers for the military than you do in a Third World country where unemployment is 50% and average pay is a dollar a day. Admittedly, this might pose a problem for morale if soldiers working side by side are being paid very different amounts. But I don't think that is a serious problem, and, in any case, the alternatives are worse. One alternative is to have an all-volunteer army with uniform pay for volunteers from all countries. But that automatically means that almost all volunteers will come from poorer countries. Then we will have the richer, more powerful countries controlling the F.O.N. and sending off people from the poor countries to die in their wars for them. Alternatively, to maintain both proportional national representation in the military and a uniform pay scale, we would probably need a permanent military draft in almost all member nations—and instituting a permanent draft would mean permanent protests and permanent dissension.*

Each member nation, then, through its F.O.N. representatives, should be responsible, independently of the rest of the F.O.N., for recruiting its fair share of F.O.N. soldiers. Likewise, each member nation, through its F.O.N. representatives, should also be responsible, independently of the rest of the F.O.N., for paying for those soldiers. The money for those soldiers should come entirely from their own nation, and the F.O.N. delegates from that nation should be entirely responsible for setting the tax rates and the type of taxes (i.e., a property tax, income tax, gasoline tax, or whatever) to raise the money.

The virtue of this system is that it leaves power with the nation itself and does not put it in the hands of foreigners. The power to recruit soldiers and determine the taxes to pay for them shifts from the national government to the F.O.N., but it stays almost completely in the hands of citizens and elected representatives of that particular nation. It is not surrendered to foreigners.**

---

*An alternative system for raising soldiers that would largely avoid the problems discussed here by combining a national quota system with a guarantee of uniform pay for all soldiers and a constitutional ban on the military draft is presented in Appendix 8-B after this chapter. Some may find that system to be better than the one proposed here. I do not, though, so I relegate it to an appendix.

**It is necessary here also to discuss what happens if the delegates from a particular nation do not perform their duty under these provisions—enlist too few soldiers or too many (recall that the purpose of the quota system was to maintain a balance of nationalities in the military, (cont.)

The Rest of the F.O.N.'s Expenses

I turn now to the rest of the expenses of the F.O.N.—the paying of judges, the purchase of weapons, the construction of prisons, etc. These expenses have no intrinsic national boundaries, and they must be decided upon by the full F.O.N., not by the separate nations. That is, the full F.O.N. legislature, not the separate nations, must decide what salaries to pay judges, which weapons to buy and what to pay for them, and so forth.

Having decided all those things, having set all the expenses of the F.O.N., the next question is, How are we going to raise the money to pay for it all?

First, let's address how the tax burden is to be divided between nations. One criterion for apportioning the tax burden could be population. Clearly that would be a bad idea, though. The most overpopulated nations also tend to be the poorest and the least able to afford more taxation. Another possible criterion could be land area. But that would be clearly unfair, too. It would place a disproportionate tax burden on large countries with low population densities like Canada and Australia. The last thing we should be doing is punishing countries for having low population densities. On the contrary, we should be doing everything possible to encourage countries to reduce their populations.

I propose that, instead, *a country's share of the F.O.N. tax burden should be directly proportional to its Gross National Consumption or G.N.C.** That is, every country would pay exactly the same percentage of its G.N.C. in taxes. This would distribute the tax burden essentially according to the ability of a nation to pay.

(cont.) so too many soldiers from one nation is almost as bad as too few) or fail to raise the money to pay the soldiers after they are enlisted. In this case of dereliction of duty, I propose that we temporarily turn the power over to the president of the F.O.N. (Art. I, Sec. 6, Prov. 1). The president has not been mentioned yet, but the argument for that office, as well as for the president's selection and powers, will be discussed in Chapter 11.

*Gross National Consumption is almost identical to the more familiar Gross National Product. The major component of both is the sum value of all goods and services both bought and produced within the nation. G.N.P. adds to this the value of exports while G.N.C. adds imports.

Some would argue that this is not a progressive enough system of taxation, that we should soak the rich. They would like to see the rich countries pay a higher percentage of their G.N.C. in taxes than the poor countries. But there are a few arguments against doing that. The first argument was brought up earlier when discussing redistributing wealth between nations. Taxing nations progressively, that is, at different rates, is merely a means of redistributing wealth between the nations;* and, as was mentioned earlier, redistributing wealth between nations cannot and should not be a purpose of the F.O.N. If that is an avowed purpose of the F.O.N., to take from the rich and give to the poor, then the rich nations simply will not join, and there won't be any wealth to redistribute anyway. Moreover, as was indicated earlier, allowing redistribution of wealth between the nations would not even really serve the interests of the poor, since, because it would decrease the number of rich nations that join the organization, it would interfere with the goal of ending the exploitation of the poor nations by the rich.

---

*Taxing all nations at a constant percentage of their G.N.C. is neutral in terms of redistributing wealth between the nations because the expenditures of the F.O.N. that go to each nation will also be approximately proportional to G.N.C. If the businesses in member nations have about the same relative chance to get contracts from the F.O.N. as from other customers, that is, if the F.O.N. is not biased in awarding contracts, F.O.N. payments will tend to distribute themselves between countries in proportion to G.N.P. (which approximately equals G.N.C.).

This turns out to be another argument for having tax revenues also proportional to G.N.P. or G.N.C., because if tax revenues are not proportional to G.N.P. or G.N.C., then the F.O.N. will be affecting the international balance of payments and flooding the currency exchanges with certain currencies. If, for instance, the F.O.N. taxes Japan at a higher rate than other countries, it will be taking in more yen than it is paying out. It will then have to use its excess yen to buy other currencies in order to pay its debts. This will flood the currency exchanges with yen, decreasing the value of the yen relative to other currencies. This of course will affect Japan's trade balance and have repercussions throughout its economy. To avoid those effects, it would be desirable if the F.O.N. took in in each currency approximately what it pays out. To do that, its taxes from each nation should be proportional to G.N.P. or G.N.C.

Taxing rich nations and poor nations at the same rate, incidentally, does not by any means exploit the poor. On the contrary, even without some system of wealth redistribution (and, as I mentioned, progressive taxation can be considered to be a form of wealth redistribution), the poor nations are still the ones that will receive the greatest benefits from the F.O.N. at the lowest cost. With taxes proportional to G.N.C., poor nations will pay the smallest amount of taxes. Yet they will actually receive the largest amount of benefits from the F.O.N. The most important achievement of the F.O.N. will be to improve the military defense of its member nations and insure their security; and poor nations, since they suffer far more invasions than rich nations, will be the ones that will benefit the most from this. In no sense are the poor nations being exploited under this system.

Another argument against taxing different countries at different rates is that this will create dissension likely to limit membership and tear the organization apart. If we tax all nations at the same rate, none will feel it has been treated unfairly. Some may not like the system. Some may feel it should be more charitable towards the poor. But none can feel it has been singled out and treated unfairly. In contrast, if we tax different nations at different rates, *all* will feel they have been treated unfairly. Whatever method we use to calculate which nation is richer than another, it will be imperfect and controversial. Several methods could be used to calculate relative national wealth or well-being. We could calculate G.N.P. per capita, the amount of time the average worker must work to earn enough to buy a loaf of bread or to pay for his housing, the size of the average home, or even illiteracy rates or infant mortality rates. But all of these methods have their flaws, and most involve either imprecise measurements or complicated calculations that are certain to be challenged. No one, in other words, is going to be happy with the rankings of which nation is richer than another.

If we tax different nations at different rates, every nation will be able to point to another that it feels should have a higher tax rate. The system will of necessity be somewhat arbitrary and unfair. This will create perennial bitterness, will not be at all conducive to union within the organization, and will almost certainly limit membership by driving away nations that feel shortchanged. It is much better just to treat every nation exactly the same, taxing all at the same rate.

The next question, if Gross National Consumption is to play such a key role in the tax system, is, How is G.N.C. to be determined? G.N.C. is not like population or land area. It's pretty easy to count people or measure distances, but economists have a much harder time precisely measuring G.N.C. So how do we get around this? Very easily. No calculation of G.N.C. has to be made at all. G.N.C. is just the sum total of the price of all goods and services bought in a nation, so *by assessing a flat percentage sales tax on the purchase of all goods and services, with the percentage being exactly the same in all member nations, we automatically tax every nation at exactly the same percentage of its G.N.C.* (Art. I, Sec. 6, Prov. 12). A 6% sales tax means every nation pays 6% of its G.N.C. in taxes.

I think this is an almost perfect system of taxation. It largely eliminates perhaps the greatest fear people have of international government—giving foreigners the power to tax them. By limiting the F.O.N. to a flat percentage sales tax, any tax those foreigners assess on us will apply at exactly the same level to themselves.

Another beautiful feature of this tax system is that it eliminates for the F.O.N. representatives all decisions about taxation except for one: what to set the percentage at. Most of us trust politicians about as far as we can throw them. And we trust politicians from foreign countries even less. But by so strictly limiting the type of taxes they can assess, this tax plan almost completely eliminates the possibility of mischief. There will be no 1,000 page tax codes that no one could possibly understand—tax codes that inevitably have so many loopholes that the rich never pay a cent. The F.O.N. tax code will contain just one sentence: "The F.O.N. sales tax will be X%."

Some might object that a flat sales tax, while perhaps apportioning the tax burden fairly between nations, does not apportion it fairly between individuals. Regardless of the distribution of taxes between nations, within a nation they would like to see rich citizens pay a much higher percentage than poor citizens. I agree with that as a goal for a total tax system, but the F.O.N. taxes will be only a small part of a total tax system. As will be discussed at the end of this chapter, the national governments will need to raise considerably more revenue than the F.O.N.

government, so if the nations do not consider the F.O.N. tax system progressive enough, they can very easily compensate for that by making their own tax systems more progressive than they otherwise would. Moreover, the flat sales tax will be only a part of the F.O.N. tax system. The other part will be taxes to pay for soldiers, which will be assessed solely by a nation's own representatives. The representatives can make that part of the F.O.N. tax burden as progressive as they like.

Printing Money

The next economic question we should address in this chapter is the question of currencies and the printing of money. It might appear that the present system of world finance, with each country printing its own currency and the relative values of different currencies floating freely on international exchange markets, would pose some problems for financing an international government. So, offhand, it might seem we should give the F.O.N. the power to coin and print money and take that power away from the national governments of the member nations.

But this chapter has said that the nations, not the F.O.N., should retain the power to regulate their economies. To do that, nations need to be able to print money.

To manipulate their economies, that is, to reduce unemployment and reduce inflation, nations have only two major tools. Those two tools are to change the size of the government's budget deficit (or surplus) and to alter the amount of money in circulation. The logic of using the budget deficit to control the economy is as follows: When the government increases its budget deficit, that is, spends more or collects less in taxes, it puts more money in the hands of the public. More money in the hands of the public means the public should, in theory, spend more money, which should stimulate economic activity and reduce unemployment (but it also should tend to increase inflation). Conversely, if unemployment is low and inflation is high, the government may choose to reduce its budget deficit so as to reduce inflation (hoping that it does not also bring on unemployment and a recession). The logic of using the money supply to control the economy is similar. By printing more money (or more commonly, by purchasing a government bond),

103

the government puts more money in the hands of the public and can thus stimulate the economy and reduce unemployment. By doing the opposite, removing money from circulation, it can reduce inflation.

If we take away from national governments the power to print money, we completely remove one of the two tools nations have for manipulating their economies—controlling the money supply. Moreover, we would make it more difficult for them to even use their other tool, a budget deficit, to manipulate the economy. This is because the easiest way to finance a budget deficit (although most nations try to avoid this approach these days) is just to print money to make up the difference, and we would remove that option. Deficits would then have to be financed entirely by borrowing.

Nations would not much care to lose the power to print money. They may handle that power badly, but they would rather handle it badly themselves than have someone else handle it badly for them.

To be less flippant though, there are three good reasons to leave the power to print money in the hands of the nations rather than to have the F.O.N. take it over. The first, as I've mentioned, is that the power to print money essentially carries with it the power to manipulate the economy. If the F.O.N. took on the job of manipulating the economies of its member nations, it would be in the position of trying to pursue the greatest good for the greatest number, and would inevitably trade off the interests of some nations for the interests of others. That is not something the F.O.N. should be doing, so the F.O.N. should not have this power.

The second argument is purely pragmatic. It is not wise to concentrate so much economic power in one institution. If the F.O.N. is to be the sole entity able to print money, it will have an unprecedented power to control the money supply for the entire world. If it makes a mistake, it is easy to imagine that it might plunge us into a global depression. Leaving the power to print money with the hundreds of nations should be a more stable system, because not all nations will be doing the same thing at the same time and their policies should tend to counteract each other.

The last argument for leaving the power to print money with the national governments is that it is the national governments that will be in most need of this power. The level of government which will have the greatest difficulty raising enough tax revenue to balance its budget is the one in the most need of the power to print money, because it may want or need to print money to make up its budget deficit. And as I will show soon, the national governments will have much greater expenditures than the F.O.N., and will therefore have a much harder time balancing their budgets.

Thus, the Federation of Nations should leave the power to print money in the hands of the nations. My proposed constitution will read:

> Article I, Section 6
> Provision 17. The Federation of Nations is prohibited from coining or printing money.

Does this leave the F.O.N. in a terrible bind—collecting its taxes and paying its expenses in perhaps dozens of different currencies? Not at all. It's an accounting nightmare, but for those of us who don't work as accountants it's not a major problem. If the F.O.N.'s expenses and revenues in each currency do not balance perfectly, that can be resolved quite easily. For instance, if the F.O.N. owes dollars to a weapons contractor and it has already spent all the dollars it collected in tax receipts, it can simply use some of its excess yen or marks or pesos or whatever to buy dollars on the currency exchanges.

The Monetary Cost and Savings of the F.O.N.

The best economic news has been saved for last.

One of the arguments people are certain to make against forming a Federation of Nations is that it would be too expensive, that, as another level of government, it would just be a huge bureaucracy soaking up even more taxes from us. Let's examine that charge.

The charge is partially correct. The F.O.N. would be another level of government and there would be a cost associated with that. We would have new legislative representatives, their staffs, judges and courts, enforcement officials, and prisons. Virtually all those people and things would be added on to the lower levels of government; they would not replace the lower levels of government.

But how much does that really cost? Table 1 shows the expenditures of the U.S. national government in 1991 broken down into different categories. All the things I just talked about that would be duplicated by the F.O.N. fall under the category of "general government, justice." That category is just 1.8% of the U.S. national government's expenditures.

The expenses in each category in Table 1 have been put under either the F.O.N. or national government according to which level of government would take over the expenses of that category in an F.O.N. member nation. As I discussed in this chapter, the F.O.N. would not take over responsibilities such as health insurance, supplementary income payments to the elderly and the poor, agriculture subsidies, education, and road construction. The only current national responsibilities the F.O.N. would take over are the military and, as will be discussed in the next chapter, some of the responsibility for environmental protection.

The table shows that the only expenditure of government that would be duplicated by the F.O.N. is "general government, justice" (environmental protection is shown in both columns, but it would be divided between the two levels, not duplicated), and this is a tiny 1.8% of the expense of national government. U.S. national government expenditures in 1991 were 23% of G.N.P., so 1.8% of that is 4/10 of 1% of G.N.P. That means the F.O.N. amounts to an additional expense of $80 for a person earning $20,000 a year. Eighty dollars a year for world peace (among many other benefits) sounds like a bargain to me.

But actually, even that figure is overstated. The F.O.N. will not even cost $80 per year. In reality it will save us money. The overwhelming majority of the F.O.N.'s expenses are for the military, and one of the major reasons for forming the F.O.N., as discussed in Chapters 2 and 7, is that it can handle military defense cheaper and more efficiently than independent nations can. For the same military power, the F.O.N. can spend much less than the nations must, and that savings will more than offset the $80 cost of having an additional level of government. Even in the early years, when the F.O.N. contains only a few nations, the savings in military expenses will more than offset the cost of having an additional level of government. But as the F.O.N. grows, those savings will really become extraordinary. Once the F.O.N. contains a solid majority of the nations of the world, the

TABLE 1
PREDICTION OF F.O.N. EXPENSES FROM A BREAKDOWN OF U.S. NATIONAL GOVERNMENT EXPENDITURES

In column 1, U.S. government expenditures from 1991 are broken down into categories. In columns 2 and 3, expenditures in each category are assigned to either the F.O.N. or national governments according to which level of government would be responsible for them in an F.O.N. member nation.

	% of 1991 U.S. Fed. Govt. Expenditures[a]	F.O.N. Expenses	National Expenses
National Defense and International Affairs	21.2	21.2	
Veterans Benefits	2.3	2.3	
Interest on Public Debt	14.3		14.3
Health	5.2		5.2
Income Security	12.5		12.5
Social Security and Medicare	27.4		27.4
Education and Community Development	3.6		3.6
Agriculture	1.1		1.1
Commerce, Housing Credit	5.6		5.6
Transportation	2.3		2.3
Energy and Science	1.3		1.3
Environment	1.4	0.7	0.7
General Government, Justice	1.8	1.8	1.8
Total		26.0[b]	75.8[b]

[a]Source: Executive Office of the President, Office of Management and Budget.
[b]Adds to 101.8% because "General Government, Justice" expenditures are duplicated in both the F.O.N. and National Government columns.

military can wither away almost to nothing, and at that point, if the United States, for example, were part of the F.O.N., the F.O.N. would be saving the average American worker about 1,500 dollars per year in taxes.*

Another of the reassuring things, for me at least, revealed by this table is that the national governments will cumulatively be considerably larger, in terms of expenditures, than the F.O.N. government. Based on the U.S. government, the table predicts a ratio of size between the national and F.O.N. governments of about 3 to 1, with this being the ratio of the taxes you would pay to your national government relative to the taxes you would pay to the F.O.N. Since the U.S., though, spends less on social programs and more on the military than any other industrialized country, 3 to 1 is undoubtedly an underestimate; the real ratio will be even more lopsided. You will thus pay much less tax to the F.O.N. than to your national government, and, as discussed above, your overall tax bill will be lower in the F.O.N. than it would be in an independent nation.

Table 1 also allows us to estimate the total tax bill you could expect from the F.O.N. According to the table, the U.S. share of F.O.N. expenses (since each country's share would be proportional to G.N.C., and G.N.C. approximately equals G.N.P.) would represent 26% of its 1991 national government budget. U.S. national government expenditures in 1991 were 23% of G.N.P., so taking 26% of 23% gives the value 6%. F.O.N. taxes, based on this calculation, would be 6% of G.N.C. The F.O.N., then, could be funded entirely by a 6% sales tax (or by some combination of a smaller sales tax and other types of taxes to pay for soldiers).

Now, before some of you start objecting that you don't want to pay a 6% sales tax on top of all the other taxes you already pay,

---

*In 1991, the U.S. government spent 273 billion dollars on military defense. Since, according to the government, there were 117 million full and part time workers age 16 and older in 1991, that works out to $2,333 per worker. Assuming, very conservatively, that a worldwide F.O.N. would allow us to reduce per capita military expenditures by 75% relative to the expenditures of the U.S., that means a savings to the average worker of $1,750 per year. Subtracting the $80 or so additional cost of the F.O.N. bureaucracy still leaves a net savings of over $1,500 per year.

let me say again that this is not on top of other taxes; it would replace other taxes. Your total tax bill in the F.O.N. would be smaller than in an independent nation.

Moreover, and more important, remember that in making this calculation I assumed no savings at all in the military, which is obviously absurd. In fact, I assumed that the F.O.N. would spend as large a percentage of its cumulative G.N.C. on the military as the U.S. spends, something that no other nation currently does. So this calculation is really a worst case scenario. In reality, even when the F.O.N. is first formed its taxes will be lower than this. Furthermore, as more countries join the F.O.N., it will be able to spend less and less on the military, by far its largest expense, and thus will be able to reduce its taxes even more. By the time most of the nations of the world have joined the F.O.N., F.O.N. taxes should be less than 2%, possibly less than 1%, of G.N.C.

In conclusion, though the F.O.N. will be an additional level of government and there will be a small cost associated with that, that small cost will be more than offset by the enormous savings the F.O.N. will create in the cost of military defense. In short, the F.O.N. will save you money, and will probably save you a lot of money.

Summary of Chapter 8

- Joining the F.O.N. will improve a nation's economic condition simply because the F.O.N. will save money for the nation and its taxpayers.

- The F.O.N. should not fund projects for economic development. Doing so would achieve little if any economic gain and only lead to bickering over these spoils that would tear the organization apart. Likewise, the F.O.N. should not attempt to regulate the economy for "maximum economic benefit for all." Any slight economic gain the F.O.N. might achieve by, for instance, abolishing tariffs and denying nations the right to regulate imports, would not justify this drastic infringement on national sovereignty and the national right to economic self-determination.

- The F.O.N. should be forbidden to deliberately transfer wealth from one nation to another.

- The F.O.N. should not adopt the powers of the welfare state and should not attempt to guarantee a minimal standard of living for the citizens of its member nations. Those responsibilities should be left with the nations.

- In my proposed constitution, the full F.O.N. legislature will establish the necessary size of the F.O.N. military. After this number of needed military personnel has been determined, each nation will be assigned a quota of soldiers, based upon its population, that it must recruit for the F.O.N. In other words, every nation will be required to recruit the same percentage of its population to serve in the F.O.N. military. It will then be the responsibility of the elected F.O.N. legislative representatives from each nation, independently of the rest of the F.O.N. representatives, to recruit their nation's quota of soldiers and to establish terms of compensation for those soldiers.

- It will also be the responsibility of the elected F.O.N. representatives from each nation, independently of the rest of the F.O.N. representatives, to assess taxes on their own nation to pay the salaries of their nation's soldiers.

- Taxes for all other F.O.N. expenses should be distributed between nations in direct proportion to Gross National Consumption. To achieve this, the sole F.O.N. tax for these expenses should be a flat percentage sales tax, assessed on all purchases of goods and services at exactly the same percentage in all member nations.

- Since the power to regulate the national economies should be left with the nations and not usurped by the F.O.N., the power to print and coin money must also be left with the nations and must be forbidden to the F.O.N.

- Critics are likely to charge that forming a Federation of Nations will mean another expensive layer of government and greater taxes for us all. That the F.O.N. will be another layer of government is true, and there will be a cost associated with that additional bureaucracy. But that cost is calculated to be just 4/10 of 1% of Gross National Product. This very small cost will be much more than offset by the enormous savings in the military achieved by forming a Federation of Nations. This will be especially true once a majority of the world's nations have joined the F.O.N., at which time the military can wither away almost to nothing. Hence, a person's total tax burden will decrease, not increase, when his nation joins the F.O.N.

Appendix 8-A
Why Nations Should Restrict International Trade

> I sympathize, therefore, with those who would minimize, rather than with those who would maximize, economic entanglement between nations. Ideas, knowledge, art, hospitality, travel—these are the things which should of their nature be international. But let goods be homespun whenever it is reasonably and conveniently possible; and above all, let finance be primarily national.
>
> *John Maynard Keynes*

In the main text of this chapter, I concentrated my argument against granting the F.O.N. the power to abolish tariffs or regulate international trade on the simple point that nations should have the right to regulate their economies. Regardless of whether it is wise for nations to enact tariffs and otherwise restrict international trade, they clearly should have the right to do that. I avoided the question of whether enacting tariffs and trade restrictions is a wise policy. Here, though, I want to confront that question.

The common wisdom among economists is that tariffs are always unwise and international trade should be completely unfettered. The giants of the past in economics, such as John Maynard Keynes, whose quote heads this appendix, David Ricardo, and Adam Smith, questioned this principle, at least to the extent of indicating that free international trade had to be conditioned on the immobility of investment capital between nations. But modern economists have no such qualms. So unanimous are economists on this position, and so stubborn are they in their refusal to even consider the arguments against it, that it almost seems they must take a religious vow upon entering their profession never to question it.

The argument for free international trade is basically that trade between nations is exactly analogous to trade between individuals. But it plainly is not. When two individuals trade with each other, we can assume that the exchange is in the interest of both parties. Otherwise, one or the other wouldn't choose to make the trade. But with nations we cannot make this assumption. The reason is that it is not nations that choose to trade with each other. Individuals and corporations choose to trade with each other. When I choose to buy a Japanese car, as when I choose to buy anything, I do it because I believe it is in my individual interest. Likewise, when a U.S. electronics corporation chooses to move a manufacturing plant to Mexico and thus buy Mexican labor, it does it because it is in the corporation's interest. International transactions are undertaken by individuals and corporations, not by nations, and they are undertaken because they are in the interest of the individual or corporation, not because they are in the interest of the nation.

The argument for unfettered international trade is that just as we can assume that any transaction freely entered into by two individuals is in the interest of both individuals, so we can assume that any transaction freely entered into by two nations is in the interest of both nations. Obviously this is wrong. The reason it is wrong is that international trade is not entered into by nations. It is entered into by individuals or corporations. In order to assume that international trade is in the interest of both nations, the decision to enter into that trade has to be made by the nations—in other words, by the national governments. For international trade to be beneficial to all nations involved, it has to be controlled by the national governments.

At this point the economists might concede that this argument is correct and that, at least in theory, when trade between two nations is entered into only by individuals and corporations, rather than by nations as national entities, it is not necessarily to the benefit of the nations. But then they will reassure us that this theoretical objection is irrelevant. In practice, they will say, unrestricted international trade always works to the benefit of the nations that take part in it. This, I suppose they would say, is due to some kind of invisible hand mechanism, whereby although the individuals and corporations are pursuing only their own profit, their actions always benefit the nation of which they are a part. (We can only "suppose" what economists would say in response to this argument, because they never actually deign to consider any arguments against free international trade.)

But is this true? Well, no. Free trade quite plainly has worked against many groups within nations and against many nations as wholes. It works, for instance, against unskilled laborers in the industrialized world as a class. There has historically been a large difference between the wages of unskilled laborers in industrialized nations and those in Third World nations. This situation existed because there was more capital in the industrialized nations, which made the workers in those nations more efficient than workers in the undercapitalized Third World. This difference in efficiency then justified a difference in wages. But today, due to the triumph of the free trade dogma, we have free international capital mobility. Thus, if an American car company finds that its Detroit laborers want $15 per hour, while Mexican laborers only want $2 per hour, it doesn't have to worry about any barriers to international trade or international capital mobility; it just moves its plant to Mexico. Because of free trade and free capital mobility we no longer have national labor markets; we have one worldwide labor market.

A worldwide labor market instead of national labor markets means that the wage rates for unskilled laborers around the world should equalize. Many people (most of them allied with the wealthy capitalists moving their plants to the Third World) have interpreted this as a good thing. Why, after all, should workers in the wealthy nations make so much more than workers in the poor nations. Indeed, this might be a good thing if it resulted primarily in raising wages in the Third World. But it does not. It primarily equalizes wages by decreasing the wages in the industrialized world. With so many unemployed in Third World nations, and with the unemployed and the poor reproducing so excessively, there is always an excess of labor in the Third World. Thus, it is almost impossible for their wage rate to go up. The wage rate will only go up when population growth comes to a halt.

Because the labor market has become worldwide rather than national, the wage rate in the United States, increasingly, is not set by the number of people in the U.S. labor market, or by historically accepted wage rates, or even by the productivity of the U.S. worker. It is set by the birth rate in Mexico City's slums.

Free trade and free capital mobility have exactly the same consequences for wage rates as free immigration. Exactly the same. If you want to be intellectually consistent and you argue for one, you must also argue for the other. Does anyone want to argue that we should eliminate all restrictions on immigration? We should allow anyone, from anywhere in the world, to come here, no matter how many want to come?

Of course, the point that free trade is not always in the interest of workers has been made before, but the workers are usually dismissed as a "special interest," not worthy of consideration. But even if we consider workers to be a special interest, there are other ways in which unrestricted free trade can and does clearly work against a nation's general interest.

In unrestricted free trade, there are winners and there are losers. The winners are those nations that run a trade surplus, and the losers are those nations that run a trade deficit. Running a trade surplus means that a nation exports more goods and services than it imports, with the exported goods and services being exchanged for imported money and capital. The reason a trade surplus is "good" is that the imported money and capital that result from a trade surplus can be reinvested in the nation to increase its productive capacity and efficiency. This investment, then, will give the nation a competitive advantage over other nations, which will give it the chance to further increase its trade surplus. Thus, a trade surplus can be self-perpetuating and self-accelerating. This situation cannot go on forever, though, because the nations running a trade deficit, if they do so forever, will eventually run out of money. Thus, they will no longer be able to buy anything, and their trade deficit will come to a halt. So, economists reassure us, there's nothing to worry about. The system is self-correcting. But what is it exactly that corrects a nation's trade deficit? It is either a fall in the value of its currency or a fall in its wages or some combination of the two. (It could also be a rise in its efficiency, but without any capital coming in it's hard to see how the nation is supposed to increase its efficiency.) Those alternatives don't sound so great. But those are actually the good alternatives. The bad alternative is that rather than accept a drop in its wages or in the value of its currency, a nation will sell off its land and capital. Thus, the nation itself, along with its productive capacity, will come to be owned by foreigners. Or, the other bad alternative is that rather than accept a fall in its wages or in the value of its currency, a nation will borrow in order to continue to pay for its imports.

These two means of financing persistent trade deficits—borrowing or selling off land and capital—are exactly what has befallen many Third World nations. Those nations unwisely chose to follow the advice of mainstream economists—breaking down their trade barriers, throwing open their borders to foreign industrialists, and plunging into the exciting world of international finance—and as a result they have come to be owned and controlled by foreign creditors. Incidentally, the United States, which is now the world's largest debtor nation, runs the same risk. If we do not end our worship of the false economic god of free international trade and begin enacting some tariffs, we are likely to continue to run trade deficits, to fall deeper into debt, and eventually to surrender some control over our affairs to foreign creditors.

Unrestricted international trade is a very real threat to the security of nations. It can and has resulted in certain nations having to surrender intolerable levels of control over their affairs to foreign creditors.

The economic dogma that international trade should never be restricted is just plain wrong. It is very much in the interest of every nation to enact whatever tariffs are necessary to have overall balanced trade. It may also be wise to ensure balanced trade with particular important trading partners. Further, in the interest of creating a level playing field, and in the interest of insuring a nation's right to protect its environment and regulate its business affairs, tariffs should be enacted against foreign competition that does not abide by the same environmental or labor regulations. Likewise, in order to prevent a nation's wage rate from being determined by the rate of population growth in the Third World, nations should restrict the export of investment capital to those nations with higher rates of population growth. It is also important for each nation to protect strategic domestic industries, such as agriculture and energy. No nation should be dependent on others for its food, and its probably not too wise for a nation like the United States to be dependent on others for its cars or computer chips either. Finally, nations should subsidize investment in, or otherwise protect, those domestic industries that produce numerous high-paying jobs. A nation should not, in the name of free international trade, allow other nations to specialize in industries that produce high-paying jobs while it "specializes" in low-paying jobs.

There are many ways in which restrictions on international trade are clearly in the interest of every nation.

Does Free Trade Promote Peace?

Another argument for free international trade that is frequently mentioned bears directly on the purpose of this book. That argument is that free trade promotes peace because nations that trade with each other don't make war on each other. I fail, however, to see any evidence in support of this idea. Germany traded with France, England, the Netherlands, Poland, and Austria before World War II. Japan traded with China and Korea. Iraq traded with Kuwait and Saudi Arabia before the Persian Gulf War.

If extensive economic interdependence reduced the likelihood of hostilities, then civil wars should be nonexistent and spouses should never murder each other. But, of course, exactly the opposite is the case. Civil wars are more common than wars between separate nations and you are far more likely to be murdered by a member of your family than by a stranger.

If anything, logic would seem to indicate that extensive economic interdependence increases the tendency for resentment to develop and increases the likelihood of war. Right now, for instance, there is extensive ill will in the United States toward Japan. This ill will has developed not in spite of the fact that we trade with each other and compete economically, but rather because of that fact. If we had no interactions with Japan, no one here would care about them.

If It Enforces Free Trade, the F.O.N. Must Enforce Other Things Also

Probably the most important point to be made about free trade for the purposes of this book, though, is that if the F.O.N. were to enforce free trade between nations, denying the nations their right to assess tariffs and regulate their economies, it would have to adopt almost all powers of government. It would have to take the primary responsibility for environmental, minimum wage, and worker safety laws, because otherwise nations would be forced to lower their standards in order to attract business. To prevent all capital, and thus all jobs, from migrating to those nations that could produce goods most efficiently, it would have to have some type of central planning system to mandate movement of capital to the less productive nations. (And as we know, central planning of the economy hasn't worked too great in the past.) Most important, though, in order to prevent overpopulation in one nation from driving down wages in all other nations, it would have to legislate mandatory sterilization around the world.

In order to prevent this ridiculous overcentralization of power, nations must be permitted to control their economies and restrict international trade and international capital mobility.

Appendix 8-B
An Alternative System For Raising Soldiers

In raising soldiers for the F.O.N. we have two contradictory problems: (1) If we pay soldiers a uniform amount and accept soldiers from anywhere, all the soldiers will come from the poorer countries; and (2) If we insist on having a fair distribution of soldiers between the nations, while at the same time having an all volunteer force, we have to accept paying the soldiers from different nations different amounts. In the text I accepted paying soldiers from different nations different amounts as the lesser of these evils. Here, though, I will propose an alternative that, at least in theory, can avoid both of these problems.

What this would require is that we use uniform pay, a national quota system, and an all volunteer force. That means we would have to set the pay high enough to attract volunteers from even the wealthiest nations. This pay, then, would be so high that we would attract far more volunteers than we would need from the poorer nations. We would have to turn the large majority of them away. (On the other hand, this competition would mean that those recruits we accepted from the poor nations would presumably be very high quality individuals.)

Under this system, the money to pay the soldiers would not come from each nation separately but just from the general F.O.N. treasury, from revenues raised by the uniform sales tax. There would be no taxes imposed on each nation separately by the nation's own representatives.

A key element of this system would have to be a constitutional ban on military conscription. Without that provision, the legislature would probably take the cheap way out and offer a medium-range pay that would attract recruits from the poor nations but not the rich nations. The soldiers from the rich nations would then be routinely raised by a military draft. I personally find the idea of routine use of the military draft to be morally unacceptable. Few people seem to notice it, but a military draft is simply a form of involuntary servitude. In other words, it is slavery. An entity is claiming to own your life and to be able to force you to perform a specific job against your will. That is involuntary servitude. The fact that the entity is a government rather than an individual is irrelevant to the conclusion that it is involuntary servitude.

On that basis, courts in the F.O.N., as in any nation that has a constitutional ban on slavery, could (and it seems to me should) find military conscription to be unconstitutional. But I wouldn't hold your breath waiting for that to happen. So if we institute this system of raising soldiers, we need to insert a constitutional clause banning the military draft. The only reason I didn't insert that in my proposed constitution at the end of this book is that with the method of raising soldiers proposed in that constitution and in the text of this chapter, the responsibility for raising soldiers rests solely with each nation separately. Thus, any military drafts that F.O.N. representatives impose will be imposed only on their own nation. That is, we wouldn't really have an F.O.N. draft but just national drafts. I thought, therefore, that the F.O.N. doesn't need to intervene. We can leave this as a subject of debate for each nation separately. (Nonetheless, I'd be quite happy if F.O.N. courts ruled, as I have indicated here, that any draft is an unconstitutional form of slavery.) But if we adopt the alternative method of raising soldiers proposed in this appendix, then we would have drafts being imposed by F.O.N. representatives on nations other than their own. In that case, we would need a constitutional ban on drafts.

In addition to the constitutional ban on military conscription, one other provision is very important if we adopt this uniform-pay method of raising soldiers. We would need to maintain the national quotas. Once we adopt a uniform-pay, all-volunteer force, it would be very easy to slip into accepting volunteers only from the poorer countries. That, again, is dangerous in terms of creating an imbalance of nationalities in the military, and is morally unacceptable. The human burden of any F.O.N. wars must fall equally on all member nations. If an F.O.N. legislator plans on starting a war, he should be certain that it will be his constituents doing the dying.

Personally, I prefer the method of raising soldiers proposed in the main text of this chapter. The reason is that the method proposed in this appendix has two dangerous slippery slopes. One is the danger of a military draft. Because of the difficulty of raising volunteers from the rich nations, it will be very tempting for the legislature to resort to imposing a draft on those nations. The other slippery slope concerns the national quota system. Because of the expense of attracting recruits from the wealthy nations, it is likely the legislature will just take the cheap way out by abandoning the quota system and accepting a military comprised solely of soldiers from poor nations. There is less danger of falling into these two traps if we use the system proposed in the main text of this chapter, whereby the representatives from each nation will be responsible for raising soldiers from their own nation. Also, that system has the virtue of leaving a greater amount of power with the separate nations.

The one advantage that the system in this appendix has is that it largely avoids the problem of paying soldiers from different nations different amounts. But even that advantage is not as clear cut as it would seem. The reason for that is that currency exchange rates are rather unrealistic. Paying soldiers "the same amount," while paying them in different currencies, presumably means that pay will be determined by the currency exchange rates. The only problem with that is that currency exchange rates, especially between the nations of the industrialized world and nations of the Third World, make some strange claims of equal value. Advocates for the poor frequently tug at our heartstrings by telling us that workers in some Third World nation earn two dollars a day, but what they don't tell us is that two dollars will buy a lot in most Third World nations.

Thus, having "uniform pay" for soldiers from all nations doesn't entirely avoid the problem of paying soldiers from different countries different amounts. It just means that now we will have soldiers from the rich nations complaining that they aren't paid as much as soldiers from the poor nations, rather than vice-versa.

Chapter 9

The Eleventh Commandment: Overpopulation and the Environment

The only problem that matters in this world is overpopulation.

That statement is, of course, an exaggeration—but only a very slight exaggeration. Overpopulation is either the sole cause or a major cause of very nearly every problem in the world. In particular, it is the root cause of all our environmental problems, which, as far as I am concerned, are the most important and urgent problems we face. We simply will not solve any environmental problems until we reduce the population. Conversely, when we do reduce the population, most environmental problems will automatically be taken care of. Nothing else will need to be done.

Are you worried about protecting the few pieces of wilderness we have left? You can pass all the laws you like protecting them, but as long as the population continues to grow, the pressure on those wildernesses will continue to grow, and the laws will one day be rescinded. Do you care about endangered species? Those species can't exist without wild and natural places, and wild and natural places can't exist in the face of ever increasing human population. Pollution? Pollution is caused by human beings. It is directly related to the number of human beings. And it isn't linearly related. It is exponentially related.* If you increase the population a little, pollution increases a lot. Likewise, if we could only decrease population a little, pollution would decrease a lot. It doesn't matter how much "cleaner" you make automobiles. If you have more people, you have more cars, more traffic jams, people trying to move farther away from the city and thus driving farther, and you have more pollution.

---

*The reasons for this effect are not obvious, so I should explain. The amount of pollution emitted increases exponentially with population growth rather than linearly basically because when society becomes larger, things that formerly could be accomplished simply and without pollution become complex and require processes that pollute. For instance, when population density is low, people live on farms and in small towns; they live near where they work; and they rarely have to travel far. So walking is their primary means of transportation. When population density becomes higher and people live in larger and larger cities, in order to see a tree once in a while and get a tolerable amount of breathing space, people move to more and more distant suburbs. They no longer live near where they work, where they shop, or where their friends live. To do almost anything—work, shop, or socialize—they must drive or use some other polluting means of transportation. The more the population increases, the further each city's population will disperse, and the further each person on average will drive. Thus, not only does population growth mean more people polluting, but it means, as this transportation example shows, that each person, on average, must pollute more. The relation between pollution and population growth is therefore not linear but exponential.

Another example to illustrate this effect would be farming. When a society's population density is low, it can feed its people by farming only a small amount of land. Also, a low population density means there is no great pressure to increase production from each acre of land. Rather, if production must be increased, it is easier to just farm more land. So farmers don't overwork the land. They leave stream banks and steep hillsides unplowed, thus reducing soil erosion and runoff pollution into the streams. They rotate their crops and graze livestock, which then provide a source of manure to use as fertilizer. They let fields lay fallow regularly. But when population densities increase, (cont.)

But it isn't just environmental problems that are caused by overpopulation. Overpopulation is at the root of most social problems as well. The problem causing starvation isn't too little food; it's too many mouths to feed. The repeated mass starvations of Africa in recent years didn't just happen. They were made inevitable by overpopulation and poor farming practices. As the population grew, people were forced to plant and graze more and more of the land to feed themselves. Soon they couldn't afford to leave any land unused. They left no natural vegetation growing, no windbreaks. They could no longer afford even to rotate crops or follow soil conservation. Yields became lower and lower and the pressure on the land further intensified. When the next drought came, and droughts inevitably come once in a while, the soil just blew away. The land became a desert. Hundreds of thousands of people were left to starve. These disasters weren't caused by nature; they were caused by man. And they weren't caused by too little food; they were caused by too many people.

How about other social problems? Poverty? The resources of this world are finite. When you have too many people, shortages are going to occur and some people aren't going to have enough. Racism? This is about as close as you can come to a problem that is not caused by overpopulation, but even here overpopulation is a significant contributor. Overpopulation means that competition

---

(cont.) these "luxuries" of sound farming practices can no longer be afforded—or so we are told. Farmers then plow right to the streambanks and plow even the steepest hills. Every inch of land must be used. No windbreaks are left standing. Crop rotation can no longer be "afforded," so the land is exhausted by planting the same crop year after year after year. To replenish it, then, more and more fertilizers are needed. But since each farm has now specialized in one particular grain, no livestock are left and no manure is available, so the fertilizers used must all be artificial. Also, the vast monocultures are much more susceptible to pests, so more and more pesticides are used. Thus, greater population density means more wind and water erosion of the soil, more pesticides and greater runoff pollution from the pesticides that are applied, and weaker soil. Population growth means more pollution from farming not just because more land is being farmed but because the land farmed must of necessity be farmed more poorly and with a greater dependence on techniques that pollute. As we found with transportation, pollution from farming increases not linearly but exponentially with population growth.

for limited resources becomes more intense, and when that happens, people feel the need to separate into groups so as to improve their competitive position and so as to be able to blame their problems on some other group.

Perhaps homelessness and the high cost of housing are the problems that most concern you. The single most important root cause of both is overpopulation. In fact, overpopulation is essentially the sole cause of these problems. It's a very simple case of the law of supply and demand. The amount of land is finite. Therefore, when the population increases, the cost of land increases—increases over and above the rate of inflation. Furthermore, when people know the population will increase, they know the price of land will rise, so land becomes a good investment. Investors then bid up the price, further adding to the rising cost of land and housing. And when the cost of housing rises, some people won't be able to afford it and will wind up sleeping on the streets.

How about war? Anthropologists tell us that in our distant hunter-gatherer past there were few enough people in the world that all could pursue a hunter-gatherer lifestyle without depleting their environment. *At that time, war simply did not exist.** When neighboring bands ran into each other, they would have what amounted to ceremonial chest-beating to establish loose boundaries and then they would go away.

---

*This idea that war did not exist in hunter-gatherer times, though well accepted by anthropologists and archaeologists, is not widely known among the general public, so I should present some of the evidence for it. The primary evidence is that among the existing or recently extinguished hunter-gatherer societies that have been studied by anthropologists, war is just never observed. It is, for instance, reported to be absent among the "Andamann islanders, the Arunta, the Eskimos, the Mission Indians, the Semang, the Todas, the Western Shoshone, and the Yahgan" (Lesser, 1968), as well as among the aboriginal Australians, the !Kung San or Bushmen, and the Mbuti or Pygmies (Lesser, 1968; Lee, 1979; Turnbull, 1962). Hence, since warfare is completely absent from existing hunter-gatherer societies, we can infer it was also completely absent from our ancestral hunter-gatherer societies. And indeed, the remains from the hunter-gatherer era do "suggest remarkably peaceful societies" (William McNeill, quoted in Schmookler, 1984).

The reason war was absent from hunter-gatherer societies is (cont.)

But then the population grew. Resources became limiting. Bands ran into each other more often. In this atmosphere of limited resources, naturally some groups resorted to force to get their way and to steal land or other resources from their neighbors. For the first time, skeletons from this period began to be buried with weapons and to show signs of being wounded in battle. War had begun, and it has been with us to this day. The reason war began was very simple. Population grew and it became necessary for societies to compete with each other for limited resources. In the absence of population growth, war would never have existed.

I don't mean to imply though that overpopulation only caused the wars of 10,000 years ago. If you were to catalog the wars of the last few hundred years and list next to each the factors historians say caused the war, without a doubt population and resource pressures would be the most common factors listed. For a clear modern example we need only consider Japan and Germany in World War II. Japan simply had and has too many people for such a small island. The Japanese felt they needed to get more resources to support their population, and that is at least one of the fundamental reasons they went to war. Likewise, a desire for more land, in particular for the farmlands of Poland

---

(cont.) that it served no purpose for them. War is waged in order to capture land, possessions, or slaves, but hunter-gatherers had no use for any of those things. They already had ample land since there was no population pressure at that time and unused land was always freely available. They had no use for extra possessions since they were nomadic and had to travel light. And they had no use for slaves since, as discussed in Chapter 2, they worked so little. Furthermore, slaves carried along for gathering or hunting in the forest would have to be largely unsupervised and would have a perpetual opportunity to escape.

I should point out, though, that in saying that war was absent from hunter-gatherer societies, I do not mean that murder and violence were absent. In fact, murder is about as common in existing hunter-gatherer societies as in our own societies. But the killings are generally committed by just one person and generally arise out of some personal conflict such as jealousy over a lover. They are not committed by large, organized armed groups, and do not arise out of a desire to capture land, booty, or slaves. They thus clearly seem to fall under the category of simple murder rather than war.

and the Ukraine, was one of the most important reasons Hitler and the Germans went to war. In fact, the need for those farmlands to feed the growing population of Germany was specifically mentioned by Hitler in *Mein Kampf.*

Overpopulation is even one of the causes of general unfriendliness. What city in the U.S. has the reputation of having the rudest and most unfriendly people? New York, of course. Is it merely a coincidence that New York also has the largest population and greatest population density? It is a popular generalization in probably every nation on earth that people in the countryside are friendlier than those in the cities. Again, is it only a coincidence that this difference in friendliness coincides with differences in population density?

To this litany of problems directly caused by overpopulation, I will add one other: traffic jams. More people means more cars and it means people have to move further away from the cities to get a little space, and that means they have to drive farther. All this adds up to more cars on the road and greater distances driven per car. The result is traffic jams. Compared to starvation, poverty, war, homelessness, the loss of wilderness, or the extinction of one-third of the species on earth, traffic jams are a trivial problem. But ironically, I have a hunch that it is traffic jams, in the United States at least, that will finally create a consensus that something has to be done about overpopulation. People are just finally going to get tired of creeping along at 5 miles per hour breathing carbon monoxide.

It is very simple. The world and its resources are limited. Therefore, our population must be limited also. This is so obvious to me. I just cannot grasp why so many otherwise intelligent people seem to have such difficulty accepting this idea. But since I know that many people do have difficulty accepting it, including many of my closest friends, I have attached an appendix to this chapter in which I discuss the two most popular arguments for why overpopulation is not a problem—the economic and "scientific" arguments—and explain why both are very, very wrong. If you still do not accept that overpopulation is, for almost all practical purposes, the only problem that matters, please read that appendix.

Whatever cause you care about, it is a lost cause unless we

solve the population crisis. War, homelessness, starvation, racism, poverty, the wilderness, pollution, endangered species, or your own economic well-being and cost of living—if you care about any of those things, you should be working to reduce the population.

Apportioning Representation in the F.O.N. Between Nations

If, therefore, overpopulation is essentially the only problem that matters, is either the sole cause or a major cause of very nearly every other problem in the world, why does it continue? Why have our societies not made a greater effort to stop it? The answer is very simple: The parable of the tribes, the competition for power between autonomous societies, has not allowed them to. As I discussed in Chapter 2, population size is one of the most important components of national or societal power. In the world in which we have lived ever since we left the hunter-gatherer state, autonomous societies have always competed for power. And since we have always had anarchy above the level of the nation or the autonomous society, that competition has been completely without restraints and has often been ruthless. In this environment of unbridled competition, the primary concern of every nation or society must be societal power and societal survival. In this environment, we do things such as build nuclear weapons; we do things that we would otherwise never ever choose to do because we believe they are necessary for our societal power and our societal survival. Societal power and survival take precedence over everything else, as indeed they must. That is why our nations have allowed population growth and overpopulation to continue.

Until now, a nation that attempted to reduce its population would be weakening itself in the competition for power. And that is tantamount to suicide, because, in the long run, as explained by the parable of the tribes, societies that weaken themselves in the competition for power cease to exist. Regardless of how horrible all the other consequences of population growth have been, and they have indeed been horrible, nations have had no choice but to allow and encourage population growth to continue because it contributes to national power.

Under the F.O.N., though, this will end. The F.O.N. will end our imprisonment by the parable of the tribes and will end unbridled competition for power between nations. This means that at last we will be free to reduce our populations. In fact, that may actually be the F.O.N.'s most important achievement. I doubt that many other people will agree with me on this, but to me the single greatest outcome of forming the Federation of Nations is not that war will no longer exist, but that we will finally be free to reduce our populations and reap all the benefits which that will create.

A big "if", however, is associated with that statement. The F.O.N. will allow us to finally reduce our populations only if we design it properly. The F.O.N. will end the need of our nations to be obsessed with national power. In so doing, it will end the one reason why nations have had to maximize their populations. It is vitally important that it not replace that with another reason.

One of the most important principles in designing the F.O.N. is that there must be nothing in its design that would encourage member nations to increase their populations. For that reason, *it is important that the legislature NOT have seats apportioned between countries according to population.* This would only encourage countries to increase their relative power in the F.O.N. by increasing their populations.

Some might object here that nations aren't likely to institute deliberate policies to increase their populations merely to get more votes in the F.O.N. That might be right. But populations don't grow just from deliberate national policies. They grow, of course, from a deliberate *lack* of national policies to stop population growth and from the many overt and subtle cultural, religious, and economic factors that encourage people to have large families. If we are ever to get control of our populations, which we must do if we are to solve almost any problem in the world, we must break this cascade of factors that drives population growth. To do that we should start by ceasing to send signals that more people is better and that growth is a good thing. Just for this subliminal effect, this signal of our change in mindset, it is important that the F.O.N. not have representation proportional to population.

Beyond that, though, it just doesn't make much sense, if you are trying to stop a behavior, to simultaneously offer incentives for it. If we are ever to get control of our populations, we have got to stop encouraging couples to have more children and encouraging nations to increase their populations.

If we do not use population as a basis for distributing voting power between the nations, though, what should we use? I propose we have a bicameral legislature, just as in the United States and many other countries, with passage of a bill in both houses of the legislature required before it can become law. One house of the legislature, which I will call the Senate, should have representation proportional to arable land area—arable land being defined as dry land that is not desert or tundra (Art. I, Sec. 3, Prov. 4).* The other house, the House of Representatives, should have representation proportional to the tax revenue received from each member nation, thus directly proportional to Gross National Consumption and approximately proportional to economic power (Art. I, Sec. 2, Prov. 2).**

The logic of making representation in the Senate proportional to arable land area is that arable land area is directly proportional to what a nation's population ought to be. So this gives, in effect, a legislative body with representation proportional to population, without actually encouraging countries to raise their populations. It also gives, in my opinion, a fair share of voting power to the

---

*To be precise, arable land would be defined as land that receives at least 250 millimeters (9.8 inches) of precipitation each year, and has an average daily temperature during the warmest month of at least 11°sC (52°F).

**The astute reader will notice that making representation proportional to tax revenue does provide a weak incentive for nations to maintain large populations, which violates my earlier statement that we must not offer any encouragement to increase population. In my defense I can only say that the correlation between economic size (and thus tax revenue) and population is weak, and in fact, when a nation is extremely overpopulated the correlation becomes negative. That is, when a nation is extremely overpopulated, a decrease in population would cause an increase in the size of the economy. Nonetheless, it would be preferable to eliminate even this weak incentive for population growth, and an alternative basis for representation in the House of Representatives that would do that is discussed in Appendix B of this chapter. I have chosen to relegate that plan to an appendix only because I think it is politically unrealistic.

Third World, or underdeveloped, nations. The Third World nations cover a majority of the land area of the world and would therefore hold a majority of the votes in the Senate under this system. The Senate would thus be the body designed to give a fair share of power to the poorer nations.

The House of Representatives, in contrast, with representation proportional to the tax revenue received from each nation, would be the body designed to give a fair share of power to the economically and militarily most powerful and important members of the F.O.N.

Before we leave the subject, two details of this system of representation in the House of Representatives need to be mentioned. First, my use of the term "tax revenue" here has been too general. I would actually advocate that for calculating representation in the House of Representatives we only use revenue from the general F.O.N. sales tax, not the revenue that each nation raises to pay its own military personnel. That way, no nation would be able to "buy" extra representation by trying to raise extra taxes. Representation would simply be proportional to the size of the economy.

Second, I should mention how relative tax revenues can be calculated when different nations are paying in different currencies. This may at first seem to be a problem, but I don't think it is a serious one. Presumably, some system of using the exchange rates of the currency exchange markets to normalize the value of different currencies would have to be adopted, but once a system is agreed upon, the calculation of relative tax revenues will be straightforward.

Since population control is so vitally important, I was tempted in designing this proposed constitution to insert specific provisions encouraging member nations to reduce their populations. I thought about proposing tax breaks for nations with declining populations or low population density, and I thought about proposing that those countries somehow receive greater voting power in the F.O.N. legislature. As you can see, though, I decided against those ideas. Specific provisions encouraging population decline shouldn't be necessary, I hope, because the formation of the F.O.N. will remove the one major factor that has always prevented nations from reducing their populations. To reiterate, a large population is a very important component of national power. For that reason, no nation has ever been able to afford to really try to reduce its population. But when nations band together in the F.O.N., the pressure on them to maintain large populations will be greatly reduced. Even at first, when there are only a few nations in the F.O.N., since the member nations will have improved their power and national security by joining, the pressure to maintain a large population will be considerably reduced. But the effect will really become decisive once the F.O.N. has grown to include a majority of the nations on earth. At that point, member nations will never have to fear attack again. They will have no reason at all to maintain large populations and, as I've explained in this chapter, countless reasons to reduce their populations.

The importance of that effect cannot be overestimated. When nations no longer are forced by the selection for power to maximize their populations, it will be one of the most important turning points in human history—perhaps the most important turning point since we left hunter-gatherer societies.

I hope and assume that at that point nations will behave rationally and do what is so obviously in their self-interest—reduce their populations. On that basis, therefore, I assume that the F.O.N. will not have to do anything specifically to encourage member nations to practice population control.

Legislating Population Control

It is to be hoped that the world's population can be brought down without coercion, that such things as tax breaks and social mores will be sufficient to induce almost all people to have no more than two children. But unfortunately, neither the tax breaks nor the social mores currently exist in most nations. The tax code of the United States, as of most other nations, still anachronistically specifies deductions—that is, lower taxes—for those with children. In other words, it actively encourages population growth. Likewise, many, if not most, religions and cultures still celebrate "fertility" and actively encourage irresponsibly large families.

These features are maladaptive vestiges of our legacy of

competition—not just competition between nations but also between religious groups, ethnic groups, and other cultural subgroups. In the past, just as we have failed to control competition between nations, we have also generally failed to control competition between groups within the nation. So those groups naturally came to fear each other and realized they needed to strengthen themselves in order to compete and survive. To strengthen themselves, they accurately realized that they needed to increase their numbers. Thus, all these groups—religious groups, ethnic groups, and others—encouraged population growth. That would have been fine except for one thing: The earth is finite.

This situation, and the maladaptive social mores that it has created, must be changed. Fortunately, in the 20th century this situation has indeed begun to change. We have recognized the importance of human rights and civil rights and have begun to guarantee them. And we have recognized the dangers of uncontrolled capitalism and, with welfare systems and antitrust laws, have stopped some of the abuses inherent in that system. In other words, we have protected individuals and groups from uncontrolled competition.

The era of uncontrolled competition is coming to an end. Therefore, the diseased vestiges of that era—the religious and cultural encouragements of population growth—should begin to fade away. Social mores will begin to change and soon ought to begin to encourage responsible limitations on the birth rate.

But it will take time for that to happen and we don't have that much time. In the short run, it will probably be necessary, at least in some places, for government to enter the fray. At the least, governments ought to be encouraging population decline through such things as tax breaks for those without children. But it may also be necessary for government to take more drastic measures, such as instituting mandatory birth control—with perhaps the newly developed Norplant for women or a nonsurgical vasectomy being developed in China for men—after a person has fathered or mothered a certain number of children.

Should, then, the F.O.N. have these powers? Should the F.O.N. be able to legislate birth control? No.

I give that answer not because overpopulation is not a serious problem or because mandating birth control is not a legitimate power of government. I give it only because the F.O.N. would be the wrong level of government to hold that power. As long as a nation can control immigration, it can control its population and need not be significantly affected by overpopulation in other countries. Under those circumstances, overpopulation is a national issue and not an international issue, and the F.O.N. need not have the power to control it.

Thus, it is crucial that the nations retain the right to control immigration. If they do, the F.O.N. need not and should not have the power to legislate population control.

My constitution, then, will read:

Article IV, Section 4
    Provision 1. Member nations shall have the right to control their immigration but not their emigration.
    Provision 2. Having children is a basic right of all human beings, so neither the Federation of Nations nor any lower level of government may restrict the right of all individuals to father or mother one child each. However, population control is and always shall be a requirement of humankind, so national and local governments are not forbidden from taking any other measures necessary to limit their birth rates. The Federation of Nations itself, however, while permitted to enact voluntary population control measures, is forbidden to enact legislation restricting the right of people to have children.

These restrictions on the F.O.N.'s involvement in population control, however, do not lessen the vital importance of the issue. In particular, they do not lessen the importance that there be nothing in the F.O.N.'s design that would encourage nations to increase their populations. Probably the single greatest thing the F.O.N. can do is to free us from the shackles of overpopulation that have been imposed upon us by the selection for power. When that becomes possible, nothing must be allowed to interfere with it.

Environmental Ethics

Before we go on to consider the specific powers and responsibilities the F.O.N. should have for protecting the environment, I want to explore the subject of environmental ethics. This will give us a better foundation for deciding what environmental powers the F.O.N. needs (and will give me a chance to lobby for my favorite issues).

The first foundation for the environmental ethics to be developed here is the theory of evolution. Since I am a biochemist I might be a bit biased, but I think the theory of evolution is the most important idea in the past 1900 years. Unfortunately, though, it has yet to be taken seriously.

The biological fact is that our species, just like every other species, evolved from similar forms of life that lived in earlier times. This means we are related to every other form of life on this planet in the same sense that you are related to your brother or sister. The only difference is that with another species you have to go farther back in time to find your common ancestor.

One of the things you would predict from that fact is that there is nothing truly unique about human beings. Any characteristic we have, some other species, probably many species, to one degree or another, must have as well. That prediction turns out to be correct. Many qualities have been put forward as the defining feature of what it means to be human, but one by one each of those qualities has fallen. Each was found to be present in other species as well. One of the earliest and most popular attempts at a defining feature of human beings was the idea that we were the only species to use tools. It didn't take long to knock that one down. Birds, chimpanzees, gorillas, monkeys, racoons, sea otters, elephants, and many other species also use tools. Several of those species even "make" their tools—that is, they do not simply use objects they find in nature as tools but modify some of those objects to suit their purposes.

The next earnest attempt was that we were the only species capable of learning language. To support that idea, an attempt was made to teach chimpanzees to speak. When they failed to speak English sentences it was gleefully reported that we are the only species capable of understanding language. Unfortunately, chimpanzees are physically incapable of making the sounds of human speech, so that experiment was akin to giving someone a written exam without allowing him to use a writing implement. To get around that limitation, a more open-minded experimenter tried to teach a gorilla American Sign Language, the language of the deaf. Koko, the gorilla in question, now has a sign language vocabulary of 2,000 words, which is about the number of words in an average sign language dictionary. She constructs simple sentences, responds to questions at about the level of a three-year old, and by most definitions not only understands but uses language.*

Along the way Koko has also destroyed another supposedly defining feature of human beings: She makes jokes. One time she was asked, for probably the 100th time that month, what color her pillow was. (It was white.) Gorillas get bored and annoyed easily, so she was tired of being asked such a stupid question and she responded that it was red. When the questioner signed that it wasn't red and asked for the real color, Koko held up a tiny piece of red lint and laughed. Yes, gorillas throw back their heads and laugh, just like we do.

Koko has even invented profanity. One time when she was being unjustly scolded by her teacher for something she didn't do, Koko responded, "You dirty bad toilet." (The story of Koko is told in Patterson and Linden, 1981.)

Dolphins also have now been shown to be able to understand human language and grammar. They, of course, are unable to speak it or use sign language, but they will respond appropriately to new sentences and different word orders, showing that they understand language and grammar. Chimpanzees and orangutans also have been taught sign language, and no doubt a few other species are capable of understanding and using language, too. Moreover, it is likely that some species, in particular probably some species of dolphins or whales, not only are capable of learning language but actually use their own languages in the

---

*Some have claimed that Koko and other nonhuman primates taught sign language do not seem to vary the meaning of their sentences with word order, and so, claiming this ability as the defining feature of language, have concluded that they do not actually use language. But this analysis is difficult, because sign order is not nearly as important in sign language as word order is in spoken language. Furthermore, Koko and the other apes do respond appropriately to questions whose meanings are varied with word order. In any case, this objection appears to have been finally put to rest with recent experiments on pygmy chimps taught to use a type of keyboard to communicate. Their language abilities are a good deal more advanced than even Koko's, and, according to preliminary results, they clearly are able to apply the rules of word order and syntax in deciphering meanings.

wild. We're just too stupid to be able to understand them.

Likewise, we are not the only species to experience such emotions as affection and grief. Many dog owners could tell you that with stories of dogs who became depressed when a child went off to college or when another dog in the house died. But if you would prefer an example from a wild species, Jane Goodall described an adult chimpanzee in the wild who, after his elderly mother died, refused to leave her body, proceeded to lose interest in food, and finally starved to death. For another example, we can ask once again the first gorilla able to talk to us. Koko displays great fear every time her teacher, Penny Patterson, jokes to her that she (Penny) might die.

Finally, perhaps the most tenaciously held "defining feature" of human beings is that we are supposedly the only species capable of consciously ethical behavior, capable of making sacrifices for the good of another. Evidence refuting that position, of course, comes to us frequently from the domestic animals around us. But it also comes from well-controlled scientific studies, such as one done way back in 1964 on rhesus monkeys (this description of the experiments is reprinted from Rachels, 1990):

> These experiments were designed to discover whether rhesus monkeys are altruistic, and the method was to see whether they would be deterred from operating a device for securing food if doing so would cause pain to another monkey. One animal (called by the experimenters the 'operator' or 'O') was placed in one side of a divided box and taught to obtain food by pulling either of two chains. Food was available only when a light signal was given (a different light for each chain), and the O was trained to show no special preference for either chain.
>
> Next, another monkey (called the 'stimulus animal' or 'SA') was put into the other side of the box, which was divided by a one-way mirror so that the O could see the SA but not the other way around. The floor on the SA's side was covered with a grid attached to a shock source. Three days were allowed for the O to adapt to the presence of the SA, and then a circuit was completed so that whenever the O pulled one of the chains to secure food the SA received a severe electrical shock. Pulling the other chain continued to give food, but produced no shock. Now, by turning on one signal light at a time, in various

sequences and at various intervals, the experimenters could determine the extent to which the perception of the SA's distress would influence the O's willingness to pull the shock-producing chain.

After numerous trials the experimenters concluded that 'a majority of rhesus monkeys will consistently suffer hunger rather than secure food at the expense of electroshock to a conspecific'. In particular, in one series of tests, 6 of 8 animals showed this type of sacrificial behavior; in a second series, 6 of 10; and in a third, 13 of 15. One of the monkeys refrained from pulling on either chain for 12 days, and another for 5 days, after witnessing shock to the SA—which means they had no food at all during that time.

Other experiments showed that status in the social hierarchy of the SA and O monkeys had no effect on whether altruism was observed or not. One factor that did affect whether altruism was seen, though, was whether the O had previously been an SA and been shocked. O's who had previously been SA's were more likely to exhibit altruism, presumably because they remembered what being shocked was like and didn't want to put anyone else through it.

All of this is not to argue that other species are as intelligent as we are, or as sensitive or as capable of ethical behavior as we are. Comparing intelligence, for instance, it is obvious that we have somewhat bigger brains in proportion to our body size and are more intelligent than other species in most respects—although the difference is not nearly as great as we like to pretend it is. Nor is this to argue that other species are equivalent to us or should be treated as having equal rights. I only assert that other species do have rights and deserve far more respect than we have given them in the past. On whatever basis you value yourself and other human beings—intelligence, the ability to appreciate beauty, the willingness to make a personal sacrifice for the good of others, or the ability to feel such emotions as affection, grief, fear, and joy—other species, to one degree or another, possess the same traits. So if we are really as wonderful and exalted as we so incessantly claim we are, it is high time we proved it by treating our fellow creatures on this earth with the compassion and respect that they deserve.

The fact of evolution most clearly has implications for our atrocious and inexcusable treatment of domesticated animals in today's factory farms, as well as our treatment of laboratory animals and occasionally of pets. But it also bears upon our treatment of wild animals and nature in general. The fact of evolution makes untenable our traditional Western ethical position that human life has infinite value and all other forms of life have zero value. Clearly, at the least, other sentient species of animals have ethical value. It is an ethical good for them to be permitted to exist and permitted to pursue their lives in freedom, just as that is an ethical good for human beings. That means, for instance, that unless we have a compelling reason for denying it to them, we must reserve land that is intended exclusively or primarily for the use of these other animals. And what constitutes a compelling reason? "Because we want the land" is not a compelling reason. That is again saying that any human interest, no matter how trivial, takes precedence over any nonhuman interest, no matter how essential. That view is inconsistent with the biological fact of evolution. How about "Because the land is needed to feed more people;" is that a compelling reason? Yes and no. Yes in the short run but no in the long run. We have a duty of course to try to feed all the people in the world. With 5½ billion people it actually is not possible to feed them all, even farming, as we do today, almost every inch of land. But certainly we must try to feed as many as we can. In the long run, however, the excuse that we need to use all the world's land in order to feed people is not adequate. Our population is not something that happens to us; it is something we choose. And we have no need to choose to have 5½ billion people in the world. In choosing to have 5½ billion people vs. 200 prairie chickens, 150 mountain gorillas, 20 California condors, and 100 ocelots, we are demonstrating that we consider prairie chickens, gorillas, condors, and ocelots to have zero value relative to human beings. If we consider them to have value, as we must, we must allow them sufficient land to have substantial numbers.

What we are talking about is sharing—a virtue we supposedly learned in kindergarten but that we still aren't very good at.

To exist in reasonable numbers and pursue their lives in true freedom, wild animals must have abundant land, must be relatively free from pollution, and must have the other species on which they depend existing there with them also. Thus, to show ethical respect for these other sentient species of animals, which the fact of evolution demands that we do, we must reserve a significant fraction of the earth's land for the primary use of other species.

It is simply not tenable to claim, as almost all our traditional Western systems of ethics claim, that all other forms of life on this earth exist solely for the use of man. What kind of a just God would create sentient beings—capable of thought, of feeling pain and pleasure, and in some cases of behaving ethically—solely for the use of another species?

I think we all instinctively realize, however, that the purpose in preserving natural ecosystems is not just to preserve playgrounds for other intelligent mammals. It is not just the species that share certain traits with us that have ethical value. Saying that only those species have value is still taking an egotistical and human-centered view because it is still saying that we only value traits present in human beings. In our hearts I think we know that other species—even plants and bacteria—also have ethical value, and that it is a good to permit a forest to exist, even if no human ever visits it and even if no intelligent mammal ever visits it. In fact, many of us would go beyond that and say that even some inanimate objects—wild rivers and topsoil, for instance—should be treated as having ethical value. But why is this? One answer would be theological.

In the Judeo-Christian tradition, the book of Genesis explains how God created the world and man—created day and night, the waters teeming with countless living creatures, plants bearing seed and fruit trees bearing fruit, birds flying above the earth, cattle, reptiles, and wild animals, and man, both male and female. This process supposedly took six days, and after each day God saw that what He had created was "good." Finally, after the sixth day, "God saw all that He had made, and it was very good."

God was being much too modest. To say that the world He created was and is "very good" is the biggest understatement of all time. At one time or another in my life, I have doubted just about everything I have ever wanted to believe, but I have never for one moment doubted that this natural world around us is very, very good.

Since, therefore, the world around us—the rocks, the soil, the air, the water, the plants, and the other species of animals—is "very good" and was created by God, it seems clear that we are called to love it and care for it. Jesus said that the first great commandment is to love God with all your heart and with all your soul and with all your mind. Clearly, if a person is to obey this commandment, if he is to love God, one of the things he must do is love and nurture God's creation.

The argument to treat all of nature as having ethical value in itself need not, however, be based solely on theology. On a secular basis the duty to protect the natural world in general comes down to the fact that life works better for all of us when we do that. We, like every other species on this earth, are completely dependent on the other species and the physical processes of the earth for our survival and prosperity. The world works best, and thus we live best, when ecosystems are as healthy as possible, which basically means as natural and undisturbed as possible. We best protect those ecosystems, and best promote our own prosperity, when we treat the natural world and its individual parts as having value in themselves, aside from any utilitarian value to us. Although this argument is basically utilitarian—we should protect the natural world because to do so improves our lives and the lives of other "higher" animals—the ethics works best when it is not practiced on a utilitarian basis. It works best when we simply view nature as having value of itself and protect it for that reason, rather than protecting it only when we can calculate some benefit for ourselves or for other sentient animals.

In part, this type of environmental ethics is on weaker footing than our human ethics or our ethics concerning the sentient nonhuman animals that share some traits with us. With humans or other sentient animals, we can ask ourselves how we would like to be treated if we were in that other being's shoes (or paws); and we can see that we wouldn't want to be robbed, or lied to, or caught in a leg-hold trap. But when we put ourselves in the roots, so to speak, of a tree, we feel that we wouldn't particularly care whether we were cut down or not. In that respect, then, environmental ethics is on shakier ground than human ethics.

But in another respect, environmental ethics rests on exactly the same ground as human ethics. The ultimate argument for our rules of human ethics is just that life is better for all of us when we agree to follow those rules. Likewise, the ultimate argument for an environmental ethics that places inherent value on other forms of life and on the natural world in general is that granting nature inherent value and behaving as though nature has inherent value improves our lives and the lives of other sentient beings.

In both cases, although there is a utilitarian basis for the ethics, the ethics must be practiced without a utilitarian motive if it is to work.

Another secular argument for an environmental ethics that treats all of nature as having inherent value is that such an ethics is more consistent with the scientific facts of ecology than is an ethics that values only human beings. From the scientific study of ecology, we now know that we depend entirely on the other species and the physical processes of earth for our existence and prosperity. We know also that in any healthy ecosystem no one species is able to dominate. All species are always observed in healthy ecosystems to coexist in moderate numbers, with each species playing only a small part in the system. These findings do not fit well with an ethics that says that only human beings matter and that all other species and all of nature exist solely for human use. Such an ethics displays an arrogance about humanity's place in the world that flies in the face of scientific facts.

An ethics that values only human beings, though, is not merely inconsistent with the facts of science. It is also in an important sense philosophically inconsistent with itself. Central to our human ethics is the idea that each of us is only one small part of society—that every other person is just as important as we are and they must be treated that way. In other words, modesty is at the core of our interpersonal ethics. Yet when the prevailing ethics turns away from human beings to look at the rest of the world, they suddenly toss modesty in the dumpster. They suddenly proclaim that we are the pinnacle and goal of evolution, that we are the jewel of God's creation, and that all other beings and all of creation exists solely for our use and pleasure. I would suggest that there is a small inconsistency here.

What does it mean in practical terms to adopt this environmental ethic? It means, for instance, that we must recycle all recyclable materials, even if it is not economically necessary. Viewing nature as having inherent worth means that we must refrain from cutting down a forest or mining a hillside unless there is a compelling reason for doing so. Just as an ethic of respect for other human beings means that we must sometimes suffer some inconvenience in order to avoid harming another person, so an ethic of respect for nature means that we must sometimes suffer some inconvenience in order to avoid harming nature. If viewing nature as having inherent worth is ethically mandatory, then recycling is ethically mandatory. Instituting recycling programs involves so little inconvenience and cost that a society could only not recycle if it views nature as having no inherent worth. A society could only refrain from recycling if it were making that decision solely on the basis of the cost of recycling vs. the cost of extracting the resources from nature. In other words, it could only refrain from recycling (assuming the cost of recycling wasn't so exorbitant as to impinge seriously on human well-being) if it viewed nature as only a collection of resources, with no inherent worth at all.

Likewise, viewing nature as having inherent worth means that a society must leave substantial amounts of all types of land in a wilderness or natural state. That is, it must leave, say, a third or more of even land that is perfectly suitable for agriculture as wilderness. Currently, in case you hadn't noticed, even in the United States, a country that is relatively advanced in terms of environmental awareness, we have virtually no arable land in a wilderness state. The only existing wildernesses in the lower 48 states are wildernesses because they are unsuitable for agriculture. This situation is inconsistent with an attitude of viewing nature as having inherent worth. Currently, by exploiting every possible inch of suitable land for human use, we are demonstrating that we believe the goal in life is to carry as many people as possible on earth (and, it might be added, to carry them in as impoverished and malnourished a state as possible). Basically, we are carrying out on a global level the old party game of seeing how many people you can stuff into a Volkswagen.

If a society views nature as having any inherent worth, then it must leave substantial areas in a natural state—*and not just areas that the society would not be interested in using anyway.* It must leave even substantial areas of perfectly good agricultural land as wilderness.

The demands of this environmental ethics can be summarized in an Eleventh Commandment, which has been proposed by Father Vincent Rossi, an Episcopal priest in San Francisco:

> The earth is the Lord's and the fullness thereof; thou shall not despoil the earth nor destroy the life thereon.

Environmental Powers of the F.O.N.

Regardless of whether you agree with this attitude about the environment, it is still clearly a legitimate function of government to regulate our behavior toward the environment. Even if you feel that other species, the earth itself, and even future generations of human beings have no inherent rights and that we have no ethical responsibilities in our actions toward them, government still has a legitimate interest in regulating our environmental behavior. The essential function of government is to regulate behaviors that, if taken by some people, will adversely affect other people. And pollution by one group of people adversely affects the health and comfort of others. Consumption of the earth's limited natural resources by one group of people affects all other people. Destruction of a wilderness or other natural state by one group of people, if nothing else, deprives other people of a recreational opportunity. So actions affecting the environment are obviously legitimate areas of governmental regulation.

The question for this book then becomes, What level of government should have the responsibility for regulating which types of environmental activities?

More so than almost any other problems societies face, environmental problems are international. Air pollution doesn't stop for customs at national borders. Manufacture of chlorofluorocarbons by a few industrialized nations destroys the ozone layer and threatens the climate and human health of all the nations. Continued killing of whales by a few outlaw nations threatens to exterminate magnificent species that, to the extent they belong to humans at all, belong to all the nations of the world, not just to the nations that are killing them. So, clearly, many of the powers of environmental protection should rest with an international government. The ensuing sections will discuss what exactly those powers should be.

Pollution

Let's start our consideration with pollution. It is an unfortunate fact of life that pollution crosses national boundaries and causes problems for the countries downwind or downstream. That has already created some very serious international disagreements, and it will only create more in the future. If for no other reason, merely in the interest of keeping the peace, the F.O.N. should have the power to regulate this. But more than that, nations simply do not have the right to dump their garbage on their neighbors' lawns any more than we individuals have that right. So in the interest also of decency and protecting what is right and fair, the F.O.N. should have the power to regulate cross-boundary pollution.

How, then, should we deal with the specifics of pollution control laws? Should the F.O.N. have the power to regulate only pollution that actually crosses national boundaries? No. If we limited the F.O.N. in that way, we would make it impossible for it to ever achieve meaningful pollution control. Every time the F.O.N. attempted to enforce a regulation on some factory, the corporation owning the factory would go to court claiming that very little of its pollution actually crosses national boundaries. The courts would be bogged down with endless testimony on chemistry, wind direction, and weather patterns by different sets of experts constantly contradicting each other. It would make a mockery of the law. So I will propose that the F.O.N. simply have a blanket power to regulate pollution:

> Article I, Section 6
> Provision 22. The legislature shall have the power to enact laws regulating pollution of the air, water, land, and outer space. All such laws shall apply uniformly to all member nations.

Land and Wilderness

The next environmental issue to consider is the use of land and the preservation of wild and natural places. Like pollution, this also is an international issue. The destruction of Brazil's rain forests, for instance, clearly affects other nations besides Brazil. For one thing, the loss of that forest affects the global climate through its acceleration of the greenhouse effect and through its probable alteration of the global water cycle and global rain patterns. For another thing, the loss of that forest is causing the extinction of countless species that, to the extent they belong to nations at all, do not belong just to Brazil but to the whole world.

The argument is frequently made in the United States when a tract of land is being considered for protection, that that land doesn't belong only to the local people, who may want to exploit it; it belongs to the whole nation. But that argument should go further. The land doesn't belong only to the nation; it belongs to the whole world. If the United States were to consider, as it did in the 1960's, damming the Colorado River and flooding the Grand Canyon, should that decision be made only by the United States? Of course not. The Grand Canyon is one of the greatest natural treasures in the world. It is visited every year by thousands of people from foreign countries, and those people should have a say in its preservation. The Grand Canyon does not belong to the state of Arizona and it does not belong to the United States of America; it belongs to the world, to posterity, and to God.

What powers, then, should the F.O.N. possess to control the use of land in its member nations? First, it should certainly have the power to protect natural areas. But even a radical environmentalist such as myself would admit that it might be unwise to grant the F.O.N. unlimited power to protect as much of a nation's land as it wishes. Such unlimited power could be abused to deny a nation and its people their legitimate right to use their natural resources to make a living. In circumventing that potential abuse, though, we should not make the opposite mistake of granting the nations the right to pick and choose which of their lands the F.O.N. may protect. That would completely destroy the purpose of giving the F.O.N. the power to protect land at all. Rather, we should limit the F.O.N. to being able to protect only a certain percentage of a nation's land. The

F.O.N. then would still have the right to protect the natural areas it feels are most important to the rest of the world and to posterity, while the nation would still have the right to use the large majority of its land any way it chooses.

The value I would suggest is 15%. The F.O.N. should have the right to protect an area in any one nation equivalent to 15% of that nation's arable land area. That may seem like a rather large percentage to some, but it is not. If a nation cannot squeak by using "only" 85% of its arable land, the solution is not to open up the remaining 15% to exploitation; the solution is to learn how to use birth control.

If the only purpose in giving the F.O.N. power to protect natural areas were to protect the world's greatest natural treasures, the most scenic and beautiful places in the world, this could be accomplished by allowing the F.O.N. to protect only 5%, or even less, of a nation's land. But the purpose is larger than that. The purpose is to protect the worldwide environment—to protect the climate and the atmosphere, to protect the oceans, and to protect not just the majestic large animal species from extinction but also plants and insects, which are frequently more ecologically important. Accomplishing those goals involves far more than saving tiny tracts of natural areas as museum pieces; it involves preserving huge areas in a rather undisturbed state, accepting that those areas are as important to our survival as our farmlands, and accepting that the species living in those areas are full members along with us of the community we inhabit—the earth.

I propose the following clauses in the constitution:

Article I, Section 6

    Provision 23. The legislature shall have the power to enact laws protecting or creating natural areas within the territory of Federation of Nations member nations. Such areas shall not exceed an area equivalent to 15% of the arable land area (as defined in Article I, Section 3, Provision 4) of the nation containing them. Such areas may be separate from or coincident with areas already protected by national or local governments. These areas may be given any degree of protection the Federation of Nations wishes, but the Federation of Nations must purchase the land from its owners at fair value or give fair monetary compensation to the owners for the restrictions on the land's use.

Provision 25. In enacting laws protecting natural areas, the Federation of Nations may only increase or keep constant the legal protections on the land already enacted by national or local governments; and after creation of Federation of Nations-protected natural areas, the national and local governments shall retain the power to enact laws giving still more stringent protection to the areas.

The only part of this clause that needs further explanation is the circuitous sentence, "Such areas shall not exceed an area equivalent to 15% of the arable land area of the nation containing them." The sentence was constructed in such an awkward manner to recognize that the protected areas may not be part of the arable land area of the nation. They might instead be desert or tundra or rivers or lakes or even a region of the ocean that is part of that nation's territorial waters.

Incidentally, this 15% (or less) of a nation's land that the F.O.N. would protect is not designed to be the end all to protecting natural areas. As we saw in the section on environmental ethics, a great deal more than 15% of the world's land should be in a basically natural state. Probably at least one-third of a nation's arable land, in addition to almost all its nonarable land, should be in a wilderness state or be left for the primary use of other species. But not all of the responsibility for protecting this land should fall on the F.O.N. Most of the protection should be done by national and local governments.

Endangered Species

The next environmental issue that is an international issue, and thus an issue in which the F.O.N. ought to be able to intervene, is the protection of endangered species. Species of life do not belong to individual nations. No nation has an absolute right to exterminate a species.

I propose this clause for the constitution:

Article I, Section 6

Provision 27. The legislature shall have the power to ban or restrict the killing or harming of particular wild or endangered species of life and to ban or restrict the trade of products derived from such species.

Note that under this clause the F.O.N. could protect not just endangered species, but any wild species. There are two reasons for that. First, the F.O.N. should not be restricted to being able to act only when a species is on the verge of extinction. At that point it is frequently too late. Second, preventing extinctions, although it is the most important reason, isn't the only legitimate reason for the F.O.N. to protect certain species. Other legitimate reasons for protecting a species might include its ecological importance, or its intelligence, or simply its beauty.

Oceans

Finally, one of the obvious things that it would seem an international government ought to have jurisdiction over is the oceans. (Likewise, it should also have jurisdiction over the other areas of potential importance that are outside the nations' borders—Antarctica and outer space.) Of course, the F.O.N. will not be able to claim to own the oceans, because presumably not every nation of the world will be a member of the F.O.N. and nonmember nations will have as much claim to the oceans as member nations. Nevertheless, the F.O.N. could and should regulate its member nations' use of the oceans—particularly their pollution of the oceans and their extraction of the oceans' natural resources. Pollution of the oceans was already covered in Provision 22. To that I would propose that we add the following provision:

> Article I, Section 6
> Provision 28. The Legislature shall have the power to regulate the use of the oceans and the oceans' natural resources by the member nations and their citizens outside of the member nations' territorial waters, which extend 10 kilometers [6 miles] from their shores, and likewise shall have the power to regulate the use of Antarctica and outer space by member nations and their citizens.

That concludes the powers the F.O.N. will need to protect our global environment.

Summary of Chapter 9

- Overpopulation is, for almost all practical purposes, the only problem that matters. With few exceptions, the other problems of the world are not diseases in their own right but are only symptoms of the one most important disease, which is overpopulation.

- Despite the fact that overpopulation is the most serious problem we face and *the* cause or *a* cause of very nearly every other problem in the world, nations have done virtually nothing to attempt to reduce their populations. The reason for this inaction is simply that a large population is a crucial component of national power, and in the world in which we live, a world of anarchy above the national level and unrestrained competition between nations, concerns of national power must take precedence over all others.

- The F.O.N., though, will protect member nations from unrestrained competition and thus will end the need for their diseased addiction to national power. Thus, for the first time since we left the hunter-gatherer state, societies will be free to reduce their populations without the fear that doing so threatens their survival. This freeing of nations to reduce their populations will be one of the most important turning points in human history.

- The F.O.N., however, will permit this epochal transformation of our world, will permit for the first time in history this reduction of our populations, only if we design it properly. Specifically, we must not allow anything into its design that would encourage member nations to increase their populations. Thus, it is crucial that the legislature *not* have seats apportioned between nations according to population.

- Instead, I propose that we have two houses of the F.O.N. legislature, one in which seats are allotted between nations in proportion to arable land area, and one in which seats are allotted in proportion to the tax revenue a nation contributes to the F.O.N. The house with seats apportioned according to arable land area would provide a fair amount of power to the poorer nations, since they hold a majority of the world's land, while the house with seats apportioned according to tax revenue would provide a fair amount of power to the wealthier, and therefore militarily and economically more important, members of the F.O.N.

- Nations must retain the right to control their immigration because doing so is essential to their ability to limit their populations. If we do not allow nations to control their immigration, overpopulation in one nation will mean overpopulation in every nation. The excess people from the overpopulated nations will spill over into those nations that limit their birth rates, nullifying the benefits the responsible nations deserve for limiting their birth rates. In this situation, to protect each member nation from the consequences of overpopulation in the others, the F.O.N. would be forced to legislate mandatory birth control.

  But by leaving the nations the power to control their immigration, we can avoid that. If that power is left to the nations, then the F.O.N. need not and should not have the power to legislate population control.

- Scientific, theological, and philosophical arguments all compel us to obey an Eleventh Commandment pertaining to our treatment of nature:

  > The earth is the Lord's and the fullness thereof; thou shall not despoil the earth nor destroy the life thereon.

- Pollution from one nation crosses national boundaries and affects other nations. The extinction of species in one nation affects other nations. And the destruction of wildernesses and natural areas in one nation affects other nations. Therefore, environmental issues are international and the regulation of behaviors affecting the environment is a proper power of the Federation of Nations. The F.O.N. should have the power to control pollution, the power to ban the killing of particular species of plants and animals, and the power to protect wildernesses and other natural areas.

Appendix 9-A

The Absurd Arguments in Favor of Continued Population Growth

The most popular arguments for continued population growth fall into two general types, the "scientific" and economic.

The "Scientific"* Argument

The "scientific" argument asserts that advances in science and technology will be able to keep up with any population growth we perpetrate on the world and allow us to feed and take care of any conceivable number of people. The tiniest bit of thought reveals that that is absurd. At the current rate of growth, in a little less than 600 years the land area of the earth will be completely covered with human beings. That's if they stand upright. It wouldn't be possible to lie down. And of course there would be nothing to eat. You have to leave some land area for plants and livestock if you want to eat.

While the image of the earth's land area completely covered with human beings is rather powerful, there is another image I am even more fond of. At the current rate of population growth, in just 6,500 years the solid sphere of human bodies covering the earth would be creating more bodies so quickly that this sphere of bodies would be expanding at the speed of light.

At some point—in fact, at some point very, very soon, certainly within the next century—population growth must stop. Any advances in science and technology are simply irrelevant to that conclusion.

Some people protest at this point that we don't have to live on the earth. We could colonize the moon or other planets, they say. That is ridiculous. Life on other planets or the moon would not be self-sustaining. It would depend on food and supplies from the earth. It would in fact add to the burden on the earth,

---

*I put "scientific" in quotes because the argument has nothing to do with real science and everything to do with blind faith in science as a religion by people who don't understand science.

not lessen it. Colonizing other planets would decrease, not increase, the total possible human population in the universe.

To a very limited extent it is probably true that technology can postpone the day of reckoning, can allow us to temporarily have a larger population than we otherwise could. After all, in general, advances in technology do allow us to generate more goods from less resources. But as far as supporting a larger population is concerned, the only good that matters is food, and technology's ability to generate more food is far more limited than its ability to generate more of other goods. Food isn't manufactured, it grows. Food is just plants and animals, and they are dependent upon their interactions with soil and with other forms of life. They don't just materialize.

Technology does have a few tools to try to increase the food supply, primary among them being the breeding of crops. But the improvement that can come from the breeding of crops is inherently limited, and we may be approaching those limits. The breeding of a crop is basically just the effort to alter the plant so it will produce more of its food part, usually the fruit or seed, and less of its nonfood parts, usually the leaves, stem, and roots. Therein lies the inherent limitation on the process. A plant cannot be all fruit or seed. It has to make a living somehow, so it has to have a certain amount of leaves and roots. Testament to the fact that this process is limited is that, despite continuous increases in the manpower and money devoted to breeding crops, the rate of improvement of almost all engineered crops has begun to decline, and further improvement of some highly bred crops has stopped altogether. Although plant breeding will continue to help increase the food supply, it is clear that it will not be able to help as much as it has in the past.

This trend of diminishing returns is even more dramatic with the second most important technological tool to increase the food supply—fertilizers. Artificial fertilizer use steadily increased in the decades following World War II and was largely responsible for the steadily increasing crop yields that occurred simultaneously. But there is only so much fertilizer you can apply to land before you reach the point of diminishing returns, and we have now reached that point. Fertilizer use has now plateaued in all industrialized nations, as well as in many developing nations, as farmers have found that they can no longer increase their yields by increasing their fertilizer applications.

Likewise, the other major technological tools that agriculture has at its disposal—pesticides and irrigation—are also yielding diminishing returns. Pesticides are just generating resistant pests, not to mention their many other unpleasant side effects, and irrigation in vast areas where it is practiced today is just generating depleted aquifers and salt-poisoned soil.

But undoubtedly the most important limitation on future increases in food production is that we have just plain run out of land. Two-thirds of the earth's land is now under direct human use, with the remaining third consisting almost entirely of Antarctica, mountains, deserts, and arctic tundra. Until about a decade ago, the amount of land under cultivation worldwide steadily increased. But that increase has now come to a screeching halt. Unless you can figure out a way to grow wheat in Antarctica, there is just no more land to cultivate. In fact, not only has the amount of land under cultivation stopped increasing, but it will probably soon start decreasing—as it already is decreasing in the United States and many other nations. It is decreasing in those nations, first, because of the spread of roads and cities that is caused by population growth, and second, because of the retreat from cultivating unsustainable, highly erodible land. That retreat is either, in the best case, a conscious decision to stop cultivating erodible land before it is turned into desert and made unfit even to support grasslands or forest, or, when that foresight is not practiced, simply the result of the land becoming desert and no longer being cultivatable.

What all this means is that the rate of increase of agricultural output is now slowing and will continue to slow. In fact, it might even reverse. In 1987 and 1988, for the first time in history, total world grain output declined for two consecutive years. While it is true that in the other years of the 80's world grain output was able to increase, it was never able to increase as much as population. World per capita food production has been in steady decline for a decade. In fact, since 1984 per capita grain output has been declining on every continent on earth. Yes, even on Europe and North America.

World food production cannot keep up with population

growth and is not keeping up with population growth.

Aside from all that, though, even if technology could magically enable us to always generate more food and other goods from less resources, why would it follow that we should continually increase the population? Where is it written that we must always carry the maximum number of people that we can feed? Isn't there more to life than avoiding starvation? Doesn't the opportunity to see other species of animals in the wild and let them stir our imaginations count for anything? Doesn't space for solitude have some value?

The Economic Argument

This argument is even more insidious than the "scientific" argument because it does not merely assert that it would be *possible* to increase population forever, as the "scientific" argument does, but actually claims that an eternally increasing population is *necessary and desirable.*

The economic argument claims that an increasing population automatically creates a healthy economy and a decreasing population automatically causes a depression. One of the many drawbacks to this argument is that there is not a shred of evidence it is true. In fact, all available evidence strongly indicates, as does simple common sense, that exactly the opposite is the case: An increasing population creates economic hardship and a decreasing population creates prosperity. Of the industrialized world, the nation with the lowest rate of population growth between 1970 and 1990 was West Germany. In exact contradiction to the theory behind this economic argument for population growth, West Germany also happens to have had, with the possible exception of Japan (another nation with a comparatively low rate of population growth), the world's most robust economy over that period. Likewise, again in direct contradiction to this argument for population growth, the industrialized nation that has had the greatest population growth over the past two decades, Israel, also has been plagued with the highest rate of inflation and perhaps the worst economy of any industrialized nation.

The story is the same among the underdeveloped nations. The tiny handful of Third World nations that have managed to hold their population growth to less than 50% over the past 20 years—a group headed by China, Sri Lanka, South Korea, and the star of the Third World population sweepstakes, Uruguay, with only a 6% population increase over that period—also happen to be almost the only Third World nations whose economies have not spiraled into oblivion. (Sri Lanka and Uruguay have suffered from civil war and political unrest in recent years, so their economies have not done as well as they might have. But those two nations have still done better economically than most Third World nations, and China and South Korea have been vastly better off than most Third World nations.)

It is well known that there is a negative correlation between national wealth and the rate of a nation's population growth. Likewise, *rate* of growth of a nation's wealth or per capita G.N.P. is also negatively correlated with the rate of growth of its population. Given that, one would logically conclude that rapid population growth (or for that matter, any population growth) harms a nation economically. Of course, we could argue about cause and effect. We know that poverty causes families to choose to have more children. So it isn't only true that population growth causes nations to be poor. It is also true that being poor causes nations to tend to have more rapid population growth. But given the persistent correlation between population growth and poor national economies, it is very strange to look at that data and then conclude that it means population growth *helps* a nation's economy. Yet this is exactly what economists do. It's like observing the large number of tall individuals in the National Basketball Association and then concluding that this data means *short* people have an inherent advantage in basketball.

When economists argue that population growth helps a nation's economy, or even that it is essential for national economic well-being, they are forced to ignore the evidence, since, as we have seen, all empirical evidence indicates exactly the opposite: The nations with the lowest population densities and the lowest rates of population growth have the highest standard of living and the biggest rate of increase in their standard of living. So the economists are forced to base their arguments on a "logical" analysis. It turns out, though, that their analysis isn't very logical.

The one and only valid point economists have when they say

that a large population is necessary for developing wealth is that a community or nation must have a certain minimum population if it is to allow economic specialization. If a community consists of just one family, every member of that family is going to spend most of his or her time working as a self-sufficient farmer. That one-family community is not likely to produce televisions, because the members of the family are not going to have the time to learn electronics, learn how to mine metal and smelt it, learn how to synthesize plastics, and then apply all that knowledge to produce a television.

To make televisions, a society needs a certain amount of specialization. But it doesn't need 250 million people (the current population of the U.S.) to develop that level of specialization. A society of 50 people can have members who specialize in medicine, religion, and military leadership. A society of a few hundred can have traders, shopkeepers, and teachers. With a few thousand people, a society can have enough teachers that they can specialize in teaching particular subjects. With a few tens of thousands, or at most hundreds of thousands, of people, a society can support enough scientists and inventors to allow them to specialize as astronomers, microbiologists, and materials engineers. With a million people, a society has sufficient population to support virtually all of the specialization that is necessary for our modern life.

Economic specialization is a central characteristic of our societies today, and it is necessary for the development of the kind of wealth we enjoy in the United States. Economists rightly point out that in order to have this kind of economic specialization, societies need some minimum population. But we are way beyond that population. If we decrease our population a bit, we are not suddenly going to find ourselves with too few people for some of us to specialize as teachers and doctors. In order to allow the kind of economic specialization needed to develop and support our current wealth in the United States, the world and U.S. populations would need to be no more than 10%, and probably no more than 1%, of their current levels.

One of the cornerstones of the economic argument for population growth is the idea that population growth increases total demand (because there are more people to buy goods). But first of all, it isn't *total* demand that matters, but *per capita* demand. According to economists, I as an author should be happy about population growth because it means there are more people to buy my book. But it also means there are more authors writing books. So it really doesn't matter. The ratio of readers to authors doesn't change. Despite population growth (and despite the fact that his book had no sex in it), Thomas Paine sold nearly as many copies of *Common Sense* during the American Revolution as Danielle Steel sells of her best-sellers today.*

Second, it isn't even necessarily true that population growth increases *total* demand. It doesn't increase total demand if the people on average become poorer and have less to spend. And since the earth is finite, population growth does have a tendency to make people poorer. It certainly has had that effect in Mexico, India, and Ethiopia.

One thing population growth does automatically do, though, is increase the cost of all raw materials. Of course, other factors also affect the cost of raw materials, so this is not to say that when population rises the price of every raw material necessarily rises with it. Sometimes, for instance, a technical advance in the extraction of a resource will decrease the cost of that resource. But that has nothing to do with the effect of population. When a technical advance allows the price of a raw material to drop despite a rise in population, you can be assured that the price would have dropped even more if population had stayed constant. In the present world situation, with moderate or high population densities in every country on earth, any population

---

*Admittedly, *Common Sense* was an unusual case. In general, it is true that population growth allows the most successful best-sellers of today to sell a few more copies than the best-sellers of earlier times. But population growth also has negative effects for authors. Since the number of books that a bookstore can carry is fairly constant, population growth, and the increasing number of authors and aspiring authors that goes with it, means that it is more difficult for any given author to get his book into a bookstore (or to get it published at all). Overall, at best this situation is a wash for authors. For the tiny number of authors who reach the top of the best-seller lists, population growth is an asset. It allows them to sell a few more books and make a bit more money. For all the rest of the authors, population growth is a hindrance. It makes it more difficult for them to get their books published and to get attention for them if they do get published.

growth automatically contributes to an increased cost of every raw material and thus hurts economic well-being.

The final and most ridiculous aspect of the economic argument for population growth is the claim that without continuous population growth we risk a labor shortage. First, except in very special circumstances, no serious labor shortage has ever existed in an industrialized country in peace-time, so it's not much of a threat. (The only serious labor shortages have been in nations, such as Germany and Japan in the first few years after World War II, rebuilding immediately after being destroyed by war.) Second, and more important, a labor shortage is not a bad thing at all but rather the best thing that could possibly happen. A labor shortage means you have a robust economy, no unemployment, and employers competitively bidding against each other for lower-class laborers, driving up wages.

The economic argument for population growth is totally wrong. It claims that an increasing population is necessary for economic health, when in fact, as all the evidence indicates and as a small application of common sense will tell us, the opposite is the case. An increasing population means less raw materials for each of us, and means we are all poorer. A decreasing population means more raw materials for each of us, and means we are all richer.

Appendix 9-B

An Alternative Basis for Representation in the House of Representatives that Avoids Providing Any Incentive to Increase Population

I have proposed in this chapter that representation for each nation in one of the houses of the legislature, the House of Representatives, be proportional to the revenue received from that nation from the general F.O.N. sales tax. As discussed in chapter 8, revenue from this tax will be directly proportional to gross national consumption (G.N.C.) or to the more familiar gross national product (G.N.P.). Since G.N.P. is somewhat correlated with population, this plan violates my desire that nothing in the F.O.N.'s design should in any way encourage population growth. It should be pointed out, however, that the correlation between G.N.P. and population is fairly weak. If a nation were to cut its population in half, G.N.P. would fall by less than one-half, would fall by perhaps only one-quarter of its original level, because there would be more resources to go around and each worker, having more resources to work with, would therefore be more productive. This means that per capita G.N.P. and per capita wealth increase when population falls and decrease when it rises. So on two counts, tying political representation to G.N.P. is not a significant encouragement to population growth. First, G.N.P. is fairly resistant to changes in population, both to increases and decreases. Second, to the extent that a decrease in population will decrease G.N.P. and decrease a nation's representation, that loss of representation will be compensated for by an increased *per capita* G.N.P. and *per capita* wealth. I think most people would rather be richer than have more votes in the F.O.N.

Nevertheless, I would prefer to have nothing in the F.O.N.'s design that gives even a weak incentive for nations to increase their populations. So as far as I am concerned, we could improve upon this provision of the constitution.

The plan I have proposed in this chapter makes representation in the House of Representatives proportional to tax revenues or G.N.P., which is the same as saying it is proportional to per capita tax revenues times the population. That sentence can be explained by the following equation:

$$\text{tax revenues} = \frac{\text{tax revenues}}{\text{population}} \times \text{population}$$

An improvement on this plan would be to make representation proportional to per capita tax revenues times what the population *ought to be,* instead of what it actually is. In theory, the populations of the nations ought to be proportional to their arable land area. So in this formulation we would make representation proportional to

$$\frac{\text{tax revenues}}{\text{population}} \times \text{arable land area}$$

instead of

$$\frac{\text{tax revenues}}{\text{population}} \times \text{population}$$

Now, if this is a better plan, why didn't I use it in the main text of this chapter and in the proposed constitution? Two reasons: (1) The plan used in the main text of this chapter is simpler, and (2) That plan is also more politically realistic.

The second reason is probably more important. Although the plan proposed in this appendix might be better, it would never be accepted by Japan and the European nations because of their small land area. Since those nations are such important potential F.O.N. members, we are likely to have to make some concessions to their wishes.

Chapter 10

Summary of the Goals and Powers of the Federation of Nations

Up to this point, we have almost completely covered what the F.O.N.'s powers should be. There is just one power left to mention, which I will mention now: In order to carry out its task of keeping the peace between member nations, the Federation of Nations must have the power to extradite criminals between nations (Art. III, Sec. 2, Prov. 7). A citizen, resident, or government official of one nation who violates the laws of another nation must not be able to hide behind the shield of national borders. Justice must be served. He must be extradited and given a fair trial* in the nation in which his crimes occurred. Without this provision, true peace between nations could not exist.

---

*Through constitutional provisions that will be discussed in the next chapter, the F.O.N. will have the ability to ensure that all trials in all member nations are indeed fair.

With that, I have now completed the list of powers that I will propose for the Federation of Nations. So now would be a logical time to stop and look back at the goals we want the F.O.N. to accomplish and the powers we have granted it to achieve those goals.

The list of goals I have chosen for the F.O.N. to try to achieve is short but sweet:

1. To keep the peace between member nations and, ultimately, when all, or almost all, the nations of the world are members, to create permanent world peace.
2. To increase the power, both in military terms and in other terms, of each and every member nation.
3. To guarantee the observation of basic human rights for citizens of all member nations.
4. To create an international situation in which nations will finally be free to reduce their populations, and thus begin to solve almost all their problems, without fearing the loss in power that reducing their populations would otherwise entail.
5. To protect the global natural environment.

In addition, I found that if the F.O.N. is to carry out the first goal, to keep the peace *between* member nations, it will have to share partial responsibility with the nations for achieving a 6th goal:

6. To help keep the peace *within* each member nation.

To achieve those magnificent goals, we needed to grant the F.O.N. only a rather short list of powers:

1. To take over the control of the militaries of all member nations.
2. To enact laws that enforce the constitutional list of basic human rights.
3. To require all member nations and all citizens of member nations to observe economic boycotts and embargoes enacted against a nonmember nation or, on occasion, against a particular offending member nation.

4. To assess one and only one type of tax: a flat percentage sales tax applying uniformly to all goods and services sold in all member nations.*
5. To extradite criminal suspects between nations.
6. To protect a small percentage of each member nation's land as natural areas.
7. To regulate pollution, especially pollution that crosses national boundaries.
8. To enact laws protecting endangered species.

Along the way, in assigning these goals to the F.O.N. and granting it these powers, we have also found that it will achieve two other pleasant goals: It will improve (one might almost say create) nonmilitary means of exerting power, and it will reduce the total cost of government, in particular will reduce the cost of defense, which is the biggest expenditure of government.

Those goals and powers that the F.O.N. *has* been given, though, are only part of the story. The other, and larger, part of the story is the goals and powers it has *not* been given. Let's recount some of those.

The F.O.N. has not been given the goal or power of guaranteeing a democratic form of government at the national or local levels for its member nations, or indeed of guaranteeing any other form of government that some might deem good. Rather, it will only have the power to insure that human rights are respected, and then it will leave it to the people of the separate nations to decide what forms of government they want.

Except for its power to legislate an occasional total embargo or boycott, the F.O.N. has not been given any power to regulate trade or the economies of its member nations. It has not been given the goal of maximizing the economic health of the whole of

---

*Technically, the F.O.N. also has another power of taxation, which is that a nation's representatives can assess taxes on their own nation to pay their nation's military personnel. I do not include that on this list of F.O.N. powers because it does not involve surrendering any power to foreigners. It is a power over a nation exerted solely by that nation's own representatives, just as exists today.

the F.O.N. or any of its parts. It has not been given the power to print money, and it will not infringe on the right of nations to manipulate the money supply for their own benefit. It has not been given the power to regulate corporations or control prices. It has not been given the power to regulate the relations between labor and management.

Also, the F.O.N. has been given the power to assess only one type of tax—a single, uniform, socially neutral sales tax. This forbids it from another very large activity of government—the design of complicated tax codes to accomplish various economic and social goals. That power is left exclusively with the national and local governments.

Except for its power to protect a small percentage of a nation's land as natural areas, the F.O.N. has not been given any power to zone land or dictate how it should be developed.

The F.O.N. has not been given the goal or power of redistributing wealth between nations.

Likewise, the F.O.N. has not been given the goal or power of redistributing wealth between citizens or of guaranteeing for its citizens a certain minimal standard of living or basic health care. Those may be laudable goals, but they should be left to the nations.

In short, almost all powers of government remain with the nations and localities. The list of real powers "given up" in any sense to the F.O.N. by the nations and people is just four: (1) control of the military, (2) the right to extradite criminal suspects between nations, (3) the right to regulate some environmental matters, and (4) a limited power to tax. The other powers of the F.O.N. listed earlier in this chapter either fall under the heading of one of those four powers or do not represent the surrendering of any powers by the nations and people.

Specifically, guaranteeing human rights is not really a power for the F.O.N. but rather, for the F.O.N. and all other levels of government, the absence of certain powers—the absence of the power to block free expression of ideas, to jail without charge, and so forth.

As for the F.O.N.'s power to legislate economic boycotts, this can be thought of as simply a part of its power to control the military. Boycotts and embargoes are just ways of exerting force such that we can avoid having to use military force. Surely, if we grant the F.O.N. control of the military, we should also grant it every available tool for avoiding having to use that military.

So, again, the nations are yielding to the F.O.N. only four real powers—control over some environmental matters, control over the military, the right to extradite criminals, and a limited power of taxation.

Despite the F.O.N.'s limited sphere of influence, though, it is a government, and consequently we must decide a great many details about how it is to operate. Those details are the subject of the next chapter.

Summary of Chapter 10

- To enjoy the many wonderful benefits the F.O.N. can provide, the nations and people will have to surrender to the F.O.N. only four powers: (1) control of the military, (2) the right to regulate some environmental matters, (3) the right to extradite criminal suspects between nations, and, in order to pay for those first three powers, (4) the right to assess a uniform sales tax.

Chapter 11

The Federation of Nations Government

This book has so far given a complete description of what the powers of the Federation of Nations should be but only very few details of what the form of the F.O.N. government should be and how it should be run. I have described an entity that could bring about universal respect for human rights, rational control of our population (which would largely solve virtually every problem in the world), a measure of morality and sanity to our treatment of the environment, and permanent world peace. The F.O.N. could, I believe, be the greatest thing to happen to mankind in almost 2,000 years.

But, to be honest, if we do not design it properly, it could also be a nightmare. The difference will be in the details. The form of the F.O.N. government and a controlled system of checks and balances between the fallible human beings who will run the F.O.N. is what will determine whether it can be the tremendous force for good that I have described. It is to those details of form that I now turn.

Separation of Powers

Probably the most important principle of government developed and followed by the framers of the United States Constitution (building upon and extending an idea originally stated by the English philosopher John Locke) is that the three basic powers of government—passing laws, enforcing laws, and judging accused violations of laws—should be separate. This means that the people responsible for these three branches of government—the legislative, executive, and judicial branches—should be separate groups of people and should derive their positions and power in different ways. It also means that each branch of government should have ways to fight back when, as inevitably happens, the other two branches try to usurp some of its powers. Those ideas are the cornerstone of a system of checks and balances to prevent tyranny.

The Legislative Branch

The first branch of government I will discuss will be the legislative. In Chapter 9 I proposed that the F.O.N. should have two legislative bodies, one of which, the Senate, would have seats distributed between nations in proportion to their arable land area, and the other of which, the House of Representatives, would have seats distributed between nations in proportion to their tax contributions to the F.O.N. from the F.O.N. general sales tax. In order to be passed into law, a bill would have to be approved by a majority in each house of the legislature.

There are two major reasons for having two houses of the legislature instead of just one. The first is that it allows a political compromise in apportioning power between the member nations. The Third World nations vs. the industrialized nations, the nations with small land area vs. those with large land area, and the nations with large populations vs. those with smaller populations will all have different ideas about how representation in the legislature should be apportioned. By having two houses instead of just one and making the basis for representation different in the two houses, we can satisfy more nations.

The second reason, and probably the more important reason, for having two houses of the legislature is to promote stability in government by making it somewhat more difficult to enact laws and ensuring that the proposed laws receive careful consideration before they are enacted. To be respected by governments of nonmember nations, against whom it must defend itself, and to be respected by the people of its member nations, from whom it must derive its support if it is to function, the F.O.N. should be fairly stable, predictable, and deliberate in its actions. New laws should not be enacted lightly. Requiring that bills be approved by two houses with somewhat different interests insures that indeed they will not be. Having two houses with somewhat different interests makes changing the law fairly difficult, and more important, slows down the process of enacting a law, so as to allow more time for consideration and more time for the public to organize and express its opposition or support for the bill.

Next, I want to discuss the terms of office for the senators and representatives. I propose that senators be elected to single eight-year terms of office and be prohibited from ever seeking election to the Senate again. This will free senators to vote their consciences and to concern themselves with the long term interests of the F.O.N., rather than having to worry about being reelected and having their actions dictated by the whim of public opinion.

To promote stability, Senate terms should be staggered so that one quarter of the Senate seats, both in the total F.O.N. and in each nation, are up for election every two years, rather than having the entire Senate change every eight years.

The House of Representatives should then serve as the more democratic body, with its members elected to two-year terms and no limitation on the number of times they may seek reelection.

Finally, one power and responsibility for the legislative branch, in addition to its power to enact laws, deserves special mention: The legislative branch must have the sole power to declare war.

The decision of going to war is, of course, the most important decision a society ever makes. It demands careful consideration, and, as much as possible, the views of all the different groups in the society should be publicly expressed and debated before the decision is made. For those reasons, the legislative branch, the branch of government that contains elected representatives representing all the groups in the society, and the branch that is designed to foster careful consideration and public debate before its decisions are made, is clearly the branch that should have the power to declare war.

The Executive Branch

The defining feature of this second branch of government is that it is in charge of "executing" (hence, "executive" branch) or enforcing the laws. That is, it is in charge of capturing and prosecuting accused lawbreakers. It is also traditionally in charge of the military and of negotiating treaties with foreign nations. The reason control of the military is granted to the executive branch is that, of the three basic functions of government—writing the law, enforcing the law, and judging accused violations of the law—enforcing the law is the only one that by its nature requires physical force. Lawbreakers do not want to go to jail. If you are going to put them in jail, you had better have more physical force than they do. So the executive branch needs to control the ultimate physical force of the society, which in the case of the F.O.N. means the F.O.N. military.

As for why the executive branch is traditionally given responsibility for negotiating treaties and handling diplomacy with foreign nations, these of necessity go along with control of the military. The threat of military action is the ultimate threat or bargaining chip any nation or society has in its dealings with other nations. Therefore, those who negotiate treaties must also be those who control the military. If we nominally gave the power of making treaties and negotiating with foreign nations to some group of people other than the people who control the military, the foreign nations would ignore them and come to the people controlling the military anyway.

There are good reasons, then, for the traditional arrangement of making the branch of government responsible for enforcing the laws, the executive branch, also responsible for commanding the military and handling diplomacy. The F.O.N. should maintain that arrangement (Art. II, Sec. 3, Provs. 2, 3, and 7). The next question is, *Within* the executive branch, how should these powers be arranged or divided? To address that question I will first point out that the discussion above showed that the powers to enforce the law, to control the military, and to handle diplomacy with nonmember nations must reside with the same group of people, which means that we can immediately throw out the possible suggested arrangement of dividing those powers among several individuals—making one person commander of the military, another the chief diplomat, and one or more others in charge of enforcing the different types of laws. The only question, then, is whether these executive powers should reside in a committee or in a single person.

The answer is probably that they should reside in a single person, as they currently do in almost every nation. The first reason for vesting executive power in a single person is that the executive branch, uniquely among the three branches, requires decisiveness and boldness. Enacting legislation is an activity that requires lengthy contemplation and wisdom, but commanding an army in war, which is the most important duty of the executive, does not allow time for lengthy contemplation (though it can still benefit from wisdom). Instead, it requires energy, imagination, and boldness. Those qualities are characteristic of individuals, not committees.

After some time, perhaps the F.O.N. will never again experience war, but it will always have a military, and any time that military is used, its leader is likely to have to act decisively. So the requirement for boldness in the executive will not go away. Besides that, the fight against criminals requires decisive and imaginative leadership just as much as the fight against military enemies, and we will most certainly always have criminals.

The second argument for executive powers resting with an individual rather than a committee is the need for secrecy in diplomacy. Negotiating treaties means making confidential offers, and when nonmember nations make those offers to the F.O.N., they will expect them to remain secret until the final treaty is announced. They can have more confidence that their secrets will be kept if they are given to a single individual than if they are given to several.

The third argument for giving executive power to a single individual is that it allows no dodging of responsibility. If executive powers resided with a committee, that committee could make mistakes and abuse power while the members of the committee could dodge responsibility by blaming everything on each other. In contrast, with a single president, when the executive branch screws up, we know who to blame and we know who to replace.*

Good government demands an energetic executive, and an energetic executive demands a single president.

Presidential Term of Office

I will propose that the president serve a single six-year term and be barred from being reelected. That will free him to make the politically unpopular but necessary decisions that any leader must make, without worrying about reelection. More important, though, it will establish that he will one day return to being a private citizen. One of the greatest checks on abuse of power is to insure that the powerful will one day lose their power and return to being ordinary citizens.

Selecting the President (Art. II, Sec. 1, Prov. 2)

The next question is, How will we select the president? At the risk of sounding undemocratic, I think it would be a major mistake to have the president popularly elected. Consider the difficulties of running a campaign for the presidency in a worldwide F.O.N. In order to reach every corner of the world, a candidate would have to campaign for years in places where he does not even know the language or anything at all about the culture. Under this system, the characteristics for which we would be selecting would be a willingness to campaign for

---

*Of late this principle has not worked like it ought to in the United States. Especially in the Reagan administration, we had a popular president who was somehow never held personally accountable for the inordinate number of scandals in his administration or even for many of his administration's unpopular policies. Somehow President Reagan managed to take credit for all his popular policies while blaming all his scandals and unpopular polices on aides. This, however, is a problem with the American press and public, not with vesting executive powers in a single person. The president is in charge of the executive branch, and he should be held responsible for everything that happens in that branch. If the American press and public refuse to recognize that, that is only a problem with them, not a problem with the constitution.

several years around the world, mostly away from his family, in pursuit of a goal he is very unlikely to achieve, and an ability to so completely transform himself and his views to suit his audience that he could appeal to peoples of totally different cultures and widely differing political outlooks. In other words, we would be selecting for shallowness, plasticity, a lack of commitment to family, a neurotic, if not psychotic, level of competitiveness, and an insatiable desire for power.

That's not exactly the person I want in control of the most powerful military force in the world.

A popular presidential election would almost certainly be a disaster. In its place I will propose something different.

Those eligible to be elected president should be the former senators who have finished their eight-year terms of office sometime in the previous six years. I will propose that the new president begin his term of office in an odd year, that is, one year after the beginning of the new legislative terms of office rather than the same year, which means that when we select a new president to begin office in year 7, those eligible to be considered will be senators who left office in years 6, 4, or 2.

One of the advantages of making only former senators eligible to be selected president is that we insure that, though the president is not popularly elected by the whole F.O.N. public, he has at least been popularly elected in his own nation. We will not be selecting someone who has not passed public scrutiny with the voters.

From this pool of former senators, in my proposal, the current senators will select two to be candidates for the presidency.* This means that the current senators will be selecting from their former colleagues. They will have experience working with these people and will know them personally. They will therefore be in a position to select for traits such as integrity, honesty, intelligence, humility, and courage. Excessive competitiveness and an insatiable drive for power, the primary traits that would

---

*When the F.O.N. is first formed of course there will be no former senators, so my proposed constitution specifies that at that time the senators will select the two presidential candidates from among themselves.

be selected for in a popular election, will be selected against in this process. The senators are likely to choose former colleagues who were more interested in cooperating than in competing and who saw power as a responsibility rather than as a trophy.

Obviously some uglier motives will also play a role in selecting the presidential candidates. But still, those who are only interested in power for its own sake are not likely to be popular with their colleagues and not likely to get the nomination. Also, two factors in the design of the F.O.N. and of this selection system will mitigate against deal-making in the selection of the presidential candidates. The first is that the candidates must be chosen from among the *former* senators. The advantage of choosing from former senators rather than current ones is that the former senators, being out of office, will not be in a position to trade their legislative votes on certain issues in exchange for the support of the other senators for their presidential candidacies. The second factor mitigating against deal-making in the presidential selection process is the almost total lack of economic powers for the F.O.N. This means that the presidential candidates will not be able to promise very many grants, loans, development projects, and other economic goodies for any particular senator's nation or district. Thus, with the senators unable to trade their vote in the presidential selection process for the votes of the candidates on some other matter, and unable to sell their vote for the promise of economic return for their district or nation, they will be left with little recourse but to choose the candidates on the merits.

With the candidates selected, the next step in this process will be to present them to the House of Representatives, which will have the responsibility for choosing between them. By making the House of Representatives responsible for the final choice, since most representatives will plan on running for reelection and will be under pressure to make their choice consistent with the will of the people in their district, we can make the process more democratic and responsive to the people.

Not only, then, is this system likely to produce two very good candidates, but choosing between those candidates will be a group of people who have been trusted with elective office by the citizens of the F.O.N., are generally well-informed on the issues, will have some personal knowledge of the candidates, will have the opportunity to explore with the candidates in detail their plans for the F.O.N.'s future, and will be responsible for their final choice to the voters. It is a system that I believe should produce very good presidents.

This system is not perfect, of course. It does not guarantee we will always have excellent presidents. But no system could. This system at least should weed out the dangerous and the power hungry and should produce better presidents than we could expect from a popular presidential election or from any other system I can think of.

Spying

Having developed a system for selecting a president, we can now discuss in somewhat more detail his powers. The first detail of presidential power I want to mention here is that the president needs the power to gather intelligence information about nonmember nations (Art. II, Sec. 3, Prov. 3). It is obviously prudent for any government to know something about the military capabilities of its potential enemies and to try to be able to predict the actions of those potential enemies. Gathering intelligence about foreign nations (which in the case of the F.O.N. means nonmember nations) is a legitimate function of any government. Since the executive branch controls the military and is the branch primarily responsible for foreign affairs, the executive branch is the branch that should be in charge of that intelligence gathering (although the legislature should also be able to control or restrict intelligence gathering through laws it may enact).

I emphasize, though, that this only authorizes the executive branch to *gather* information, not to act on it. This only authorizes the executive branch to *predict* the actions of nonmember nations, not to try to control those actions. Attempting to control the actions of nonmember nations, in particular attempting to do so in secret, is the subject of the next section.

The Military and Covert Actions

Among the most crucial questions we will have to answer in forming the F.O.N. is exactly how and by whom will the military be controlled and military actions initiated.

On this subject, two points have already been made. The president must be the commander-in-chief of the military and the legislature must have the sole power to declare wars. The logic of making the president commander-in-chief of the military is essentially that, first, to prevent tyranny the military must of course be under civilian control, and of the three branches of civilian government, the executive branch, since it requires force to carry out its duty of enforcing laws, is the branch that needs to control the military. The logic of making the legislature, rather than the president, responsible for declaring war is that this most important of decisions should not be made by just one human being, but by a large group of people selected to represent the broad spectrum of interests in the society, and should not be made quickly and in secret, but rather should be made by an open vote after lengthy public debate.

That much is easy. Now we get to the hard part. A crucial advantage to any military action is surprise. If we require that any F.O.N. military action against our enemies be preceded by public debate in the legislature and a public declaration of war, we weaken ourselves militarily. Someday, when the F.O.N. contains most of the nations of the world and is vastly more powerful than any potential enemy, that may be a price worth paying. But initially the F.O.N. will not be able to afford it. The F.O.N. will need some procedure for attacking in secret.

In the U.S. the procedure for secret attack is simply that the president orders it. Congress is not included at all. The result has been a three-year undeclared war in Korea, a 13-year undeclared war in Vietnam, a military fiasco in Beirut, embarrassment before the world when the U.S. violated international law and mined Nicaragua's harbors, and the desecration of our Constitution by the continual flaunting of its central provision that Congress alone has the power to declare war.

Clearly, that procedure is not acceptable.

I propose the following procedure instead. I propose that we require that any secret actions, military or otherwise, taken against a nonmember nation must be approved in advance by a majority vote of a Security Committee, which would be composed of the president and 14 legislators, seven from the Senate and seven from the House (Art. II, Sec. 4, Provs. 1 and 2).

After a secret action is approved by the Security Committee, a reasonable amount of time should be allowed for it to be carried out, which I will propose should be one year. Then the Security Committee vote and the precise action that was approved must be automatically revealed to the public.

There are two purposes to this procedure. First, it is designed to allow the F.O.N. to use the element of surprise and to keep actions it may take against its enemies secret from those enemies. In conjunction with that purpose, the committee would, of course, be meeting in secret, and when an action is approved, we must make it illegal and a very serious crime for the committee members who may have opposed the action to reveal it before it can be carried out.

But the second purpose of this Security Committee procedure, even more important than the first purpose, is to insure that any and all secret actions that this government may have to take are publicly revealed very soon after they are taken. The idea behind secret actions is that those actions should be secret from our enemies, not from the voters. Democracy cannot function unless all the government's actions are publicly revealed and debated. Thus, in conjunction with this purpose, it must also be illegal and a very serious crime for any member of the Security Committee to attempt to prevent the public release of its votes and the actions it approves within one year of the approval of those actions. Likewise, it must also be a serious crime for the president to attempt to take a secret action without prior approval by the Security Committee. Those three crimes—revealing an approved secret action before it can be carried out or attempting to keep it secret beyond one year or the president's taking a secret action without prior Committee approval—should all carry a mandatory sentence of at least 10 years in prison with no possibility of parole.

This Security Committee procedure should cover any secret action that could be construed as a violation of the sovereignty of any nonmember nation, including but not limited to: secret attacks or other military actions, assassinations, false propaganda, secret attempts to affect elections or affect the choice of leaders, and secret efforts by F.O.N. agents to influence governmental actions of nonmember nations.

This procedure, though, does not apply to actions taken

toward or within member nations. Any actions toward member nations must be openly debated and openly carried out.

A History of Covert Actions

Some will say that I am being naive with my demand that all covert actions be publicly revealed almost immediately after they are taken. They will gleefully remind us that the world is a "dangerous place," and say that those who would place any restrictions on covert actions are living in an idealized world, a world of make-believe. But they couldn't be more wrong. It is rather those who so blindly believe in the ease and efficacy of covert actions against foreign governments who are naive and are living in the world of make believe. They have been watching too many James Bond movies.

However, since this naive belief in the importance of covert actions is so pervasive, I feel compelled to write here a brief but complete history of all the most important covert actions that the U.S. government has taken in peacetime since World War II. This history should put to rest any ideas that covert actions are either effective or necessary.

Covert actions are defined here as acts taken by the executive branch without the knowledge of Congress or the voters to influence events in a foreign nation with whom we are not at war, and taken with the general intent that not only will Congress and the voters not know about them in advance, but they will never find out about them. Excluded from this, then, are actions against an enemy in wartime—after all, all is fair in love and war—and acts such as surprise invasions, which may be secret in advance but are taken with the awareness that they will immediately become publicized.

Before I begin, let me say that when I first looked into this history of covert actions, I expected its lessons to be equivocal. After all, the lessons of history are almost always equivocal. I expected to find that some covert actions were spectacular successes and others were spectacular failures. But, as you will see, that is not what I found at all. Rather, what I found is that the first U.S. postwar covert action was a modest success, but that after that, every major covert action, with exactly zero exceptions, not only failed but failed abysmally.

In 1948 the Central Intelligence Agency (C.I.A.) funnelled U.S. tax dollars to the Christian Democrat Party of Italy to help that party in its campaign to defeat the Communist Party in Italian elections. The Christian Democrats won that election, and U.S. money for the party remained a secret until after the election. So this operation could be considered a success, although it is very unlikely U.S. money was actually a decisive factor in the election outcome.

Iran, 1952. Mohammed Mossadeq, a wealthy landowner, was selected prime minister, in accord with the Iranian constitution, by the more-or-less democratically elected Parliament. Mossadeq was not a communist, but, like virtually all Iranians at the time, he supported the "radical" idea (to the U.S. government) that Iran's resources belonged to Iran rather than to Great Britain. This meant he wanted to nationalize the oil industry, controlled entirely at the time by the British company Anglo-Iranian. Nationalizing the oil industry meant only that Mossadeq and the Iranians wanted to require Anglo-Iranian to keep a percentage of its profits in Iran and hire Iranians for a certain percentage of its technical employees, but the U.S. looked at those reasonable demands and concluded that they were proof Mossadeq was a communist. So the C.I.A. hatched a plot to overthrow Mossadeq and the government. They convinced the figurehead monarch of Iran, the Shah, to dismiss the prime minister and declare for himself the power of government. That he did, but Mossadeq responded that this act was a coup attempt, which was correct since the Shah did not have the constitutional authority to dismiss a prime minister. As a result, the Shah was forced to flee the country.

Then, as now, Iran was an unruly place, with violent mobs frequently controlling the streets and the government unable to stop them. So the U.S. took advantage of the situation and paid some thugs to go into the streets, chant "long live the Shah," and drag from their cars and beat anyone driving by who did not have a picture of the Shah in his windshield. With the help of bribes to the police and the military, this tactic proved surprisingly effective. "Popular" support for the Shah materialized amazingly quickly. With the police and the mobs turned against him, Mossadeq went into hiding and later surrendered to police. The

Shah triumphantly returned and began a ruthless regime that murdered and tortured thousands of citizens over the next 25 years.

But Iranians never forgot what the U.S. had done to them, and when they finally overthrew the Shah, they became the United States's most intense enemy.

On the heels of what they saw as a remarkable success in Iran, the C.I.A. and the Eisenhower administration turned their attention to Guatemala. In 1952, Jacobo Arbenz was the democratically-elected president of this Central American nation. He was a liberal and may have been a socialist, but as the C.I.A. itself stated, he was clearly not a communist. The communists held only four of the 52 seats in the Guatemalan congress and Arbenz had no communists in his cabinet. Communism by no stretch of the imagination was a threat in Guatemala.

At this time, United Fruit, a gigantic U.S. corporation, owned virtually everything in Guatemala. But in 1952 Arbenz enacted the Agrarian Reform Law, which nationalized two-thirds of the land United Fruit owned, and paid for it exactly the value United Fruit had declared for it on its tax returns. Of course, United Fruit had understated the land's value on its tax returns, so in a sense this was not fair compensation. But then again, turnabout is fair play. The United States, however, did not see it that way.

Many top officials in the Eisenhower administration were former United Fruit employees, and some of these zealots were able to convince their colleagues that Arbenz's action proved that he was a communist and a threat to U.S. national security. So they hatched a plot to overthrow Arbenz. The man they chose to replace him was an inconsequential colonel named Castillo Armas. To support Armas, the U.S. hired 300 mercenaries and Guatemalan dissidents to engage in sabotage and form a fictitious invasion force, and gave these men a dozen airplanes. Rebel radio stations in Nicaragua and Honduras were also established to broadcast into Guatemala propaganda that attempted to demonstrate Arbenz was a communist. Then, on June 18, 1954, rebel radio announced that Castillo Armas had invaded. In fact, he had driven across the border in a station wagon followed by about 100 of his men. Continued broadcasts from rebel radio greatly exaggerated the strength and deeds of this fictitious "invasion force," while, in order to make those reports seem more believable, the planes were being used to drop dynamite on targets like oil tanks in Guatemala City—targets selected for their ability to create a lot of smoke and noise that would be seen and heard by a lot of people. With that tactic, the fictitious reports of an invasion did become more believable, and, miraculously, Arbenz actually thought his government was in danger. But he didn't trust his right-wing military to defend him, so he ordered the military to distribute arms to the peasants. The officers, however, refused and demanded that Arbenz relinquish power. Unable to control the army, Arbenz resigned and gave power to a general who quickly handed it to Castillo Armas.

This farcical tale might be funny were it not for the fact that it overthrew a democratic, moderate government and replaced it with a military dictatorship, which continues to this day, with the worst human rights record of any nation in the Western Hemisphere. Because of this action, the United States bears partial responsibility for the murder and torture of more than 100,000 Guatemalans over the past 35 years.

The next national government the C.I.A. and the Eisenhower administration decided to overthrow was that of Indonesia and its president, Achmed Sukarno. This government was democratically elected and Sukarno was by no means a communist—in fact, he had outlawed the communist party. But he was the leader of the movement of nonaligned nations, and the U.S. could not tolerate that any nation would not choose sides between the U.S. and the Soviet Union. So in 1957 the C.I.A. apparently authorized an assassination attempt against Sukarno by its Indonesian contacts. Five grenades were thrown at Sukarno as he left a school in the company of children. Ten people were killed and 48 children injured, but Sukarno escaped. Next, the U.S. gave weapons, advice, and intelligence information to a group of colonels in the Indonesian military who declared themselves independent of the central government's command and ostensibly wanted greater local control of the many islands of this archipelago. Soon this revolt expanded to an attempt to overthrow the central government. Rumors began to spread that the U.S. was aiding the rebels, but Eisenhower and his Secretary of State publicly denied them. Immediately after their denials, though, a U.S. plane bombing Indonesia was shot down and the American pilot captured along with his Air Force identification cards, proving the lie of the U.S. denials. Meanwhile, the Indonesian central government easily crushed the rebellion. Thus, the outcome of the U.S.'s bungled overthrow attempt, lies, and violations of international law was only to kill a few children and strengthen Indonesia's government.

Choosing to ignore the failure in Indonesia, when Fidel Castro took control of Cuba in 1959, the C.I.A. instead dwelled on its "success" in Guatemala to plot an overthrow attempt. They first conceived that another tiny fictitious invasion force would trigger the Cuban military to switch sides and overthrow Castro in a process similar to what worked in Guatemala. When reality set in and they realized that could not work, they decided to expand the operation to a small but significant force of 1500 men, and deluded themselves into believing that with an operation of that size U.S. involvement could remain a secret if it failed. The invasion was finally launched, and a new phrase, "Bay of Pigs," was added to the American vocabulary to mean fiasco.

Not content with that failure, John Kennedy and the C.I.A authorized at least eight plots to kill Castro. All eight failed.

In 1970, Salvador Allende, a socialist, was democratically elected the President of Chile. The C.I.A.'s own reports up to that time and in the ensuing years stated that Allende was not a Marxist, was not interested in close ties with Cuba or the Soviet Union, and would not interfere in the affairs of other countries in the region. But the Nixon administration decided that he was too liberal for their tastes anyway and that they had more right to select Chile's government than did the Chilean people. So U.S. agents began secretly discussing the possibility of a coup with Chile's military officers and offering U.S. aid for the effort. Those efforts initially found very little support, though. In particular, Chile's top military official, General Rene Schneider, staunchly supported his nation's constitution and opposed a coup. Since he was such a stumbling block, the C.I.A. decided to remove him. They helped military officers plan to kidnap Schneider and gave them logistical information and weapons. However, instead of kidnapping Schneider, the officers killed him. The C.I.A.

personnel involved do not appear to have let their consciences be unduly troubled by this murder that they brought about, for after it occurred they continued to try to provoke a coup until in 1973 it finally occurred and Allende was killed. Although the C.I.A. did not actively direct the final successful coup effort, it had known about it in advance and encouraged it.

After the coup, Augusto Pinochet became the dictator of Chile, where he exercised his rule with ruthless terror until 1990. In 1990 he was nominally removed from the presidency, but he continues at the moment as head of the armed forces.

Angola, 1974. Portugal in this year gave up its colonial rule of Angola, leaving three equally popular and powerful factions to vie for control. All three were socialist and all were openly hostile to the U.S. But the Soviet Union supported one faction, so out of knee-jerk opposition to the Soviets, the Ford administration secretly funnelled money to another faction. As the commitment grew, however, it became more and more difficult to keep the fact of American support a secret. Finally, in 1975 South Africa entered the war, backing the same faction the U.S. supported, and the fact that the U.S. and South Africa were working on the same side in this war became public. Because of that embarrassing position, the U.S. had to withdraw.

Nicaragua, 1980's. Much of the U.S. effort to overthrow the Sandinista government in Nicaragua was called covert but was being publicly debated in Congress, so obviously was not. That, therefore, does not concern us here. But two aspects of the effort were truly covert in that they were concealed from Congress and the American people and were intended to remain secret forever. One was the mining of the Nicaraguan harbors. This was an act of war without the approval of Congress, in violation of the Constitution, and was a violation of international law. Nicaragua took the case to the World Court, which found the U.S. guilty, forcing the Reagan administration to take the extremely embarrassing position that it refused to recognize the validity of international law.

The second truly covert action was the effort to fund the overthrow of Nicaragua's government by selling arms to Iran, a terrorist nation and the U.S.'s most impassioned enemy in the world, in exchange for the release of hostages. That episode received huge amounts of publicity in the U.S., caused enormous embarrassment for the Reagan administration, and even caused some loose discussion of actually impeaching President Reagan. Since it is so well known, I probably do not need to further recount the details here, but suffice it to say that it was a fiasco.

The lesson of the history of covert actions in a democracy could not possibly be any clearer. Virtually without exception, covert actions not only fail, but fail abysmally. Anyone who contends otherwise is living in a fantasy world of spy novels. In the entire history of the United States, the lone example of a covert action that was not a total fiasco was the U.S. financial assistance for the democratic campaign against communism in the Italian elections of 1948. Not coincidentally, that is also the only major covert action that could have been easily justified to Congress, the public, and the world. The legacy of the rest of U.S. covert actions is: the creation of our most dedicated enemy in the world in Iran; embarrassment before U.S. and world opinion for our government's actions in Angola and Nicaragua; a magnificent public relations tool for Fidel Castro, around which he built popular support and further entrenched his power; the murder of two honest and admirable leaders in Chile, among many others around the world; permanent damage on more than one occasion to our avowed goal of promoting democracy in Latin America; and the creation of ruthless dictatorships around the world that have murdered and tortured literally millions of people.

At this point the die-hard spy novel fans may object that this picture looks so bad because covert action successes have been kept secrets. Nonsense. First, any important covert action, as with all of these examples, involves a fairly large number of people, and any time a large number of people know something other people might be interested in, it comes out soon enough. Second, people tend to brag about successes. Part of the reason we know so much about the Iran and Guatemala operations is that the people involved viewed them as successes and wanted to brag. (In fact, Kermit Roosevelt, the chief architect of the overthrow of Prime Minister Mossadeq in Iran, actually had the audacity to write a book bragging about this "secret" operation in 1979, at the height of the crisis involving the American embassy hostages in

Iran—a crisis that was the direct consequence of his actions (Roosevelt, 1979)). If there are any major operations that remain secret, you can bet they remain secret because they were even bigger failures than these (if that is possible).

Covert actions do not merely fail at their initial goal. They almost invariably go far beyond that to create a great deal more damage than could possibly have occurred from doing nothing at all. Really, if you think about it, that should not be a surprise. The same rule of thumb applies to "covert actions" we take in our personal lives. Think back to any action you took in your life that you knew when you took it would have to remain a secret forever. Did that action in any sense succeed? Of course not. If you know before you do something that it will have to remain a secret forever, the reason must be because you know it is either stupid or immoral.

Thus, there are two fundamental reasons why no branch of the F.O.N. government should ever be allowed to take policy actions that the voters will never be aware of. The first is that, as I explained in Chapter 5, the F.O.N. must be a democracy. We would be insane to surrender any powers to it if it were not. And the theory of democracy is that the ultimate authorization for the government's actions comes from the voters. But if the voters don't know what those actions are, they cannot authorize them. In that case, it doesn't matter whether the officials are elected or not, the government is no longer a democracy. So if we allow the F.O.N. to keep some of its actions secret indefinitely, it would not be a democracy, and we would be foolish to surrender any powers to it.

The second fundamental reason why we should require that all F.O.N. policy actions be revealed to the public soon after they are taken is even simpler: If the government is allowed to take actions that it will not reveal, those actions will be disasters. The historical record could not possibly be any clearer on this.

Now, having said all that, I want to make it clear again that I am not saying the F.O.N. should give up the element of surprise. It is possible for an act that must be secret when it is taken to still be moral and wise. Certainly if we need a military, and we always will, we should allow a way to use it with the element of surprise. And even the other types of covert action mentioned in this history, despite being stupidly used by the United States, can on occasion be ethical and wise policy options. The problem is that these covert actions have been used with the intention that they never be revealed to the voters. Any action, whether taken by an individual, a group, or a government, that is intended when it is taken to remain a secret forever, is, almost by definition, stupid or immoral.

Covert actions can have a place in the F.O.N., but only if they are always revealed to the voters almost immediately after they are taken. By the provisions described above, I hope to allow the F.O.N. to successfully exercise its power and compete with nonmember nations with every legitimate tool available to it. But I also, by those provisions, hope to protect us from the abuses that are guaranteed to occur if we do not have strict limitations on the use of covert actions, abuses that would threaten our freedom, weaken, not strengthen, the F.O.N.'s exercise of power, and ultimately jeopardize the very existence of the F.O.N.

No One Is Above The Law

It must be made clear in this constitution that no one in the F.O.N.—neither the president, nor the Supreme Court judges, nor anyone else—is above the law. It must be absolutely clear that anyone who violates this constitution or violates the law will be prosecuted, will be removed from office, and will suffer the appropriate criminal penalties.

The first step is making it clear that the constitution must be obeyed.

Violating This Constitution

In order to mean anything, a constitution has to have some teeth. It has to be clear to government officials and to everyone else that no one can violate the constitution, and that anyone who attempts to will pay dearly for it. I think this was a serious oversight in the U.S. Constitution. Violating that constitution is not in itself a crime, so government officials are free to attempt to violate it, because even if they don't succeed, they suffer no consequences. Among the dire results of this oversight have been: President Andrew Jackson's unconstitutional theft of land from the Cherokee Indians in Tennessee and North Carolina and the genocidal forced march of those Cherokees 1,000 miles on foot to Oklahoma; the flagrantly unconstitutional imprisonment of Japanese-Americans just on the basis of their race during World War II; and the waging of the Korean and Vietnam wars, and many other military actions, on presidential orders alone, in direct violation of the Constitution's central provision that only Congress can declare war.

I do not want the F.O.N.'s constitution to be so casually violated. So Article V, Section 1, Provision 1 reads:

> Any willful violation or willful attempted violation of this constitution by a Federation of Nations senator, representative, judge, military officer, president, vice president, or top executive branch official in the exercise of his or her office is a crime. Conviction of that crime shall carry a penalty of immediate removal from office, even if an appeal of the verdict is planned (the official shall be reinstated in office if the verdict of guilty is overturned on appeal), and permanent disqualification from holding Federation of Nations office, and shall carry a mandatory sentence of at least 10 years in prison with no possibility of parole or early release.*

Prosecuting Criminals and Removing Them From Office

The deliberate violation of the constitution by the highest government officials is, short of treason, the most serious crime that can be committed against any nation or society. So the above constitutional provision specifies that that crime must be dealt with very, very harshly. But that crime is not the only one that should earn a person disqualification from holding public office in the F.O.N. We would probably all agree that the commission of any serious crime (under which I would include most violations of the constitution, whether deliberate or not and whether committed by top officials or low-level officials) should be grounds for removing a person from public office and barring him from ever holding office again. Thus, Article I, Section 6, Provision 30 of my proposed constitution specifies that conviction of a felony crime (and the F.O.N. legislature could define what exactly is to be a felony crime) is grounds for

---

*More discussion of this provision can be found in Appendix B.

removing people from office in the F.O.N. and in national and local governments, as well as removing them from the F.O.N. military and national guard and police forces. This is the clause that was discussed in Chapter 6 as being the crucial F.O.N. tool for removing dictators and tyrants from office and for guaranteeing that all national and local governments respect human rights. It would thus, as explained in Chapter 6, largely end any need for violent rebellion in member nations and prevent the large majority of all civil wars.

That clause is fine as far as it goes. We can probably all agree that convicted felons should not hold government office in the F.O.N. But it, as well as the previous clause concerning deliberate violations of the F.O.N. constitution, only specifies that people will be removed from office *after they are prosecuted and convicted.* The question we must now address is, Will F.O.N. officials ever be prosecuted?

This question is especially acute for the F.O.N. president. In the United States, a flaw in the Constitution has turned out to be that the president is essentially above the law. The president and the executive branch, under the U.S. Constitution, have the sole responsibility for enforcing the law and prosecuting those who violate it. No one else—neither the legislative branch of government, nor the judicial branch, nor even ordinary citizens—ever has the right to prosecute someone. What that means is that the president is above the law. He can never be prosecuted because only he has the right to prosecute himself. This also means, effectively, that the president's friends, advisors, and political allies are above the law.

Recently, in the wake of Richard Nixon's Watergate scandal, Congress has attempted to address this problem by establishing that it can on occasion appoint a special prosecutor to prosecute executive branch officials. That is an improvement (although it may violate the U.S. Constitution), but it still has the flaw that it makes prosecution a political process. By requiring a majority vote in both houses of Congress, the procedure insures that only unpopular officials will be prosecuted. Popular officials will still be shielded by their popularity.

I want to establish in the F.O.N. that anyone who breaks the law, regardless of his position or popularity, will be prosecuted, convicted, and suffer the consequences. To do that, I am proposing in Art. II, Sec. 3, Prov. 1 that 10% of the senators or 10% of the representatives may initiate a prosecution of any current or former F.O.N. government official, whether in the judicial branch, the legislative branch, or the executive branch (including the military), for crimes believed to have been committed while the person was in office. This ought to insure that anyone who violates the law will be prosecuted, because no matter how popular a person is, he's certain to have at least 10% of the current senators or representatives not like him. At the same time, the provision is designed to insure that F.O.N. officials won't constantly have to fend off frivolous prosecutions. Ten percent is still a fairly large number of senators or representatives, so it is unlikely very many prosecutions will be launched solely from personal vendettas rather than from a legitimate reason to believe laws may have been broken.

That provision, I believe, is one of the most important in this constitution. We must establish in the F.O.N. that no one is above the law. To do that, we have to guarantee that any government official who breaks the law, regardless of his position or popularity, will be prosecuted. This provision guarantees that.

Pardons

In the U.S., the chief executive officers—the president of the nation and the governors of each of the states—all have the power to pardon persons convicted of crimes under their jurisdiction. I suppose the logic of giving the executive this power to pardon is to make the justice system more merciful, but as far as I can tell it is a wholly unnecessary and very dangerous power. It is unnecessary because there are plenty of other opportunities in the justice system for the application of mercy—the prosecutor can choose not to prosecute, the jury can return a verdict of not guilty (even if they believe that technically the person violated the law), the judge can apply a lenient sentence, and the parole board can grant early parole. It is dangerous because more often than being used to show mercy for the downtrodden, the pardon is used to show that the powerful—the chief executive and his friends—are above the law. This cannot be tolerated. In order to create an organization worthy of our trust, worthy of surrendering powers to, we must insure that the F.O.N. is a government of laws, not of men and women. No one, including the president, can be above the law. So the pardon has no place in the F.O.N., and ought not to have a place in any government. When you examine the proposed constitution at the end of this book, you will not find any power of pardon.

The "President of the World"

One of the reasons people fear to institute a world government is that they fear the idea of a "President of the World." It seems that is too much power for any one person to have. It seems that it would automatically corrupt whoever held the position. But I think if we examine carefully the position of president of the F.O.N. described in this book, we will see that those fears are groundless.

First, the system of selecting the president was designed so that those interested in power and personal aggrandizement will not get the position. Rather, our democratically elected representatives will select, from a large pool of qualified people they have known personally, one person with the necessary responsibility and ethical standards to hold the position. Rather than people seeking the F.O.N. presidency, the F.O.N. will seek a president.

Next, the powers of the F.O.N. are quite limited in scope—limited to enforcing basic human rights, controlling the military, extraditing criminals from one nation to another, and enforcing some environmental regulations. Even if the president could arrogate all of those powers for himself, he would be hard-pressed to tyrannize us.

But the president does not control all those powers. He has only a fraction of the F.O.N.'s power, which is clearly divided between the three branches of government. He can only prosecute accused law-breakers; he cannot write the laws and he cannot judge the cases. He cannot declare war and he cannot take any military action without the consent of a Security Committee of legislators.

Furthermore, even if the president does somehow violate those provisions, extend his power beyond its proper reach, and violate laws, it will be fairly easy to prosecute him, punish him, and remove him from office.

Still, some will argue that these are all mere parchment provisions. In the real world, they will say, these provisions could all be ignored. Indeed, those people are right. These are all parchment provisions. It is up to each of us to see that they are obeyed. The ultimate security against tyranny always has been and always will be with each of us and our individual actions. Individual soldiers must take responsibility for their actions and disobey unconstitutional, illegal, or immoral orders. Jurors must refuse to convict innocent men and women. Each of us must vote for responsible senators and representatives who will uphold this constitution. We can only be tyrannized if we allow it.

Any government can become despotic if we allow it. Nothing you or I or anyone could write into a constitution could entirely prevent that possibility. All we can do is install the constitutional safeguards we think are necessary, and then trust that we and our fellow citizens will collectively demonstrate enough wisdom and courage to uphold those safeguards.

The Bill of Rights

A constitutional bill of rights is the cornerstone of freedom and good government. In this section I will attempt to lay that cornerstone by presenting my idea of a good bill of rights for the F.O.N.

Part of the bill of rights was already presented in Chapter 5— the rights having to do with freedom of expression. Those rights were freedom of speech, freedom of the press, freedom of assembly, and freedom of religion. To those rights I will now add in this section a list composed primarily of the rights of defendants in law enforcement. The reason we need these rights is that governments can very easily use the need for law enforcement, or the need to "fight crime," as a pretext for oppression. The rights listed in this section are the limitations on government that we need in order to prevent that oppression.

The rights I will list here are placed into two groups: those essential rights that must be observed by all levels of government—F.O.N., national, and local—and the important, but not absolutely essential, rights that should be demanded of the F.O.N. but that can safely be left as optional for the national and local governments.

Article IV, Section 2

The provisions in this section are the ones that must be demanded of all levels of government—F.O.N., national, and local.

> Section 2. The provisions in this section are to be observed by the Federation of Nations government, by all national and local governments in the Federation of Nations, and by all individuals in the Federation of Nations.
>
> *Provision 1.* No person may be detained or arrested without being immediately told the reason, and no person may be jailed for more than 24 hours without being charged with a crime and informed of the accusations against him.
>
> *Provision 2.* No person may be deprived of life, liberty, or property without due process of law.
>
> *Provision 3.* No person may be denied equal protection and equal treatment under the law.
>
> *Provision 4.* In all criminal prosecutions the accused shall enjoy the right to a speedy and public trial, to be informed of the nature and cause of the accusations against him, to have compulsory process for obtaining witnesses in his favor, and to have the assistance of counsel for his defense throughout the legal process.
>
> *Provision 5.* Excessive bail shall not be required, nor excessive fines imposed, nor cruel and unusual punishment inflicted.
>
> *Provision 6.* No person may be held to answer for a crime without reasonable basis for the charge, nor may any person be detained or jailed unless for reasonable cause.
>
> *Provision 7.* No *ex post facto* laws may be either made or enforced. [*Ex post facto* laws are laws that apply retroactively, that stipulate punishment for actions that were not crimes when they were committed.]
>
> *Provision 8.* Neither slavery nor involuntary servitude, except as punishment for a crime whereof the party shall have been duly convicted, shall exist in any member nation or any territory of the Federation of Nations.

Explanation of the Provisions of Section 2

Provision 1. It is a rudimentary principle of liberty and justice that people cannot be jailed unless they are charged with a crime. Any society that permits that is by definition unjust. I have written this right, however, in a way that allows the authorities to perform the necessary functions of detaining witnesses to a crime long enough to get their testimony and detaining a suspect for questioning before deciding whether to actually charge him with a crime.

Provision 2. This provision serves to make murder, kidnapping, and theft illegal.

Provision 3. This provision serves to make racial and sexual discrimination illegal.

Provision 4. The right to a speedy trial is necessary because otherwise a suspect can be held in jail for a very long time (or be deprived of a very large amount of bail money if the authorities are generous enough to release him on bail), and thus in reality be punished for the crime, without having ever been convicted of actually committing it.

The right to a public trial is necessary because otherwise no one knows whether or not the defendant's rights were violated and whether or not he received a fair trial. Tyranny thrives on secrecy and darkness and shrivels in the light of day.

The defendant's right to be informed of the nature and cause of the accusations against him is necessary because, in order to prepare his defense, the accused obviously needs to know what he is charged with and why the authorities believe he committed the crime.

Likewise, for a fair trial, the defendant obviously must be allowed to present his case. This means he must be allowed to call any witnesses he needs.

Finally, the right to legal counsel is necessary for two reasons. First, in any civilized nation court procedures and criminal statutes are complex. To have a fair chance at victory a person needs someone on his side who is familiar with the rules. Second and probably more important, without counsel we would ordinarily never find out when a person's rights are violated. The lawyer is necessary simply as a witness to what happens to the defendant in the police station, the jail, and the courtroom. Some might say that the right to legal counsel is only a Western cultural tradition and should not be imposed on all F.O.N. member nations, but I disagree. I believe it is essential to any notion of fairness and justice, and I know it is essential to our discovering 90% of the instances of abuse of people's rights.

Provision 5. This provision is intended to prevent the use of torture and maiming as punishments and to prevent such punishments as 35 years at hard labor for shoplifting.

Provisions 6, 7, and 8. These provisions need no explanation.

These eight provisions represent the minimal standards of justice that we must expect from every member nation. By specifically invoking these rights in the constitution, we give the F.O.N. the power to prosecute those who violate them. We thus allow the F.O.N., as explained in Chapter 6, to peacefully overthrow dictators and despots, and we give the F.O.N. a powerful and necessary tool for promoting in its member nations peace and justice—two qualities that are inextricably entwined.

Article IV, Section 3

These are the provisions that I think are not necessary to ask of every member nation but that the F.O.N. itself needs to obey.

> Section 3. The provisions in this section are to be observed by the Federation of Nations government but are not required of national and local governments.
>
> Provision 1. The right of the people to be secure in their persons, houses, records, and effects, against unreasonable searches and seizures, shall not be violated, and no warrants shall issue but upon probable cause, supported by oath or affirmation, and particularly describing the place to be searched and the persons or things to be seized. Any evidence gathered by Federation of Nations officials or by anyone else in violation of this provision shall not be allowed in Federation of Nations courts.
>
> Provision 2. No person shall be subject for the same offense to be twice put in jeopardy of life or liberty.
>
> Provision 3. In all criminal prosecutions, the accused shall enjoy the right to trial by an impartial jury of the nation and district wherein the crime shall have been committed. For crimes that did not occur within any member nation, the legislature shall have the power to determine where the trial shall take place.
>
> Provision 4. No person shall be held to answer for a felony crime unless on indictment of a grand jury, except in cases arising in the military forces when in actual combat.
>
> Provision 5. All civil and criminal trials shall begin within

100 days of when the suit or criminal charges were filed, unless it is ruled that the defense needs more time to prepare its case. The Federation of Nations legislature is also empowered to enact time limits for the filing and deciding of appeals.

Provision 6. No person shall be compelled in any criminal case to be a witness against himself or to offer evidence against himself.

Provision 7. In all civil suits in which the value at controversy shall be a large amount of money, the right of either party to insist on trial by jury shall be preserved, except in cases in which the Supreme Court shall have original jurisdiction. No fact or award tried by a Federation of Nations jury shall be otherwise reexamined in any Federation of Nations court than for an error in the original trial with respect to the law or constitution.

Provision 8. The burden of proof in a criminal trial shall be with the prosecution, and no person shall be convicted of a criminal offense unless he has been proven guilty beyond reasonable doubt.

Provision 9. The Federation of Nations may not take private or governmental property without just compensation.

Provision 10. No soldier shall in time of peace be quartered in any house without the consent of the owner and tenant, nor in time of war but in a manner prescribed by law.

Explanation of the Provisions of Section 3

Many of these provisions will not be discussed here or will be discussed only very briefly. However, further discussion of those provisions can be found in Appendix B.

Provision 1. In essence, this provision recognizes a right to privacy and a presumption of innocence. That is, unless there is some specific reason to believe otherwise, we are all presumed to be innocent and the police have no business searching our bodies and belongings for evidence of crimes.

Provision 2. This is an ancient principle, going back at least to the Romans. It is based on the idea that once a decision is reached it should be final, and that people should not be continually harassed with a charge they have already proven once to be false.

Provision 3. The jury* is at the core of the concept of

---

*An explanation of the jury may be in order for those readers (cont.)

democracy. The jury insures that the final and most important act of government, the conviction and punishment of individuals for breaking the law, be decided and approved by the people, by the governed rather than the government. It is the ultimate safeguard of liberty and responsible government.

The F.O.N. should be, and must be, a government of the people, by the people, and for the people. And, with the exception of specifying that all legislators are to be chosen in free and democratic elections, the single most important provision we could ordain to insure that is the right to trial by an impartial jury.

Provision 5. This is included to put some teeth behind Provision 3 of Section 2, the right to a speedy trial. As the saying goes, "Justice delayed is justice denied." And, as experience with the U.S.'s monstrously inefficient court system demonstrates, without specific time limits, justice will be delayed indefinitely.

Provision 8. The presumption of innocence until proven guilty is the cornerstone of the justice system of the U.S. and other countries, and I believe must be central to the justice system in any truly free society.

Any system of justice is imperfect. Guilty people will sometimes go free and innocent people will sometimes go to jail. But it is far more of a tragedy for an innocent person to be punished than for a guilty person to escape punishment. Judges must follow the same credo as physicians: "First of all, do no harm." A justice system should not compound crimes by committing further crimes. The requirement for proof beyond a reasonable doubt is designed to insure this. Notice, however, that

---

*(cont.) from nations that don't use juries. The jury is a panel of 12 ordinary citizens, selected at random from the population and then screened by the defense and prosecution to determine that all the jurors can be impartial in this particular case. These 12 jurors then decide the issue of guilt or guilt or innocence in a criminal trial. The trial is supervised by a judge, who insures that constitutional and legal principles are obeyed in the trial, rules on such things as the admissibility of evidence, and instructs the jury on what the law is and on what basis they should decide whether the defendant is guilty or innocent. But after hearing the evidence in the case and being told by the judge what the relevant law is in the case, it is the jury that decides whether the defendant is guilty or not guilty.

the requirement is for proof beyond a "reasonable doubt," not beyond a "shadow of a doubt." It is almost impossible to ever prove guilt beyond all doubt, and such a provision would cripple the justice system.

Provision 10. Would you want a dozen armed men to show up at your door one night and throw you out of your home?

Now, if these rights and limitations on power that are described in Article IV, Section 3 are so important, why have I chosen to impose them only on the F.O.N. itself and not on all national and local governments? The answer is that each of the provisions in this section, although it represents a tremendous safeguard of freedom and justice, is not absolutely essential to the existence of freedom and justice. I wanted to impose on member nations the minimal number of standards—only those standards or rights that are absolutely essential to the existence of a just society.

The Judicial Branch

Article III, Section 1

Provision 1. The judicial power of the Federation of Nations shall be vested in one Supreme Court and in such inferior courts as the legislature may from time to time establish. The judges, both of the Supreme and inferior courts, shall hold their offices during good behavior for up to 20 years, and shall, at stated times, receive for their services a compensation, which shall not be diminished during their terms in office. Judges who complete their full 20 year terms of office shall continue to receive an undiminished compensation for the rest of their lives unless convicted of violating a felony statute.

Provision 2. The Supreme Court shall consist of a panel of eleven judges. If there are eleven or more member nations in the Federation of Nations, no two Supreme Court judges may be citizens of the same nation. If there are fewer than eleven member nations, the number of Supreme Court judges shall be divided between the nations as evenly as possible.

The biggest inherent danger in democratic governments is that the majority, which by definition rules, will trample over the rights of the minority. The branch of government we must rely on to protect us against that is the judicial. For that reason, judgeships should be rather undemocratic positions. Judges should be protected against the will of the majority, because the will of the majority can sometimes turn into the will of the mob. Judges should therefore probably not be chosen by democratic elections in the first place (I will discuss the method of selecting judges later), but however they are chosen, it is vital that they not depend on popular election to continue to hold their offices. They should hold office for a long time and should be bound only by their consciences and by the constitution, not by the will of the majority. Only in that way can they be most free to carry out their duties of doing justice, defending the constitution, and defending our rights.

Because of that logic, the framers of the U.S. Constitution specified that judges be appointed for life. For reasons that are discussed in Appendix B, my proposed constitution makes a minor change in that provision—specifying that judges be appointed to serve for 20 years rather than for life. However, though I suggest that we limit judges to 20 year terms, we should not limit them to only being paid for 20 years. An important advantage of lifetime appointments is that it frees judges from concern about making a living after leaving the bench. This, again, frees them from having to satisfy the popular will or satisfy any potential future employers with their rulings. We should keep this advantage by guaranteeing that judges will be paid for the rest of their lives even though we limit them to 20 year terms.

Appointing Judges (Art. III, Sec. 1, Prov. 3)

How should judges be selected? As I already indicated, since the judicial branch must protect minority rights against majority will, it would be unwise to select judges directly by the "majority will," by democratic elections. Rather, in order to separate the selection of judges from the majority will, judges should be appointed by other government officials. In the United States, judges are appointed by the president and then must be approved by the Senate before they can take office. I will suggest that the F.O.N. keep that arrangement with slight modifications. The first modification is that appointment should require approval not just by the Senate but by majorities in each of four different groups of legislators: the senators from the nominee's own nation, the senators not from his own nation, the representatives from his own nation, and the representatives not from his own nation. This assures that the appointment must pass muster both with the group of legislators most likely to know and understand the nominee—those from his own country—and with the group of legislators most likely to distrust and fear the nominee—those from other countries.

The second modification is that the president's power of appointment should not be unlimited. That is, if the person he appoints for a particular judgeship is rejected by the legislature, then the power of appointment for that judgeship should pass to the Senate. A problem in the U.S. has been that the president has the sole and unlimited power to appoint judges. Because of that, the Senate hesitates to reject his judicial appointments. They understand that if they reject an appointment, the president will just nominate someone equally bad to replace him. To correct that problem and give meaning to the legislature's right to reject judicial nominees, I am specifying that if the president nominates someone who is rejected by the legislature, then the power of nomination shall pass to the Senate. This will force the president to nominate qualified judges and will give the legislature reason to reject unqualified ones.

Judicial Jurisdiction

Article III, Section 2

Provision 1. The judicial power of the Federation of Nations shall extend to all cases, in law and equity, arising under this constitution, under the laws of the Federation of Nations, and under treaties made by the Federation of Nations; to all cases affecting ambassadors, public ministers, and consuls of nonmember nations in member nations or in Federation of Nations territory; to all cases of admiralty and maritime jurisdiction involving the Federation of Nations, Federation of Nations member nations, or citizens of Federation of Nations member nations; to controversies to which the Federation of Nations shall be a party; to controversies between two or more member nations; to controversies between a member nation and citizens of a different member nation; to controversies between citizens of different member nations; and to controversies between a member nation or citizens thereof and a nonmember nation or citizens thereof.

The most important part of this provision to notice is that the F.O.N. courts will have jurisdiction over controversies between different member nations or the citizens of different member nations. This will be an important basis for the F.O.N.'s ability to keep the peace between member nations because it will provide a peaceful way for nations to settle their disputes. Of course, the claim of providing a peaceful way for nations to settle their disputes has been made before, by the League of Nations and the United Nations, but the difference is that in those cases their decisions were not enforceable. The decisions of F.O.N. courts, though, will be enforceable. They will be backed up by the F.O.N. military.

In practical terms, all this provision necessarily means is that the F.O.N. will rule on extraditing criminal suspects between member nations, a power that was already mentioned in the last chapter. But if F.O.N. law permits it, this provision could also be used to allow the government or citizens of one nation to sue the government or citizens of another nation.

F.O.N. Laws Must Be Supreme

Article 3, Section 2

Provision 3. This constitution and the laws of the Federation of Nations that shall be made in pursuance thereof, and all treaties made by the Federation of Nations, shall be the supreme law of the land in every member nation; and the national and local legal systems in every member nation shall be bound thereby, anything in the constitution or laws of the member nation notwithstanding.

Provision 4. The Federation of Nations judiciary shall have appellate jurisdiction over the legal systems of member nations in claims arising under this constitution, under the laws of the Federation of Nations, and under treaties made by the Federation of Nations. Federation of Nations rulings in such cases shall be binding upon the legal systems of national and local governments of member nations.

For the F.O.N. laws and constitution to mean anything, they must be binding on member nations and F.O.N. courts must have jurisdiction over the legal systems of member nations. If, for instance, the guarantee that no person may be jailed for 24 hours without being charged with a crime is to mean anything, then you have to be able to appeal to F.O.N. courts when you *have* been jailed for 24 hours without charge.

Judicial Review

> Article III, Section 2
>
> Provision 5. The Federation of Nations judiciary shall have the right and the duty to review whether the laws in cases that come before it are consistent with this constitution. Any laws found to be inconsistent with this constitution, whether laws of the Federation of Nations or of national or local governments in member nations, shall be declared null and void.

Again, this provision is essential if this constitution is to mean anything.

Obeying and Enforcing Court Decisions

The most serious threat to the Union and to our democratic form of government in the United States is generally considered to have been the Civil War. But I think that assessment just might be wrong. The most serious threat might have occurred in the years 1831-1838 when President Andrew Jackson decided to order the army to move the Cherokee Indians from their homes in North Carolina, Tennessee, Georgia, and Alabama to Oklahoma, 800 miles away, so that white people could move onto their land. This action, of course, violated treaties the United States had made with the Cherokees, guaranteeing them this parcel of land in the four Southeastern states, so the Cherokees fought the removal order in court, ultimately appealing to the U.S. Supreme Court. The Supreme Court sided with the Cherokees, ruling that they had a right to their land. But Andrew Jackson then said, "John Marshall [the Chief Justice of the Supreme Court] has made his decision; let him enforce it now if he can," and he and his presidential successor, Martin Van Buren, ordered the removal of the Cherokees anyway. The forced march that ensued is known as "The Trail of Tears." On it, one quarter of the Cherokees died.

This episode illustrates one of the most serious problems with separating the three branches of government. That problem is that the judicial branch controls no physical force whatsoever and therefore is entirely dependent on the executive branch for the faithful execution of its decisions. That weakness in our

American system of government means that occasionally the president and other executive branch officials simply do not enforce court decisions with which they disagree—the most heinous example of that being this case of Andrew Jackson and the Cherokees. But if the courts must rely on the charity of the president to enforce decisions only when he feels like it, the courts, and therefore the rule of law and our system of government, cannot properly function. So if any F.O.N. president ever tries to pull a stunt like Mr. Jackson's, I want to make sure he suffers severe consequences for it. To see that he does, I have written into my proposed constitution the following clause:

> Article III, Section 2
> Provision 6. The president, all other executive branch officials, and all Federation of Nations citizens must faithfully execute all Federation of Nations court decisions, whether or not they agree with them.

In conjunction with Article V, Section 1, Provision 1, that willful violations of the constitution by top F.O.N. officials will carry a minimum punishment of 10 years in prison, this clause guarantees that a president or top executive branch official who refuses to carry out a court order will indeed suffer severe consequences.

Miscellaneous Constitutional Points

The Right to Bear Arms

An important deterrent to tyranny is the possession of weapons by the general population. The Chinese government, for instance, might have been unable to so brutally crush the pro-democracy movement in 1989 if the people had had guns. So the right to bear arms needs to be protected. But it is obvious that this cannot be an absolute right. Certainly, for instance, no government can allow people to own nuclear weapons or anti-aircraft guns. And any reasonable person would want to prohibit criminals from owning any kind of weapons. So the following provision is included in my proposed constitution:

> Article I, Section 6
> Provision 10. The legislature shall have the power to ban or

regulate the manufacture, sale, and/or possession of firearms and weapons but must allow and may not regulate or restrict the manufacture, sale, and possession of at least some types of firearms. The Federation of Nations may, though, ban or regulate the possession of any type of weapon by persons convicted of felony violations of Federation of Nations, national, or local laws. This provision restricts only the Federation of Nations and not national or local governments.

Note that this provision applies only to the F.O.N. and not to national and local governments. That distinction grows out of the following principle of gun control and the right to bear arms: The level of government that controls the military should not be allowed to disarm the populace because it could use that power to pave the way for its own military dictatorship. But the other, lower, levels of government can be trusted to be impartial in the question of gun control, because, lacking control over the military, they cannot use gun control to set up their own dictatorships.

Military Courts

The world's military forces have always had their own legal and judicial systems for punishing offenses of military personnel. As far as that goes, that is fine. The military needs a high level of discipline and needs observance of some standards that are not necessary in civilian life. When a person joins the military, he accepts some restrictions on his freedoms. But sometimes military legal systems unnecessarily abuse the basic rights of the accused and sometimes the existence of a military legal system is construed as granting military personnel immunity from civilian prosecution. Too often it seems that military justice is to justice as military music is to music.

So I have included the following provision in the constitution.

> Article III, Section 2
> Provision 8. Although the Federation of Nations military may have its own judicial and legal system, all military personnel are fully accountable at all times to the Federation of Nations constitution, laws, and civilian courts, and convictions or legal actions under any military legal system may be

appealed to Federation of Nations civilian courts. Moreover, it shall not be considered a violation of Article IV, Section 3, Provision 2 of this constitution for a person to be tried in civilian courts for a criminal offense after having answered for the same offense to the military judicial system, even if he was convicted and punished for the offense under the military judicial system.

I want to make it clear by this provision that this constitution is not suspended during wartime and is not suspended because you happen to have a gun in your hands.

Amendments To This Constitution

Obviously, no constitution is perfect for all time, so we must allow ways to change the constitution. But we must also remember that changes should not be undertaken lightly or enacted easily. To balance those concerns, to allow amendments to the constitution while still making them reasonably difficult to enact, I propose the following procedure:

Article V, Section 7

Provision 1. Amendments to this constitution shall take effect only when ratified within a ten year period by majority votes in general referendums in three-quarters of all Federation of Nations member nations, collectively comprising at least three-quarters of the arable land area or three-quarters of the population of the Federation of Nations. If it wishes, the Federation of Nations legislature may propose amendments and require that referendums be called on them in every member nation, but approval by the Federation of Nations legislature shall not be required for enacting amendments.

Summary of Chapter 11

- In designing the F.O.N. government, we must follow the principle of separation of powers. Separation of powers means that the three functions of government—legislative, executive, and judicial—must be divided between separate branches. Those who write the laws, those who enforce the laws, and those who judge accused violations of the laws, must be separate groups of people. This principle of separation of powers is perhaps the most important idea ever developed for preventing tyranny, protecting liberty, and guaranteeing responsible government.

- The legislative branch must have the sole power to declare war.

- The executive branch must be under the charge of a single person, the president. The president, in addition to being in charge of enforcing laws, must be the commander-in-chief of the military.

- It would be a serious mistake to choose the president by direct popular election. Because of the difficulties of campaigning in the diverse cultures of a worldwide F.O.N., direct popular election would almost certainly give us very poor and very dangerous and power-hungry presidents. So I instead propose that the president be chosen by the legislature in a system in which only former senators would be eligible to be selected president.

- The president should not be allowed to launch secret attacks or other covert actions against nonmember nations on his own. Secret attacks and covert actions should instead require advance approval by a Security Committee, consisting of the president, several senators, and several representatives. Also, since the use of covert actions is very dangerous in a democracy and can very easily be abused, it is essential that all covert actions be revealed to the public almost immediately after they are taken.

- It must be a very serious crime, automatically bringing severe punishments, for government officials to willfully violate the

F.O.N. constitution. Without that provision, a constitution becomes nothing but an unenforceable set of recommendations.

- We must insure that no one in the F.O.N., including the president, is above the law. To do that, we need a provision in the constitution that will guarantee that any person who commits a crime, regardless of his position or popularity, can and will be prosecuted. To guarantee that, I have inserted a provision in my proposed constitution that specifies that 10% of the F.O.N. senators or 10% of the F.O.N. representatives can initiate a prosecution of any current or former F.O.N. official.

- A bill of rights is the cornerstone of freedom and good government. Part of the F.O.N.'s bill of rights, the rights having to do with freedom of expression, was discussed in Chapter 5. (Another part, having to do with population issues, was discussed in Chapter 9.) In this chapter I add the remainder of the bill of rights, which primarily involves the rights of the accused in legal proceedings. These rights comprise eight rights that are essential to liberty and must be observed by all levels of government—F.O.N., national, and local—and an additional ten rights that the F.O.N. must observe but that can remain optional for national and local governments.

- F.O.N. laws and the F.O.N. constitution must be supreme over the laws and constitutions of national and local governments, and F.O.N. courts must have appellate jurisdiction over the courts of national and local governments.

Chapter 12

Culture and Ethics in the Federation of Nations

The Federation of Nations, I believe, will energize us, revitalize our spirits, and open up all the choices that have been taken from us because of the unceasing and inevitable evolution of societies towards greater power. But that will only happen if we have the courage to take individual responsibility for our actions. The success of the Federation of Nations will depend on each of us facing up to our own magnificent importance and our own crucial role in making this world a better or a worse place.

That paragraph, as you will see, is a short summary of this chapter. This chapter is about the changes in our cultures that will occur under the Federation of Nations, changes that will occur because the Federation of Nations will destroy the selection for power between autonomous societies. When autonomous societies compete with each other, as the parable of the tribes explains, a selection for power naturally arises. That selection for power is the overriding factor that has directed cultural evolution. It has directed not only that we have large standing armies and that we develop advanced and deadly weapons, but has directed, or at least played a role in directing, most other features of our cultures as well. For instance, it is largely responsible for cultural attitudes that encourage large families and thus create population growth. It is largely responsible for the protestant work ethic—for the attitude that work is virtuous and leisure is suspect and should be allowed only in very small doses. And it is largely responsible for Western culture's reverence for the modern and technological, and its disdain for the simple and traditional. All of those cultural traits—the protestant work ethic, the encouragement of large families and of population growth, and the glorification of technology—promote the competitive power of the society that holds them. They are therefore selected for by the selection for power.

Obviously, there are other factors that also affect what cultural traits our societies develop. But the selection for power provides an overall steering mechanism that over the course of centuries and millenia gradually winnows out most, if not all, cultural traits that are not conducive to societal power. Thus, the selection for power is *one* of the most important causes, if not *the* most important cause, explaining our cultural traits.

The Federation of Nations, though, will put an end to the selection for power. The selection for power operates by selecting between separate autonomous societies that are competing with each other without outside restraints. But under a worldwide F.O.N., there will effectively no longer be separate autonomous societies. There will only be one worldwide society. Thus, the selection for power will be dead and our cultures will suddenly be free, for the first time in 10,000 years, to evolve in *any* direction we choose, rather than in only those directions that increase societal power.

In the past, when we have chosen in which directions to move our societies, our choices have been limited. We have only been able to choose those directions that increased societal power. An example of this would be the choice to develop and hold nuclear weapons. When we in the United States chose to develop nuclear weapons, chose to use them in two instances, and continue to choose to threaten to use them, we were not and are not really making free choices. Certainly we do not enjoy living under constant threat of global suicide. But our choices were limited. We could only choose the direction of increasing national power. We correctly realized that if we had not chosen the direction of nuclear weapons, had not chosen the direction of increasing national power, we would have soon been at the mercy of Hitler or Stalin, who in all probability would have developed nuclear weapons whether or not we had developed them first. And if we had chosen that direction, our nation and the world might not have survived to this point.

Our hands have been tied by the selection for power. Choices have been taken away from us. But under the F.O.N. the selection for power will be dead, and the choices it stole form us will be restored. Thus, as I said, we will suddenly be free to move our societies and cultures in *any* direction we choose, rather than in only those directions that increase societal power.

Under the F.O.N., then, there will be profound changes in our cultures. This chapter is an exploration of those changes.

Diversity

A common fear of instituting a world government is that it would homogenize our societies. But in reality the F.O.N. will do exactly the opposite. It will inevitably promote diversity and promote tolerance for diversity. It is the selection for power that has been making our societies more and more similar. The F.O.N. will break that process.

The selection for powerful societies has driven our societies to share more and more common characteristics because those characteristics promote power. Among those are: an attitude toward the land as something to be used and exploited for personal and societal gain, rather than as a sacred heritage to be revered, protected, and passed on; large populations; modern farming practices with chemical fertilizers and pesticides in order to feed the large populations, though at the cost of long-term stability of the land; large peacetime militaries with common use of the military draft; a reverence for and reliance upon technology and science; long working hours; representative democracy; and a mixed economy with some free market features but with an effort to protect a minimal standard of living for the poor.

Obviously not all those characteristics are bad. Certainly it was fortunate that representative democracy and a mixed capitalist-socialist economy happened to promote prosperity, happiness, and freedom as well as promoting the society's power. But many of the other characteristics of our societies that have been selected by the selection for power are not as desirable. Forming the Federation of Nations will eliminate this competition for power and will free the member societies to abandon those characteristics. When that happens, I think there are several cultural changes that we can predict will occur: Societies will evolve more benevolent attitudes toward the natural world; the overall size of the global military will shrink; the cultural attitudes encouraging large families will change and populations will tend to decrease; the glorification of physical aggression, which has been encouraged because it tends to promote national power, will probably decrease in many nations; and some societies, in view of the more undesirable effects of technology, will begin to de-emphasize technology and advocate simpler lifestyles.

One other cultural change we can be certain of is that, since nations no longer will need to fear other nations, xenophobia will decrease. That is not to say that patriotism will necessarily decrease; I expect patriotism in general to continue to thrive in most nations. But I expect more healthy and rational types of patriotism, instead of the xenophobic, militaristic, and bigoted brands that have thrived in the 20th century. In some places, however, the allegiance to nation probably will begin to fade. Many people may feel a stronger allegiance to the F.O.N., the world, or their local region, rather than to the nation. For that reason, some nations will almost certainly fragment. Over the course of history, nations have tended to consolidate into fewer and fewer and larger and larger nations, and clearly that process was primarily driven by the selection for power and the need to compete with other nations. Under the F.O.N., without the selection for power, we can expect that process to reverse.

Another cultural change we can be almost certain of under the F.O.N. is that the work week will begin to shrink. Throughout the last century, advances in technology have meant that the efficiency of each worker has exploded, which should have allowed us to work fewer hours. That didn't happen for two reasons, both of which were forced on us by the selection for power. First, the increasing population during the same period meant that each of us had less resources at our disposal, so we had to work more efficiently or for a longer time just to maintain the same level of wealth. And second, the competition for national power meant that over that same period an ever increasing proportion of our work went to producing military goods and other goods that increased the society's power but that, since they did not have any productive civilian use, did not increase individual wealth or raise the standard of living. Under the F.O.N., though, nations will finally be free to use increases in efficiency to improve people's lives rather than to threaten other nations. Thus, standards of living will rise and we will work less.

Some of the unpleasant consequences of the selection for power, I should point out, have already begun to reverse themselves even without the F.O.N. For instance, the destructive and antagonistic attitudes toward nature have begun to change. However, this can be explained as only a response to changing conditions and not a repudiation of the race for national power. As circumstances changed in the 20th century, the cultural attitude that nature is an enemy to subdue, though it was useful in previous times and contributed to societal power, suddenly became maladaptive. In the 20th century, total victory over nature became possible, and when that became possible nations recognized that total victory would not only destroy nature, but also destroy themselves and destroy their national power. So they modified their cultural attitudes toward nature from ones that advocated abuse or reckless use of nature to ones that advocate regulated, moderate use of nature. From the standpoint of national power, though, the optimal cultural attitude should still be that nature exists to be used by man, albeit used wisely, rather than that nature has ethical value in and of itself. To take that next step, to grant nature full ethical value on its own rather than value primarily as a collection of resources, will probably require the F.O.N. That is because as long as we have separate competing nations, threatening to make war on each other and attempting to exert power over each other, any nation that sees nature as something sacred, to be protected and revered regardless of other circumstances, will be at a competitive disadvantage against a nation that takes a more utilitarian view and sees nature as basically just a collection of resources for human use. Only in the F.O.N. will our cultures be truly free to recognize and respect nature's true sacred value.

To summarize, under the F.O.N. the societies of the world will adopt diverse approaches to all these characteristics. No longer will the selection for power put a straitjacket on societies, forcing them all to adopt every newly developed technology, to use enormous chemically dependent agribusinesses instead of small family farms, to have large peacetime armies and militaristic cultures, and to have cultures that urge sacrificing today, the only day we ever have, for the good of tomorrow, a day that always recedes into the future. Instead, some societies will prize technology and all the latest developments, and some will prize simplicity and tradition. Some will see nature and the land as deities to be worshipped and as the basis for our being, while others will merely see them as valuable and important objects to be used wisely—but none will see them as enemies to be subdued. Some will celebrate physical strength and appropriate aggressiveness, and others will celebrate meekness and the courage to turn the other cheek. Some will still use large farms to produce their food, and others will use backyard gardens. Some will speak English and others will, unfortunately, speak French. *Vive la difference.*

Tolerance and Democratic Values

To pay for some of the characteristics that the F.O.N. will encourage or allow in us, other characteristics will be demanded of us. For starters, since diversity will thrive in the F.O.N., tolerance for diversity must also thrive. Fortunately, tolerance should indeed thrive, because in at least a couple of ways the F.O.N. will tend to nurture it. First, the citizens who will most urgently need to demonstrate tolerance—the F.O.N. legislators and military personnel—should develop it from having to constantly work with and cooperate with those from different cultures. Second, the other citizens of the F.O.N. should tend to develop tolerance simply through the F.O.N.'s elimination of war. That is because when war dies, fear will die too—member nations will no longer need to fear attack from their neighbors—

and since fear is the father of hatred and bigotry, when fear dies, hatred and bigotry also should begin to wane. So as our differences grow under the F.O.N., our tolerance for differences should at least keep pace.

Other characteristics that will be demanded under the F.O.N. are what might be called democratic values. For the F.O.N. to function, as I have explained in Chapter 5, it must be a democracy—the officials must be chosen by the people, and the actions of the government must be open and publicly debated. As with any democracy, the F.O.N.'s success will depend on a strong foundation of democratic values in the people—with democratic values meaning the belief in and support for the principles upon which democracy rests, such as freedom of speech, freedom of the press, one person/one vote, the right to trial by jury, and so on. Fortunately, a large number of countries share those values now, and those that historically have not shared them are rapidly adopting them. In that sense, the need for democratic values will not be a problem in the F.O.N. But in another sense it could be. I am concerned that many of the nations that supposedly adhere to democracy do not seem to understand what democracy means. In Israel, for instance, people have for years been thrown in jail for the crime of simply talking to Palestinian Liberation Organization representatives—not for plotting the overthrow of the government or plotting any other illegal activities or revealing state secrets, but simply for talking to people to whom it is illegal to talk. Talking to people cannot be a crime in a democracy.

In the U.S. recently, President Bush and others proposed a constitutional amendment to ban burning the flag. Until then, burning the flag, since it is clearly intended as a symbolic political statement, had been protected by the right to free speech. But Bush and the others apparently felt that free speech is only O.K. as long as it does not involve statements or displays that some people find distasteful—like burning the flag. They felt that free speech is fine, I suppose, but only as long as it is speech that we all agree with. But that is not what free speech means. That is not democracy.

In Britain, the Official Secrets Act lets the government keep any policy or action it wishes a secret from its own people, and lets it jail anyone who has the audacity to discuss those particular actions. While that can occasionally be justified, as in keeping military capabilities or espionage plans secret, the act is also commonly used for purposes that cannot be justified. It is commonly used simply to hide unpopular governmental decisions from the people. That use of the Official Secrets Act is clearly inconsistent with the idea of democracy. A democratic government cannot operate in secret, and any government that does operate in secret is not a democracy.

For the F.O.N. to really thrive, these democratic principles—freedom of association, freedom of speech, the right of the people to know what their government is doing, and so on—are going to have to be better understood and better accepted than they sometimes seem to be today.

A New View of Ourselves

One of the most important consequences of the F.O.N. will be that it will change our psychological view of ourselves. Most people today, I think, have a very negative view of mankind. And that should not be surprising. It is very easy to look at human behavior and the course of human history and conclude that we are simply a worthless species and deserve anything bad that happens to us. After all, a lot of awful things happen in the world, and humans are responsible for virtually all of them. But as I have explained in this book, nearly all of those awful things are caused at least in part by the selection for power and the need of our societies to compete with other societies. In the F.O.N., that selection for power will be dead. When that happens, many of our problems, headed by war and overpopulation, will dissipate or disappear. We will then discover, to our great relief, that we did not choose war, poverty, and most of the other embarrassments to mankind; those things happened to us. Under the F.O.N., they will stop happening to us. We can then stop blaming ourselves for them. The psychological consequences of that, I think, will be tremendous. Having achieved permanent world peace, we will rightfully believe that we can achieve anything. We will be energized and will begin to stop the self-destructive behaviors that so plague us now. We will see that maybe there's a reason why God loves us after all.

Individual Responsibility

The most important way the F.O.N. will affect our cultures will be to demand of us and to nurture in us a sense of individual pride and individual responsibility for our actions.

It is not the F.O.N. that will bring about permanent world peace, and it is not this constitution that will bring about permanent world peace. It is we individuals and the sum of our individual actions. Ideas are passive. Pieces of paper are inert. Actions are what matter most. And not just the actions of "important" people, of the leaders. Their actions mean nothing without yours or mine, because leaders are only leaders if they have followers. In other words, it is not the actions of the leaders per se that matter, but rather the actions of the thousands of followers.

This idea of the importance of ordinary individuals is, I believe, the great lesson of the 20th century. The most important villain of World War II was not Adolf Hitler. The most important villains were the millions of ordinary citizens who helped Hitler. Naziism was not forced on the Germans; they chose it or chose to tolerate it. Too many encouraged it, voted for it, fought for it, and killed for it. And too many others were too cowardly, unconcerned, or filled with self-interest to try to stop it. It is these, who helped Hitler or tolerated him, who are most to blame for World War II.

The success of the F.O.N. will depend on ordinary people. It is our actions, the actions of each and every citizen, that will decide the F.O.N.'s fate. The citizens must vote to join the F.O.N., and afterwards they must refrain from voting to leave. The citizens must vote for responsible, courageous, and ethical senators and representatives. The jurors of the F.O.N. must do justice. If a defendant is innocent, they must follow their consciences and acquit him, even if their neighbors are screaming for the man's hide. The good, intelligent, and moral people of the F.O.N., who will always constitute a majority, must follow their consciences and must defend the democratic and human rights of the F.O.N. constitution. Those rights, such as the rights to trial by jury, to not be jailed without charge, to vote, and to freedom of speech, will be unpopular at times. But the good and intelligent people of the F.O.N. must have the courage to defend them anyway, accepting the condemnation of their neighbors, because it is the right thing to do. Finally, the soldiers of the F.O.N., and indeed all F.O.N. officials and all F.O.N. citizens in their daily jobs, must refuse to obey unconstitutional, illegal, or immoral orders. They must follow their consciences first, the F.O.N. constitution second, the F.O.N.'s laws third, and only last and most definitely least must they follow their orders.*

This will demand courage. I make no bones about it. Living an ethical life demands courage. It always has and it always will. Disobeying orders because they are unconstitutional, immoral, or unlawful will have consequences. Breaking immoral laws will have consequences. You may go to jail. You may suffer even worse than that. But that is what we are called on to do.

To illustrate what I mean by the call to disobey immoral orders, and how important that is, I relate the following story about Israeli soldiers fighting the Palestinians in the occupied territories in 1988. This story is from a column by Yossi Sarid in the May 4, 1989, issue of the Israeli daily newspaper *Ha'aretz*, reprinted in the September 1989 issue of *Harper's* magazine. The names, unfortunately, have been deleted to protect the guilty.

> On the morning of January 29, 1988, Captain A, a commander of the supplemental unit of one of the most famous battalions, was summoned to headquarters for a briefing by Lieutenant Colonel M, the officer in charge of the Nablus area, and his commanding officer. The lieutenant colonel gave specific orders about the procedure for making arrests in the village of Hawwara, near Nablus. Upon hearing the orders, Captain A protested, telling his commander that, in his opinion, such orders could not be reconciled with army ethics, and would be detrimental to the harmony and peace of the region. The lieutenant colonel replied that this was a new policy, dictated from above, and that it had to be carried out.
>
> ...Extremely agitated, Captain A demanded to know whether he was being directly ordered to carry out this mission. If so, he said, he would do it despite his conscientious objection....
>
> [The night of the mission], the company, forty soldiers and four officers, gathered at a civilian bus and were joined by three

---

*For further discussion of the conflict between allegiance to conscience and allegiance to law see the discussion of Art. III, Sec. 2, Prov. 9 and Art. V, Sec. 1, Prov. 2 in Appendix B.

more officers in two jeeps....

The bus and jeeps arrived in Hawwara at approximately 11 P.M. Major G proposed that, instead of the soldiers conducting a house-to-house search, he would order the *mukhtar* [village leader] to gather the men. Within a short time, and with no apparent difficulties, the men were brought to the village's central square. They offered no resistance.

The soldiers shackled the prisoners' hands behind their backs and led them to the bus....Shortly after, the bus pulled up to an orchard some 300 yards from the village. The "locals" (army jargon for the Palestinians) were taken off the bus and were led into the orchard in groups of three (four groups in all, each accompanied by an officer). Captain A found he was emotionally incapable of participating directly in the act but made sure from afar that it was carried out in accordance with army orders.

In the darkness, inside the orchard, the soldiers tied the legs of the shackled Hawwarans and laid them on the ground. An officer urged the soldiers to "get it over with quickly, so we can leave and forget." Then the soldiers stuffed flannelette (cloth Israeli soldiers use for cleaning their guns) into the mouths of the Arabs to keep them from crying out. The bus driver gunned the engine in order to muffle the noise.

The soldiers then meticulously proceeded to carry out the orders they had been given:

* Use clubs to break both hands and both legs of Arabs;
* Do not hit the head area;
* After breaking hands and legs, untie the wounded and abandon them;
* Leave the legs of one of the locals unbroken, so he can run to the village and get help.

The mission was carried out in full. Most clubs were broken in the process. Soldiers who adamantly refused to take part in the beating were allowed to remain on the bus to guard the prisoners.

[No charges were ever filed in connection with this incident, although Lieutenant Colonel M was dismissed from the military after this account was published.]

It is nice that Captain A protested his assignment. I suppose that's better than nothing. But it is not enough. Merely protesting beforehand that you disagree with an illegal or immoral order is inadequate. You must flatly refuse to carry it out. That is your ethical and legal duty. Jews, of all people, should know that. The great moral lesson of World War II is that following orders is not a defense. "Never again," the Israeli credo about the holocaust, means that never again can we allow "I was just following orders" to be used as any kind of an excuse or defense for one's actions. The soldiers who carried out this act against the Palestinians are torturers, and in the F.O.N. their kind must be treated as such.

So I now introduce the last clause of the F.O.N. constitution to be discussed in this book, and one of the most important clauses in the constitution:

> Article V, Section 1
> Provision 2. All individuals in the Federation of Nations are fully responsible for their actions and for defending this constitution. In keeping with that principle, whether or not a person may have been following orders is irrelevant to his legal responsibility for his actions and shall not be recognized as a defense or a mitigating factor in Federation of Nations courts. Also in keeping with that principle, no soldier or other person in the Federation of Nations may be punished for refusing to carry out an unconstitutional or illegal order. If a person is punished, he may seek redress in Federation of Nations courts from those who punished him.

Individual Importance

Not all the news about the F.O.N. and individual responsibility is so demanding. One of the most important effects of the F.O.N. is that it will elevate our sense of individual importance and self-esteem.

It seems to me that in many respects our societies try very hard to convince us that we don't matter, that each of us as an individual is unimportant. In part, society doesn't have to try too hard to convince us of that, because in nations of several million people, any rational person tends to conclude on his own that one person doesn't matter all that much. But that fact alone does not explain the epidemic we see of low self-esteem and feelings of inadequacy. That epidemic, I think, arises because more often than not society's efforts are designed to add to, rather than alleviate, our feelings of insignificance.

The first place we are taught that we don't matter is in the schools. In the United States and most other Westernized societies, classrooms generally have a large number of students, usually 20 or more; and students change classrooms and teachers at least every year and commonly every hour. In other words, teachers have a large group of students and little time to get to know them as individuals. Their top priority under these conditions has to be to maintain order and discipline, or they could not accomplish anything. Any boisterousness, any individual eccentricities, are quickly interpreted as threats to order and are punished. Students quickly learn that the most important lesson in life is to get in line and not make trouble. Meanwhile, what is being taught is necessarily limited to "facts" and the skill of how to take a test. The skills of thinking originally and creatively are not taught because they require getting to know the students and understanding how they think before they can be taught effectively. In fact, not only are thinking and creativity not taught, they are often actively discouraged, because any originality tends to be interpreted as a threat to order or a threat to the teacher's authority.

In other words, schools teach that you are just another person, just one out of twenty or a hundred or a million, and if you try to be more than that, you will be punished.

Why did this happen? It didn't happen by accident, and it didn't happen because the people designing our schools simply made a mistake. Our schools were rationally designed in response to the needs of the nation, and they have served their purpose very well. A modern nation needs a large body of docile and cooperative citizens in order to be powerful. It needs workers who will spend eight hours a day doing meaningless, boring, repetitive tasks without complaint. It needs soldiers who will unthinkingly obey an order without questioning the morality of it. And it needs citizens who will almost all accept without question the agreed upon cultural lies of the society—whether those lies be that capitalism is absolutely good and socialism evil and the United States has never waged an unjust war, or that socialism is absolutely good and capitalism evil and the Soviet Union has never waged an unjust war.

The selection for power among nations dictated that we design our schools to maximize the nation's power, design them to create a docile body of cooperative citizens. It is no accident that when you hear people talk about the mission of schools, they usually say it is to create good citizens—in other words, good servants of the state. Much less often do people say that the mission is to create fulfilled individuals.

Now, however, the demands on a powerful nation have changed. Now a nation's power depends more on its responsiveness to changing situations and on its technical innovativeness. Those skills require thought and creativity. So all of a sudden people in the U.S. complain now that our schools have failed, that they don't teach people to think or be creative. But our schools didn't fail. They weren't supposed to teach people to think and be creative. They were supposed to teach them to be unthinkingly cooperative and to fit in with the crowd.

Schools, of course, are not the only institutions in society that try to crush individual spirit. Other examples of this effort are everywhere. Boot camp for new soldiers, for instance, is basically just an intense effort to crush any latent individualism and independence that might have survived the educational system and might interfere with the recruits' subservient following of orders. Large corporations, for another example, preach self-sacrifice for the good of the organization and have little tolerance for anyone who disobeys orders from above. In fact, in job interviews at those large corporations we are often forced to lie about the obvious fact that we might later take a better job offer from outside the company, that our primary loyalty is to ourselves and our families rather than to the company. Finally, almost all advertising and much of popular entertainment is devoted to subtly convincing us that we are too fat, too skinny, too poor, too weak, too dumb, too smart, or too ugly.

It is important to emphasize, though, that I am not saying people are consciously trying to degrade or belittle other people. Teachers, for instance, are doing their best to help and to educate children, and advertising executives are likewise just trying to do their jobs. But teachers, because of the design of schools in our societies, are put in a position where maintaining order will be the top priority, and they will inevitably tend to quell most attempts to assert individuality or creativity. Likewise, because advertising executives have a product to sell, even if they do not consciously try to degrade people, they will still inevitably tend to send the message that you are inadequate unless you buy this product. Societies send the message that we as individuals are unimportant and inadequate because of the structure of society, not because most people intentionally do anything to degrade other people.

Forces everywhere in our societies try to convince us that we don't matter. They do this, again, because of the selection for power between societies. To be powerful, a society needs a large, docile work force, a large, docile body of soldiers, and a large, docile body of citizens who will follow their government's orders. Therefore, societies exert enormous effort to convince us we are unimportant and to make us docile. They need to exert so much effort because our hearts constantly rebel against the message. In the F.O.N., though, societies will no longer need to compete for power; so they will no longer need to crush our spirits and make us nothing but tools of the society. The resilient individual spirit will then well up and defeat those forces arrayed against it and remake our cultures into ones that glorify rather than degrade the individual.

The key, once again, is that the F.O.N. will secure nations against the selection for power.

A System of Ethics for People Who Believe They Are Important

Perhaps the most crucial way we are taught that we individuals are unimportant is through the systems of ethics that most of our religions and societies extol. In this section I want to explain how those systems of ethics tend to belittle the individual and to fail us in other ways, and explain the characteristics of alternative and better ethical systems that are likely to develop under the F.O.N.

The system of ethics I hope to see prosper under the F.O.N. centers on the proposition that each of us is important and our actions matter. They matter a lot. Beginning with that proposition, we ask then what we are called to do in our actions. The traditional answer is that we are called to make the world a better place. Wrong. That is putting the cart before the horse. First, we have to stop making the world a worse place.

There is a difference between the two. It does little good to shower your child with love and affection at the end of the day if earlier in the day you were beating him and yelling at him.

The first thing that is demanded of us is that we take responsibility for our actions and stop being part of the problem. The absolute minimal ethical standard has to be that each of us do our best always and everywhere to not hurt God and not hurt our neighbor. If you say you care about endangered species, then don't buy a leopard coat; don't buy ivory. If you say you care about the environment, and it is demanded of us that we do care, then recycle your newspapers. Walk when you don't have to drive. Don't use pesticides on your garden or your farm (or, if you must use pesticides, at least minimize the amounts you use). Don't use aerosol spray cans that destroy the ozone layer. Produce only as much garbage as you have to, only as much pollution as you have to, only as much toxic chemicals as you have to. If you say you care about racism, then don't tell jokes about other races. And don't laugh when you hear such jokes. Instead, tell the speaker that the joke was offensive. If you fail to do that, you are contributing to the problem. You are sending the message that racism is acceptable.

Finally, don't yell at people. Don't insult them when they are trying to do their best. And for goodness sake, don't yell at a child. Most of the problems in this world stem from the fact that most of us, to one degree or another, have low self-esteem. We have low self-esteem because so many people have yelled at us and insulted us and ignored us, probably without even realizing it was a sin. You are important and valuable and your neighbor is important and valuable. We are called upon to treat each other as such.

Those demands aren't all easy. We all will fail to hit the mark sometimes. We all sin. But too often the fact that we all sin is used as an excuse not to try to do better. Yes, we all sin, but it is essential to recognize it when we sin and try to do better next time. We have to try to be aware of our sins. We have to ask, "Is what I am doing contributing to making the world a worse place?"

The primary ethical demand of us is not to cure problems; it is to stop causing them. Surely, that is the minimum that must be demanded of us.

But what about going beyond this minimal standard and actively trying to make the world a better place? Surprisingly, although we have all been taught otherwise, that really isn't very important. It is much more important to not make the world a worse place than to actively attempt to make it better. It is a good deal more important to recycle your newspapers, drive a fuel-efficient car (or better yet, ride a bicycle or take the bus), and not apply pesticides to your garden or farm, than it is to pick up litter. It is much more important to be a credit to your religion by your actions every minute of your life than to give generously to the church. It is infinitely more important to treat your child with patience and love, constantly reminding him that he is unique and valuable, so that he grows up to be a self-confident and loving person, than it is to donate your time to counsel emotionally disturbed adults. After all, if everyone treated their children that way, there would hardly be any emotionally disturbed adults.

The primary demand in this ethical system that I favor is to take responsibility for our actions, to ask ourselves which of our actions might be sins, might be contributing to hurting another person, hurting ourselves, or making the world a worse place, and then to confront those sins and try to stop them.

Now, contrast this with today's prevailing ethical systems. The concept of sin seems almost to have completely vanished from today's prevailing ethics. According to Karl Menninger, as of 1973 no U.S. president had publicly uttered the word sin since Dwight Eisenhower in 1953 (Menninger, 1973). I don't recall it happening since 1973 either. Instead, the preeminent demand has become a call to self-sacrifice, a call to actively serve others. Two political examples of this would be John Kennedy's, "Ask not what your country can do for you; ask what you can do for your country," and George Bush's "thousand points of light," extolling the virtues of volunteering. A social example of this prevalence of the ethic of self-sacrifice would be that, according to the myriad charitable organizations we all constantly hear from, to solve any conceivable problem in the world, from starvation to homelessness to the loss of topsoil to the decay of sexual morals, the most important thing for us to do is to give these organizations our money.

That is fine as far as it goes. A willingness to give of yourself for the good of others, either through your time or your money, is certainly an admirable trait. But the problem is that self-sacrifice is generally treated as not merely admirable but as a duty. It is not a duty. Your life is your own, not someone else's. You don't have a duty to give it up.

Self-sacrifice is undoubtedly a virtue, but it makes a lousy central virtue. The primary reason it makes a lousy central virtue is that self-sacrifice or selflessness, the desire to go out and "do good for others," has very limited ability to actually effect change, to actually improve the world. Henry David Thoreau wrote, "If I knew for a certainty that a man was coming to my house with the conscious design of doing me good, I should run for my life." I'm inclined to agree. For the most part, we can only really improve our own lives. If other people don't want their lives "improved," you can't improve them. Our first ethical duties should be to improve our own lives and merely to *allow* others to improve their lives. Our primary duty is not to actively help other people, though it might be nice if we want to do that also, but to allow people to help themselves, to get out of their way, or, in other words, to stop sinning against them.

Another problem with elevating self-sacrifice to the central virtue is that it is not even an absolute virtue. In excess it is a sin. If you always choose to sacrifice yourself, then you place no value on your own life. And surely your own life is as valuable as anyone else's. So failing to care about your own life is a sin. Besides that, if you do not value your own life, why would you value anyone else's? It is philosophically inconsistent. If your own life doesn't matter, why do theirs? Jesus said, "Love your neighbor *as* yourself," not love your neighbor *instead* of yourself. God so loved you that He gave you a life on this beautiful earth to cherish and enjoy. Don't refuse that gift.

These problems with making self-sacrifice the central virtue, though, are not even the most serious problems with the prevailing ethics. The most serious problem with the prevailing ethics is their emphasis on curing or alleviating problems instead of preventing them. I suppose it's more glorious to be a martyr and save the world from impending disaster, but it's more important and effective to prevent impending disasters from arising in the first place. The prevailing ethical systems treat the problems of the world as though they just dropped from the sky and we had nothing to do with them. But they didn't drop from the sky. Except for disease and natural disasters, all the problems in the world are caused by us. They are all caused by sin.* Yet in the prevailing ethical systems, sin is barely mentioned. When it is mentioned at all, it is either in the context, from the liberal viewpoint, that everyone sins, so sins don't really matter, or in the context, from the conservative viewpoint, that only other people sin, never us.

To summarize, the prevailing ethical systems seem to emphasize curing or alleviating problems after they have happened, rather than preventing them from arising, and in that context they emphasize self-sacrifice as the only way to cure problems and de-emphasize the fact that those problems are caused by our sins. In contrast, the ethical system I try to abide by says that trying to cure problems after they have arisen is generally fruitless, but that we can achieve much better results by addressing the causes of those problems and trying to prevent the problems from arising in the first place. In that context, then, self-sacrifice is unimportant. You are free to enjoy your own life without feeling a duty to sacrifice it for others. But you must take responsibility for your actions and you must constantly ask yourself how your own actions might be sins, might be causing problems in the world.

In some respects, the ethical system I advocate is much more demanding than the prevailing ethical systems. It imbues many actions or decisions every day with great moral significance and thus insists that we constantly demand morality of ourselves. The concept of sin is extended from just the big ones, such as adultery and murder, to everyday lapses such as losing our tempers or

---

*Earlier in this chapter, I indicated that most of the problems in the world are caused by the selection for power, so I should reconcile these two positions. They are not in contradiction. They are merely opposite sides of the same coin. They are merely the proximate and ultimate explanations.

Sins are the immediate causes of all our problems. But the selection for power creates an environment conducive to sin. It makes or has made such things as holding slaves, raping the environment, and waging war profitable behaviors for societies and individuals. The selection for power dictates, in many if not most cases, the extent to which the sins that cause our problems will spread and thus how bad the problems they cause will become. Sins, though, are still the immediate causes of our problems.

throwing something in the garbage that could have been recycled.

But in other ways this ethical system is much more liberating and uplifting and much easier than the prevailing ones. By turning several actions every day into moral choices, it makes every day of your life part of the great struggle between good and evil. This has great effects in endowing your life with a feeling of importance and focusing your attention on the present moment. People in the modern world frequently complain that life is devoid of meaning and adventure. Well, it's not devoid of meaning and adventure when you recognize that every day of your life is part of the great struggle between good and evil. Moreover, this approach to life tends to create tremendous pride. It is commonly pointed out that we all sin, but the equally important fact that most of the time we don't sin is rarely mentioned. When people are given a choice between doing what is right and what is wrong, and when they recognize that that is the choice (or, I should say, *force* themselves to recognize that that is the choice), nine times out of ten they will choose to do what is right. Since the ethical system I advocate presents you with that choice several times every day, in practicing it you discover that most of time you will choose to do what is right. Noticing that, you will develop a lot of pride in your actions and in your life. And that pride will tend to inspire even better actions in the future.

In contrast, the prevailing ethical systems emphasizing self-sacrifice, by ignoring sin and ignoring what you do with the bulk of your life—the time when you are earning a living and doing other ordinary chores—send the message that your life is unimportant. After all, what you do with 90% of your time doesn't really matter. Then, on the rare occasions when these systems make a demand of you, they demand something that, by definition, is difficult: self-sacrifice. The name says it all. These acts are sacrifices. (Some activities that we casually call self-sacrifice are actually things that we really want to do. In these situations we say that we got more than we gave, and although we are doing something for the good of others, we are doing it primarily because we want to. So I will define this as not being true self-sacrifice and as being accommodated equally well by an ethical system emphasizing sin as by one emphasizing true self-sacrifice.)

Since the ethical systems emphasizing self-sacrifice, by definition, demand something that you don't want to do, most of the time you are going to fail. This produces guilt, and in fact guilt becomes one of the primary tools for inducing compliance with the ethical system. The other primary tool for inducing compliance is even more devious. Since you are being asked to give something up, the systems minimize the importance of what you are giving up: your life!

The primary goal of any sensible system of ethics has to be to maximize the total enjoyment of people's lives, both the enjoyment of those practicing the ethical system and of those they practice it upon. On both counts, ethical systems emphasizing self-sacrifice, which I think are the predominant ethical systems in existence today, fail very badly. First, by using guilt as a major motivator and by minimizing the importance of your life, both as a tool to motivate compliance and as a consequence of ignoring what you do with the bulk of your life, these ethical systems poison the enjoyment of your life. Second, because they use negative emotions—guilt and the feeling that your life is insignificant—to induce compliance, and because they ask something very difficult—sacrificing yourself—they can never be very successful in inducing ethical behavior.

In contrast, the ethical system I advocate doesn't rely on such devious tactics. It says your life is valuable. It is the most valuable thing there is in this world. Enjoy it. That's why God gave it to you. And it says likewise that your actions are important. It is your actions that determine what kind of world we have, and by your actions we can solve any problems we face. When you treat people that way, they take pride in their actions and behave ethically. Just as a person who owns a valuable car will take care of it and take pride in it, a person who believes he owns a valuable life will take care of it and take pride in it. He will behave ethically because he feels proud of his life and proud of his actions.

Finally and most important, even if ethical systems emphasizing self-sacrifice could induce compliance, because of their emphasis on alleviating problems after they have already happened, they would have little effect on improving the world. It does little good to lock the barn door after the cows have already escaped.

If ethical systems emphasizing self-sacrifice are so inferior to other ethical systems, though, why have they spread so widely? Because, of course, they increase a society's power. They do this, for instance, by producing soldiers who, being already attuned to the importance of self sacrifice, and having already been taught by their ethical systems that their own lives are unimportant, are only too willing to give their lives for their country—the most extreme examples of this phenomenon being Japan's kamikazee pilots and Iran's legions of soldiers and terrorists so eager to be martyrs for Allah. Another way an ethics of self-sacrifice helps increase a nation's power is by creating compliant workers and citizens who, having never been taught the importance of sin and the importance of taking individual responsibility for their actions (not to mention having never been taught the importance of their own lives) are willing to dutifully carry out the directives of their government and their employers without asking themselves what it is they are doing and whether perhaps they should not be doing it. In these ways and others, an ethic of self-sacrifice tends to increase a nation's power.

Under the F.O.N., though, this competition for power will no longer be necessary, and healthier and more effective ethical systems will develop.

Giving Self-Sacrifice Its Due

In the previous section I oversimplified a bit when I created this dichotomy between ethical systems that emphasize sin and individual responsibility on the one hand, and those that emphasize self-sacrifice on the other. I said that ethical systems that emphasize sin and our own individual responsibility for correcting our sins are addressing the causes of problems—sins. And as with medicine or any other endeavor, actions that attack the causes of problems are much more effective than those that only address the symptoms. In this sense, since self-sacrifice is generally only aimed at the symptoms of problems and not their causes, ethical systems that emphasize sin and individual responsibility are clearly superior to those that emphasize self-sacrifice.

But my oversimplification has been in characterizing self-sacrifice as always addressing symptoms and never diseases.

Much, and probably most, self-sacrifice does indeed only address symptoms, and is therefore almost totally ineffective in curing or even alleviating the world's problems. But some self-sacrifice is aimed at causes, is aimed at eradicating sin, and this is often spectacularly effective. Two examples of movements of self-sacrifice that were aimed at eradicating sin in the United States were the pre-Civil War abolitionist movement, aimed at eradicating the sin of slavery, and the 1950's and 60's civil rights movement, aimed at eradicating the sin of racial discrimination. The people involved in those movements were going beyond correcting their own sins. They did not own slaves and they did not discriminate on the basis of race themselves, so they had taken the first ethical step of taking individual responsibility for their actions and not sinning. Now they went beyond that to prevent other people also from sinning. The way they did that was through self-sacrifice. They sacrificed their time to write, speak, and march for the things they believed in. And they sacrificed their bodies and their freedom in actively violating unjust laws and then being beaten, killed, or jailed for that. But by doing that, they ultimately changed the laws and morals of the nation to stop the sin of slavery and greatly reduce the sin of racism. In so doing, they profoundly improved this nation.

Some self-sacrifice is successful in correcting problems and improving the world. But when it is successful, it is invariably because it is addressing the causes of problems rather than the symptoms. It is invariably because it is aimed at eradicating sin. For example, another successful instance of self-sacrifice, though less spectacular and well known than the abolitionist or civil rights movements, was the movement to end the use of lead as an additive in gasoline. After World War II, tetraethyl lead began to be added to gasoline in order to increase the gasoline's octane rating and thereby prevent "engine knock" and give better engine performance. The only problem was that lead is toxic. In high doses it causes severe brain damage, and in lower doses it causes a slight but very measurable decrease in mental ability. With all this lead in gasoline, lead was present in the air and, after settling from the air, in the soil—particularly in inner cities. Hence, children, who tend to play in the dirt and then lick their fingers, were accumulating lead in their bodies. This, it could be shown, was causing a significant decrease in their mental abilities.

A traditional approach to this problem, addressing the symptoms rather than the causes, might have been to raise government money for extra tutors for children found to have high lead concentrations in their bodies, to try to compensate for their decreased mental abilities. Or it might have been to launch a public education campaign to tell parents they should not let their children play in the dirt. In fact, the latter approach actually was one of the approaches taken. (Pretty shocking, isn't it? I mean, what's the point of childhood if you can't play in the dirt?) But fortunately, another approach was also taken. The problem was attacked at its source. Through the tireless lobbying of a few, lead was gradually removed from gasoline, ultimately being almost completely banned. Between 1975 and 1987, lead emissions decreased by 94% and the lead levels in children's bodies showed similarly dramatic decreases. The lead problem was solved by attacking it at its source, eradicating the sin of adding lead to gasoline.

I'm sure many readers laughed at my hypothetical solution to the lead problem of hiring extra tutors for children found to have high lead concentrations in their bodies. But I do not think that approach differs much from the approaches our governments and charitable organizations take toward most of the problems in the world. Consider the drug problem and the associated crime it causes. The "solutions" our government proposes for this all only address the symptom—more crime. Those solutions are just more police, more courts, and more jails. Only a few look beyond the symptoms of the drug problem, in particular crime, to see at least one cause of the symptoms—which is that these drugs are illegal—and ask, Do all of these drugs really have to be illegal? Could we at least legalize some of them and thus eliminate the crime associated with those drugs? And almost no one looks beyond that cause to see the ultimate cause of the problem, which is that we have created a society from which so many want to escape.

For even clearer examples of how our societies and our prevailing ethical systems address the symptoms of problems rather than their causes, we can look at the problems of hunger and homelessness. Hunger is fundamentally caused by just one thing: overpopulation. There are of course other contributing factors, chiefly poor farming practices that destroy the soil and turn arable land into desert, and unequal distributions of wealth that leave some people too poor to buy food even when it is available. But the basic problem is just that with the amount of land in the world and our current agricultural technology (or for that matter any agricultural technology we are ever likely to develop) it is just not possible to feed 5½ billion people an adequate diet. Furthermore, to the extent that destructive farming practices and unequal distribution of wealth contribute to the problem, these are largely caused by overpopulation anyway. Destructive farming practices arise primarily because of the need to feed a too large population and the need to desperately try to produce more food from a parcel of land than the land is capable of sustainably producing. While unequal distribution of wealth is a more complex problem, it too is largely caused by overpopulation. Overpopulation means a shortage of resources, and when there are shortages of resources, people are not going to share equally. People are going to say, "I'm going to get what I need, and to hell with my neighbor."

Overpopulation, therefore, can be considered for most practical purposes to be the sole cause of hunger. Yet, of the hundreds of Western charitable organizations devoted to fighting hunger in the Third World, I don't know of a single one that devotes even a tiny fraction of its efforts to fighting overpopulation. All these organizations ever do is attack the symptom. To all appearances, it has never occurred to them to ask why these people are hungry in the first place. Thus, since this effort is devoted entirely to the symptom and not at all to the disease, it has had no effect whatsoever on reducing the amount of starvation in the world.

The actions taken against homelessness here in the United States also seem to address symptoms rather than causes and also have had little if any effect on the problem. Homelessness arises, very simply, because land and housing cost too much. Like any other commodities, the price of land and housing is determined by the law of supply and demand. Since the amount of land is constant, when population rises you have more people pursuing a constant amount of land, and the price rises. Therefore, the only way to reduce homelessness is to reduce the cost of land and housing. And, although government subsidies could temporarily and artificially reduce the cost of land and housing, at least for the poor, the only way to permanently reduce these costs is to reduce the population.*

Overpopulation in the United States is basically the sole cause of homelessness here. Although specific governmental policies could alleviate the problem and could have delayed the onset of the problem, continual population growth guaranteed that at some point homelessness would become a serious problem in the U.S. But in all the articles about homelessness I have seen, I have never even seen a mention of overpopulation. The advocates for the homeless devote their energy to the symptom—they devote their energy to finding shelter for a small fraction of the homeless on a small fraction of the nights they are homeless. They do not devote their energy to solving the cause of the problem, to curing the disease itself. They do not devote their energy, or devote very little, to reducing the cost of land and housing, and of the little energy they may devote to that, none of it is aimed at reducing population, which is ultimately the only way the cost of land and housing will permanently come down. As a consequence, the fight against homelessness has been completely unsuccessful so far.

That was a long digression, but my point is that self-sacrifice can be effective in correcting the world's problems and, thus, it does have a place in a healthy system of ethics. But self-sacrifice can only be effective in any large way when it is directed at eradicating the causes of problems, at eradicating sin. It is almost completely ineffective when it is directed, as most of the self-sacrifice in the world today is directed, at alleviating the symptoms of problems without attacking the sins that cause them.

---

*Technically, some might point out here, the price of land is determined not by the number of people available to buy the land but by the total amount of money those people have to buy the land. So if we reduce the total wealth of the nation, if we all choose to live in poverty, that also would bring down the price of land. But I don't think many people would favor that solution. Reducing the number of people rather than their wealth seems like a more viable option. Besides, reducing the total wealth of the nation isn't even a solution. Although the price of land would come down, since we would all be poorer we still wouldn't be able to afford it.

As I said, self-sacrifice can have a place in a healthy ethical system. But it must be secondary to a sense of individual responsibility for our actions and a sense of courage to recognize and confront our sins and stop them. Our first ethical duty must be to as much as possible stop our sins, to stop making the world a worse place. Then, having done our best at that, some may want to go further and actively make the world a better place. To do that will require self-sacrifice—specifically, it will require self-sacrifice that is aimed at eradicating the sins of others or the sins of our societies, not self-sacrifice that is aimed at simply giving things away or aimed at treating symptoms rather than diseases.

Self-sacrifice is decidedly secondary in this ethics. It can only come after mastering the basics of ethics, and the most important part of ethics, which is a sense of individual responsibility for our actions and the courage to confront our sins. And even then, even after we have taken responsibility for our actions, have had the courage to confront our sins, and have reduced our sins as much as possible, I do not believe that self-sacrifice is required. That is, self-sacrifice is only optional in this ethics. We are under no duty to practice it. There are a lot of problems in the world, and if it were our ethical duty to attempt to eradicate them all, we would never have time to do anything else. To quote once again my favorite writer, Henry David Thoreau, by whom this ethics is inspired: "I came into this world not chiefly to make this a good place to live in, but to live in it, be it good or bad." Our primary calling is just to live and enjoy life. And that is enough.

The Ethics of Population

I will now demonstrate my total lack of tact and diplomacy by offending just about everyone. I do not do this because I enjoy offending people, but because it has to be said.

The ethic of population growth and birth control must change. As I explained previously, under a system of independent nations, a nation's power is tied to its population, so no nation could wholeheartedly attempt to control its population. No society could declare that it was a moral responsibility to practice birth control. Under the F.O.N., though, that will no longer be the case. Nations will suddenly be able to afford to control their populations, and societies must change their ethics in this matter.

We've got about 5½ billion people in the world today. Hundreds of millions of them starve to death or die of malnutrition every year. Billions of them live in abject poverty. Hundreds of millions live without adequate shelter. Species are going extinct at a greater rate than has ever happened in the history of life on this planet. Soil is being lost due to bad farming practices so rapidly in most countries on earth, including the United States, that in less than 100 years at the current rate it will be gone entirely from vast areas of what is currently our most fertile farmland. Wilderness is vanishing. Pollution is poisoning every corner of the world.

All of those problems are the direct consequence of the fact that we have far, far too many people in the world.

Overpopulation is the one and only significant cause of starvation, homelessness, the high cost of housing and land, and about half of the world's environmental problems. Overpopulation is not *a* cause of those problems, not *a major* cause, it is *the* cause. Any other contributing factors are so trivial in comparison they should not even be mentioned.

In addition, overpopulation is a major cause, if not the most important cause, of all the environmental problems for which it is not the sole cause, of poverty, of racism, of war, and of almost every other problem in the world.

None of those problems are going to get better until we reduce our population. And I mean reduce it drastically, reduce it from 5½ billion to at the most 1 billion people. There are three ways that could happen, and it *will* happen one way or another: We could all die of starvation, we could all die prematurely of disease, or we could all choose to have two or fewer children. I prefer the last of these.

No longer can it be viewed as O.K. to have five or more children. In fact, in our time, when drastic population decreases are necessary, it is not O.K. to have even three children.* Some

---

*I emphasize that this particular cutoff point, where even three children is unacceptable, is only for our time in history. Obviously, if no one ever had three or more children forever and ever, we would eventually go extinct. So someday—when we have reduced our population to a level at which we have abundant wilderness, at which we can afford to practice sound farming techniques and soil is being gained (cont.)

will say it is a right to have as many children as you like. Nonsense. I'll tell you what a right is. It's a right not to starve to death. It's a right to have a roof over your head. It's a right for children to have wild and natural places to dream about and to grow up in. It's a right for other species merely to exist. Those are rights. Having ten children isn't a right; it's a crime.

Having three or more children in today's world is a sin. I don't say, "In my opinion it is a sin," because I don't feel it is merely my opinion. It is an observable fact. The traditional sins are not sins because God arbitrarily chose to chisel them in stone. They are sins for observable, logical reasons. Murder is a sin because it takes away a person's right to his life and because, by creating fear and distrust, it poisons all social interactions even for the survivors. Adultery is a sin because it creates jealousy and distrust that again poison the productive social interactions necessary for the functioning of any society, and because, as we are being reminded by the AIDS epidemic, it spreads disease. Lying is a sin because, again, it creates distrust that poisons society.

All those things are sins because they have observable bad consequences. Likewise, having three or more children has not just bad consequences but utterly horrendous consequences. It directly causes almost every serious problem in the world. So unless one wants to claim that our prohibitions against the sins of murder, stealing, or lying are just arbitrary cultural quirks, one has to admit that having three or more children is also a sin. In fact, one has to admit that it is at least as serious a sin as most of the sins proscribed by the Ten Commandments.

Birth control is the greatest moral question our societies face and perhaps the greatest moral question most of us will ever face as individuals. Not including that in our moral codes is an ethical blind spot the size of the sky. To illustrate just how great a moral question that is, consider the case of Mother Teresa. She is a person whose life is so exemplary she is almost universally

---

(cont.) rather than lost, at which pollution is no longer a problem, and at which starvation and homelessness no longer exist—it can be viewed as O.K. for some to have three children, and possibly even four. But for today and for the next two or three centuries, population decline, not population stabilization, is what is needed, and it is wrong to have even three children.

considered to be a living saint, an opinion with which, in terms of her single-minded devotion to God, I wholeheartedly concur. Yet, because of her personal opposition to birth control and her encouragement of large families, there can hardly be any doubt that she has caused more suffering in India than she has alleviated. The question of population control dwarfs all other moral issues.

The preeminence of birth control ethics among all moral issues has several consequences. It means it is hypocritical to say that you care about the environment and then to have three or more children. It is hypocritical to say that you care about starvation and then to have three or more children. It is hypocritical to say that you care about homelessness or poverty or war or almost anything and then to have three or more children.

In fact, it is actually hypocritical to say that you love your children if you are choosing to have three or more children, because by your actions you are doing your best to insure that the world they inherit will be a worse place.

I do not mean, though, by this discussion, to condemn those, such as my parents, who have already had three or more children. What's done is done. The important thing is to change our behavior in the present and in the future. Besides, those in the past who have had three or more children, in a sense, have an excuse for their irresponsible actions (and yes, I do consider having three or more children to have been an irresponsible act, even 30 years ago) because no one told them to do otherwise. Until very recently, almost no one pointed out the horrible consequences of overpopulation and the fact that we are clearly suffering gravely from that disease. And even in recent years, the few who have belatedly pointed out these obvious facts have not pointed out the equally obvious moral consequences of those facts. But today, no longer can any thinking person fail to recognize the overwhelming role of overpopulation in almost all our problems. And recognizing that role, there can no longer be any excuse for failing to recognize the moral demand on each of us to limit our reproduction.

I know this discussion has offended some people—in fact, it has probably offended most people. But we've got some major problems in this world, and I think it's high time we started offending the people responsible for those problems, instead of offending others by starving them to death.

The reason I have chosen to discuss population control ethics in this book is that the F.O.N. will not long survive, and certainly will not achieve its full potential, unless we decrease our populations. And we will not decrease our populations until it becomes widely accepted that birth control is morally required. We have it in our power, through the F.O.N., to achieve permanent world peace, prosperity, and ecological sanity. We have it in our power to reach the promised land in our time, to achieve the dreams that mankind has always dreamed about, but generally believed could never be achieved. But it cannot happen unless we control our populations.

Summary of Chapter 12

- The selection for power is one of the most important factors, probably the most important factor, directing what cultural traits our societies develop.

- Under the F.O.N., the selection for power will be dead. Thus, for the first time in 10,000 years we will suddenly be free to move our societies and cultures in *any* direction we choose, rather than in only those directions that increase societal or national power.

- The death of the selection for power will free our societies to diverge more in culture. The selection for power has put a straitjacket on our societies, forcing them to become very similar and to adopt the same cultural traits, to adopt the cultural traits that promote a society's power. Among those traits are the protestant work ethic, the glorification of technology and "progress" and the denigration of simplicity and tradition, the encouragement of large families and population growth, militaristic attitudes and the possession of large peacetime armies, and the attitude that nature exists solely to be used by man or, even worse, that nature is an enemy to be subdued. Under the F.O.N., this staitjacket of the selection for power, which has inflicted all this cultural sameness upon us, will be removed, and as a consequence, many of these cultural traits will be reversed and diversity will thrive.

- The F.O.N. will give us a new and more positive view of ourselves. Having achieved permanent world peace, we will rightfully believe that we can achieve anything. We will be energized and will begin to stop the self-destructive behaviors that so plague us now.

- The most important lesson of the 20th century is the importance of individual actions and of taking individual responsibility for our actions. In keeping with that principle, whether or not a person may have been following orders should be irrelevant to his legal responsibility for his actions and must not be recognized as a defense in F.O.N. courts.

- Our cultures teach us in many ways that we ordinary individuals are unimportant. They do that because, to be powerful, societies need a large, docile body of workers, soldiers, and citizens who will follow orders—and persons too aware of their individual importance are not sufficiently docile and subservient in following orders. Under the F.O.N., though, the need of societies to compete for power will be over, so societies will no longer need to degrade the individual. The resilient individual spirit will then well up and defeat those forces arrayed against it and remake our cultures into ones that glorify rather than degrade the individual.

- The prevailing ethics seem to focus on self-sacrifice and ignore sin. But sins are what cause all of the world's problems. To really improve the world, we must attack and, as much as possible, eradicate our sins.

- In that context of confronting sins, we absolutely must finally have the courage to confront the one great sin that is responsible for very nearly every problem in the world, and that yet, by some miracle of blindness, cowardice, and irresponsibility, is rarely or never mentioned. That sin at the societal level, where it is rarely mentioned, is overpopulation. That sin at the individual level, where it is never mentioned, is having three or more children. It is absolutely, positively *morally wrong* to have three or more children.

Chapter 13 | **A Possible Danger?**

In this chapter I want to confront what I expect will be the most powerful argument against forming the F.O.N. That argument is the danger of a military coup and a worldwide military dictatorship. At first glance, it might appear that this would be a serious danger. After all, in a worldwide F.O.N., the F.O.N. military force will be the only military force in the world and in theory there would be nothing to stop it if it (speaking of the military as a single body with a single mind) decided to overthrow the civilian government and establish a military dictatorship over the world.

The situation, however, is not that simple, and I think there is no danger that this could happen.

A few facts have to be kept in mind. First, far from being a single body with a single mind, the F.O.N. military will comprise officers and soldiers from all over the world. These people will come from extremely diverse cultural backgrounds, speak different languages, in fact speak the entire range of different languages in the world, and represent the entire spectrum of political outlooks of all the peoples of the world.

Second, it is a great oversimplification to say that the F.O.N. military in a worldwide F.O.N. will be the only military force in the world. National guard and police forces in the F.O.N. will still exist, and in fact, in cumulative manpower, these forces will greatly outnumber the F.O.N. military. Furthermore, since my proposed constitution states that the F.O.N. must allow the ownership of guns, the people themselves will also be armed (although it will be possible that in some nations the national governments will forbid gun ownership).

Also, remember that in a worldwide F.O.N., the F.O.N. military should, if the civilian government is responsible, be very small. There will no longer be any external enemies to defend ourselves against, so the military need only be large enough to ensure that F.O.N. laws can be enforced and to guard against the possibility that one member nation, with its national guard and police forces, could attack another member nation.

What all this adds up to is that a successful military coup would be almost impossible, and that even if a successful coup somehow occurred, it would be even closer to impossible to translate that into a worldwide military dictatorship.

First, the diverse languages and worldwide scattering of F.O.N. military forces will make it, in practical terms, impossible, even if all military personnel were to agree to it, to organize a coordinated coup attempt without the civilian authorities being aware of it in advance. Second, the military personnel will not all be in agreement on a coup. The extremely diverse cultural backgrounds and political outlooks of the soldiers and officers in a worldwide force insure that a very large fraction of the force will resist a coup attempt and will stand ready to lead a rebellion if a successful coup occurs.

Third, even if a successful coup somehow occurs, the national guard and police forces around the world, which as I said will enormously outnumber the F.O.N. military, will be armed and ready to fight against any dictatorship. Moreover, the civilians will also be armed, and national and local governments, unconnected to the F.O.N. government and representing the diversity of political views around the world, will already be in existence and will be ideally positioned to organize resistance fighters.

In short, there is very little danger of a military coup in the F.O.N., and no danger at all of a worldwide military dictatorship.

Finally, before I leave the subject of a military overthrow, I want to return to a point emphasized in the last chapter. That point is that the ultimate safeguard against a coup, as against any unconstitutional actions, is individual responsibility. We must emphasize to each soldier, as my proposed constitution does, that he is responsible for his actions and that he has a legal duty, not merely a right but a *duty*, to disobey any unconstitutional or illegal order. And we must further emphasize, as my proposed constitution does, that whether or not a soldier may have been acting under orders from his superiors in carrying out a coup, or in performing any other illegal or unconstitutional act, will not be recognized as a defense in F.O.N. courts and will not even be recognized as a mitigating factor in sentencing. Colonels and generals cannot carry out a coup on their own; they need privates. In any coup attempt, the privates who carry out the coup are every bit as guilty as the colonels and generals who organize it. All of those people are guilty of treason. Therefore, they should all, and I do mean all, receive the most severe punishment that we permit in the F.O.N., whether that be execution or life imprisonment. When the privates of the F.O.N. army understand that, I do not believe we will have any coup attempts.

Summary of Chapter 13

- The small size and worldwide scattering of the F.O.N. military force, the extremely diverse cultural backgrounds of the military personnel, the diverse political outlooks of the military personnel, and the variety of languages spoken by the military personnel, will all combine to make it extremely difficult, perhaps even impossible, to organize and execute a successful military coup against the F.O.N. government.

- Those factors, along with the civilian right to own weapons, also mean that even if by some miracle a coup occurs and is successful, there is no possibility that it could create a worldwide military dictatorship. The small segment of the already small F.O.N. military that executed the coup would be lucky if it could continue to control the seat of the F.O.N. government, let alone control the world.

- The best safeguard against a coup will be to stress individual responsibility, stress to soldiers that they have a duty to disobey unconstitutional orders, and hold soldiers fully accountable for their actions.

Chapter 14

How the Federation of Nations Will Happen

Now let's turn to the question of how the F.O.N. is going to happen—or, in fact, whether it is going to happen.

Early in Mahatma Gandhi's campaign of civil disobedience to achieve India's independence, he sat down with some of the British officials of India's colonial government, and they mockingly asked Gandhi, "You don't think we're just going to walk out of India, do you?"

Gandhi replied: "Yes, that is exactly what you will do." The British laughed uproariously, but in the end that is exactly what they did. They did it because it became in their own self-interest and because they had no choice.

Similarly, I am sure some who have read to this point would mockingly or disbelievingly ask me, "You don't think the nations of the world are just going to voluntarily give up control of their militaries, do you?"

My response is: "Yes, that is exactly what they will do." They will do it because it is in their own self-interest and because eventually they will have no choice.

Today it is already very clearly in the interest of virtually every nation on earth to be among the first founders of a federation of nations that closely follows the constitution I have proposed here and to give up its military to that organization. Not someday in the distant future, but today.

To document that assertion, I will describe how joining an F.O.N. would be in the national interest for members of all three major groups of nations—the lone remaining superpower, the other industrialized nations, and the nonindustrialized or Third World nations.

First, let's look at the Third World nations. One argument for why it is in the interest of Third World nations to form or join an F.O.N. is the simple power and national security argument. Third World nations are the least powerful nations and the nations that suffer the largest number of invasions from their neighbors (or from the U.S., the former Soviet Union, and the other great powers) and so have the most to gain from the increase in military power and national security that the F.O.N. can offer. By banding together among themselves in an F.O.N., and even more so by banding together with some industrialized nations in an F.O.N., any Third World nations could greatly increase their military power and greatly increase their ability to deter or resist invasion.

But perhaps the most appealing feature of the F.O.N. for Third World nations is the promise it would hold for ridding them of the military coups, military dictatorships, and human rights abuses that many of them continually suffer. Many Third World nations, in trying to make the transition to democracy and civilian government, have had to promise their former oppressors that they will not be prosecuted for their heinous human rights abuses, as in the case of Argentina, or have had to allow the former dictator, when he relinquishes the presidency, to retain control of the military, as in Chile. Thus, in these countries, their military oppressors have not been disarmed and punished, and the people live in continual danger that these tyrants could rise up and regain control.

The F.O.N., though, particularly if it included some of the world's more militarily powerful nations and some stable democracies, could provide for these Third World nations outside courts and enforcement procedures, and outside military forces, that would allow them to destroy their military oppressors once and for all and create stable democratic reforms and lasting respect for human rights.

Next, let's consider the position of the industrialized powers that are not superpowers. Like the Third World nations, these nations also have clear incentives to form an F.O.N. The primary incentive is simply that by banding together in an F.O.N., they could greatly increase their power and their control over their own affairs. For the past 45 years, Japan and the Western European countries, as well as countries like Canada, Australia, New Zealand, and Israel, have often felt dominated by the two superpowers. In particular, since they are allies of the United States, they have felt dominated and controlled by the United States. Certainly, that situation is beginning to change. But it could change even more if they banded together in an F.O.N. By joining together in an F.O.N., these industrialized nations could at least equal and probably eclipse both the U.S. and the Commonwealth of Independent States in economic and military power.

Fine, you say, but what could the United States possibly have to gain from joining an F.O.N.? A lot. First, no nation stays on top forever, and the signs have been abundantly clear for some time now, despite the U.S.'s recent success in Kuwait, that the U.S., like the former U.S.S.R., is past the days of its greatest power. Since no nation stays on top forever, the U.S. would be very wise to get out, to negotiate an F.O.N., while it is still on top. If it is among the founding members of the F.O.N., it will be the most important member and it can negotiate the F.O.N. constitution to fit its needs. But if it waits too long to join, the F.O.N. and its member nations will increase in power, while the U.S. will decrease in relative power and will have little with which to negotiate when it finally joins (as it inevitably will eventually).

Another reason for the U.S. to join the F.O.N. is economics. The arms race and the desire to police the world have destroyed the Russian economy and haven't exactly done wonders for the American economy either. If the U.S. is to compete in the worldwide economic race, it will have to stop wasting so much money and talent on making weapons. The F.O.N. would allow it to do that. One of the greatest achievements of the F.O.N., as explained in Chapter 8, will be to drastically decrease the cost of military defense. The U.S. would be the prime beneficiary of that. Moreover, this smaller cost of defense will be shared equally among all member nations, creating even greater savings for the U.S., which currently bears the cost of defense not only for itself but also for its innumerable allies.

The final reason it would be in the interest of the U.S. to join the F.O.N. is that, despite its great power and influence, it could actually achieve its foreign policy goals better as a member of the F.O.N. than as an independent nation. The major avowed foreign policy goals of the U.S. are to spread democracy and to promote respect for human rights. (You frequently wouldn't know that from the U.S.'s actions, but those supposedly are the goals.) Looking first at the human rights half of the U.S. foreign policy goals, what better way to promote human rights than through the F.O.N.? The F.O.N. will be able, through the force of law, to *guarantee* the observance of human rights in all member nations, which eventually will include virtually every nation in the world. As for spreading democracy, the F.O.N. will guarantee in all member nations the cornerstone of democracy, which is freedom of speech, and will give the member nations practical experience with democracy through the democratic elections for F.O.N. offices. Short of the use of physical force for its imposition, which would be somewhat contradictory to the democratic philosophy, I see little else the F.O.N. could do to promote democracy. Thus, the U.S. could accomplish its avowed foreign policy goals of promoting democracy and respect for human rights much more effectively as a member of the F.O.N. than as an independent nation.

These arguments for why it is in the interest of the United States, the lone remaining superpower, to join the F.O.N. would also have applied equally for the Soviet Union while it was still considered to be a superpower—and they apply today for Russia or the Commonwealth of Independent States. Even the argument that it could achieve its foreign policy goals better as a member of the F.O.N. than as an independent nation applies for Russia and would have applied for the Soviet Union. The Soviet Union's avowed foreign policy goals were to guarantee its own security against the perceived threat of attack from Europe and China, and to promote the spread of socialism over capitalism. Promoting the spread of socialism seems to no longer be much of an objective since Russia and the other nations of the former Soviet Union, as well as virtually all other nations in the world, are adopting economies that are a mixture of both socialism and capitalism. But to the extent that promoting socialism might still be a Russian foreign policy goal, the F.O.N. would at least free nations from illegitimate outside interference in their affairs and allow them to choose socialism if they so wish. As for the more important goal of guaranteeing Russian (or before that, Soviet) national security, I have tried to explain at great length in this book how the F.O.N. will improve the national security of any and every member nation, including Russia.

In a sense it is too late for Russia now. Although I am inclined to think that the reports of its decline in power are exaggerated, certainly it is not an equal superpower with the United States. It therefore would not have nearly as much negotiating strength in forming the F.O.N. and shaping its constitution as it would have had a decade ago. But it is not too late for the United States. We are now the preeminent power in the world, and we would be wise to take advantage of that position (which will not last forever) to negotiate the formation of a democratic federation of nations of the sort that I have described in this book.

The U.S., Russia, the other industrialized nations, and the Third World nations all have it very clearly in their own self-interest to join the F.O.N. Virtually every nation on earth has it in its self-interest to join the F.O.N. But even with all that, the beauty of this plan to achieve permanent world peace, unlike all previous ones, is that it doesn't demand that everyone agree to it. All that is required is that three or four countries start the ball rolling by forming the first F.O.N. and making it clear that they welcome any other nations that wish to join. After that, those F.O.N. nations will have a selective advantage in power over the independent nations, and the irresistible selection for power will cause the organization to grow and grow, until it eventually includes almost every nation on earth.

Forming a worldwide F.O.N. doesn't demand that 160 nations agree at once to the organization's principles. It doesn't demand that 50 do. It doesn't even demand that ten do. All it demands is three or four. Those three or four nations don't have to be geographically contiguous. They don't have to have common cultures. All they have to do is want to increase their power—as most nations do. After that, the impersonal and irresistible selection for power will take care of the rest, and we will achieve permanent world peace in our time.

I cannot even imagine how this process could be stopped, even if you wanted to stop it. But who would want to stop it? Permanent world peace, universal respect for human rights, much greater ability to protect the global natural environment, and the likelihood that nations will finally choose to reduce their populations and thus largely solve almost every problem on earth. We can have it all. We can reach the promised land in our time.

The inevitability of this process, once it begins, is one of its most beautiful features. Surely at least three or four nations will choose to increase their power and form an F.O.N., and once that happens the process will spread and cannot be stopped. Because nations will recognize this inevitability, there is a strong incentive to be among the first to form the F.O.N. The founding nations, after all, get to determine the constitution.

Guess what that means. A peace race! Isn't that a refreshing change of pace from hundreds of years of arms races. Seeing that the F.O.N. is inevitable, nations will rush to be the first to form one. It makes the process even more inevitable.

There is a danger to a peace race, though. The danger is that several rival F.O.N.'s could simultaneously arise. I hope that doesn't happen, but if it does it should not be viewed as a disaster. Several rival F.O.N.'s would still be a more stable and secure system than 200 independent nations. Nonetheless, one worldwide F.O.N. would be greatly preferable to several smaller organizations, so if more than one F.O.N. arises, I can only urge here that they continually negotiate toward the goal of fusing and forming a single worldwide federation.

The Effect of the Current Surge of Democracy on F.O.N. Formation

Several aspects of the current point in history, naturally, will bear upon the founding and growth of the F.O.N. But the most obvious of these, and the only one I will discuss here, is the surge in democracy around the world.

When a national government allows its nation to join the F.O.N., that government is giving up some powers. It is giving up relatively few powers (if the constitution I have proposed here is followed), and the powers it is giving up are all powers that, for the good of the nation, should clearly be surrendered to this international organization, but still, it is giving up powers. And the leaders of governments don't like to give up their power. The primary concern of 99% of the top officials in any government, whether that government is democratic or not, is to maintain or strengthen their hold on power. That is not an indictment of their character; it is just a statement about human nature. Most government officials also genuinely want to help their countries, but human nature means that their top priority is to maintain their personal power.

National leaders, whether in a democracy or not, will almost never voluntarily surrender any power to the F.O.N. The key word there is "voluntarily." In a democracy they won't have much choice. In a democracy, the leaders' power derives from the people. If the people overwhelmingly want something, it cannot forever be denied. If the people overwhelmingly want a referendum on the question of joining the F.O.N., the leaders will have to give them that referendum, will have to agree to surrender a *part* of their power to the F.O.N., because if they do not, they will be kicked out of office and will surrender *all* of their power.

Even in a nondemocracy, the government sometimes has to bow to the wishes of the people, as we have seen recently in Eastern Europe, but the process is much more uncertain than in a democracy. So in the initial years of the F.O.N., the only nations likely to join will be democracies. Thus, since the F.O.N. will be largely limited to democracies in its early years, the current surge in democracy will be a large help to the F.O.N.'s early growth and power.

However, while the spread of democracy is a boon to the F.O.N., it is not essential to the F.O.N. Even if the reforms in the communist bloc and in several former right-wing military dictatorships were all reversed tomorrow, there would still be plenty of democratic nations to form a powerful core of F.O.N. members. From this core, the F.O.N. would still grow and would still eventually encompass virtually the entire world. The core democracies would have plenty of power as an F.O.N., through the use of economic boycotts and coercion, and possibly the threat of military action, and through the inevitable selection for power, to gradually induce the remaining nations to respect human rights, to join the F.O.N., and to adopt democratic reforms.

On the whole, then, as you would expect, the current surge of democracy should aid formation and growth of the F.O.N. and aid the hope for achieving permanent world peace. In one sense, though, the spread of democracy and the refreshing changes in the communist world could actually decrease the likelihood of forming an F.O.N. and decrease the hope for world peace. There is a danger that those changes will make us complacent. Even today, the feeling is sometimes expressed that permanent world peace has already been achieved. (Or at least it was being expressed until the Persian Gulf War and the Balkans War disproved it.) A Bush administration official, for instance, proclaimed that with the triumph of democratic values we have reached "the end of history."

That attitude is seriously mistaken. Even if democratic reforms in the former Soviet Union and Eastern Europe are permanent, it is not the end of history and it does not insure peace. Even were all the nations on earth to agree on the same basic political and economic philosophies—adopting free speech, free elections, and mixed capitalist-socialist economies—it would not mean peace. It is a terribly ignorant view of history to believe that wars are caused primarily by differences in political philosophy. Civil wars, it is true, are often caused by clashes of political philosophies, but not wars between separate nations. In all of human history, it is debatable whether there has ever been a war between independent nations that was caused primarily because they disagreed about political philosophy.

Nonetheless, I fear that out of this ignorant view of history, some will argue that the changes in the communist world make it superfluous and unnecessary to form the F.O.N. That view, as I have indicated, is tragically in error. The changes in the communist world in no way decrease the need for the F.O.N. Whatever the shape of national governments in the future, nations will continue, as they always have and inevitably must, to attempt to increase their power, coerce other nations, and improve their security. In this competition, wars will happen. Even if no nation wants war, they will occasionally misinterpret each other's signals, feel threatened, and initiate a war out of self-defense. Only in an F.O.N. will permanent peace be achieved, because only in an F.O.N. will nations be unable to wage war.

Equally if not more important, only in an F.O.N. will nations be free from this insane continuous race for national and societal power that has haunted us for 10,000 years and has shaped nearly every aspect of our cultures (generally for the worse). Only in an F.O.N. will nations be truly free to treat their people as something more than just tools for the nation's power.

Fusing the National Militaries

Perhaps I have still not adequately confronted the psychological difficulty of fusing the national militaries, of surrendering control of our own nation's military to an international organization. By far, the single most difficult step in forming the Federation of Nations will be fusing the national militaries. But that is also by far the single most important step.

This book has explained in great detail why, for any given nation, fusing its military with the militaries of other nations, that is, surrendering its military to the control of an international organization, is clearly in the nation's self-interest. That step will increase the nation's military power, improve its security, allow it to use the nonviolent means of economic boycotts and embargoes to effectively exert power over other nations, decrease its cost of military defense, decrease its taxes, allow the guarantee of human rights such as freedom of expression in its own and other nations, allow it to protect the global environment by exerting some control over the environmental behavior of other nations, allow it to participate in the creation of permanent world peace, and, by guaranteeing its national security, allow the nation to decrease its population and thus solve the problems of environmental degradation, starvation, homelessness, and poverty. Fusing the national militaries is the one essential step to solving basically every problem in the world. And it, along with the decrease of population that it will permit, *will* largely solve almost every problem in the world.

But, still, I expect considerable opposition to that step. The reason, once again, is the selection for power of the parable of the tribes.

The parable of the tribes means that for the past 10,000 years, the societies of the world have always competed against each other and have always attempted to exert power over each other. As a result, it has become ingrained at the very core of our cultures and national psychologies that our own nation must be number one, that no other societies are to be trusted, and in essence that all other nations are the enemy. To surrender our military, then, to joint control with other nations is unthinkable. Our psychologies and our cultures will be screaming at us that to do so is to surrender ourselves to the enemy. Many, therefore, will adamantly oppose that step.

But fusing our militaries with other nations' is not surrendering to them. It is, as I have detailed in this book, just a rational step to strengthen ourselves, militarily and otherwise, and to improve our lives. Moreover, it is the one absolutely essential step for creating peace. We have it in our power to create permanent world peace in our lifetimes. To do that, we really only have to do one thing: We have to fuse our militaries with those of other nations and share with them control of the single resultant force. That is the *sine qua non* of world peace. Many will oppose that step, but if you oppose that step, you oppose peace, for there is no other way to achieve it and never will be.

Summary of Chapter 14

- To those who would disbelievingly ask me, "What do you expect, that the nations of the world will just voluntarily give up control of their militaries to the F.O.N.?," I answer, "Yes, that is exactly what they will do." They will do it because it is in their self-interest and because eventually they will have little choice.

- Being among the first nations to form the F.O.N. and surrendering its national military to the F.O.N. is already today very clearly in the interest of essentially every nation on earth. But even with that, the beauty of the F.O.N. and of this plan to achieve permanent world peace is that it does not require that all the nations of the world, or even a majority of the nations of the world, agree to it. All it requires is that three or four nations, or possibly even only two, deciding to increase their power, take the rational and inevitable step of fusing their militaries and forming the first F.O.N. After that, the selection for power will take care of the rest, and the organization will inevitably grow and grow until it encompasses virtually the entire world.

- The selection for power has imposed on all of us cultures and national psychologies that tell us to fear and distrust all other nations and societies. Because of that, it will be very psychologically difficult to fuse our national militaries, to surrender our national militaries to the F.O.N. Many, therefore, will adamantly oppose that step. But that is the one essential step for forming the F.O.N. and the one essential step for creating peace. If you oppose that step, you oppose peace, for there is no other way to achieve it and never will be.

Chapter 15 | Nuclear War

So far in this book, I have proposed that nearly every problem we face, including the great problems that human beings have always faced, is rather easily solvable and that by taking just two concrete steps—surrendering control of our national militaries to a democratic Federation of Nations and reducing our birth rates—we can begin to solve those problems in our own lifetimes. But in discussing all those problems and how to solve them, I have somehow managed to avoid mentioning what many consider to be the single most serious problem we face. So I will mention that now.

Yes, I believe that the Federation of Nations can and will largely solve even the problem of nuclear war. Within a century the Federation of Nations should be able to come about as close as we could ever come to eliminating the possibility of the use of a nuclear weapon.

The reason I hedged my bets a little there, saying that the

F.O.N. will "largely" solve the problem of nuclear war and "come close" to eliminating the danger of nuclear weapons, is, of course, that we can never unlearn how to make a nuclear explosion. But what we can do, what the F.O.N. specifically will be able to do, is destroy every existing nuclear weapon in the world and make it very close to impossible for anyone to build another one. This chapter will describe exactly how that can be done.

The first step toward destroying every existing nuclear weapon in the world is to get the present nuclear powers to join the F.O.N., especially to get the United States and Russia to join. Fortunately, the list of nuclear powers is still manageably small: the U.S., the Commonwealth of Independent States, Great Britain, France, China, India, Pakistan, Israel, and South Africa (although South Africa claims to have destroyed its weapons). So there is a reasonable possibility that all could join the F.O.N. within two or three decades of its founding. Then, once all those nations have joined, the F.O.N. would control every nuclear weapon in the world and could, if it wished, destroy them all.

But at that point, destroying all nuclear weapons might not be wise, because the existence of nuclear weapons is only part of the problem. The other part of the problem is the existence of nuclear energy plants. If a nation has the ability to harness nuclear reactions for energy, then it has the ability to harness them for bombs. Fuel for a nuclear reactor is fuel for a bomb, and if you have a reactor, it will only take a few weeks to make a bomb.

To control all nuclear weapons production in the world, the F.O.N. needs to contain, or at least to control, not just the nations that have nuclear weapons, but also those that have nuclear reactors. This provides an additional 30 or so nations the F.O.N. will have to worry about. Before the F.O.N. can seriously attack the danger of nuclear weapons, it will have to include as members nearly all of these nuclear powers.

At that point, then, what should the F.O.N. do to eliminate the threat of nuclear war? It will not be enough just to destroy the existing nuclear weapons themselves. The F.O.N. must also eliminate the ability to make nuclear weapons. And yes, that can be done. The reason that can be done is that the fuel for a nuclear weapon must be one of two substances—either a rare isotope of uranium, uranium-235, or the man-made element plutonium—and the production of both of those substances requires large and complex industrial processes that can be easily detected and easily prevented.*

Uranium-235 is only 0.7% of the uranium in the earth's crust, and to make a nuclear weapon, the uranium-235 must be purified; it must be "enriched." But doing that is difficult. It requires one of a few rather complicated industrial processes that would be difficult to conceal from F.O.N. authorities. Moreover, to get enough uranium-235 to make even a small nuclear bomb requires a few tons of uranium ore. Since the ore is concentrated in a few locations—it is approximately as abundant as silver—the mining or acquisition of that much ore should be difficult to conceal. As for plutonium, it is made only by the nuclear reactions of uranium. Plutonium is a major waste product, the most troublesome waste product, of nuclear power plants. So if we simply shut down the nuclear power industry, which, as I will explain in a minute, is what we must do, we eliminate the supply of plutonium. Moreover, we end the unconscionable crime of continually producing more and more of one of the world's most hazardous substances, a substance that must be stored for about a million years before it will be safe.

Once the F.O.N. includes as members all or nearly all of the world's nuclear powers, it will not only be able to destroy all existing nuclear weapons, but will also be able to almost eliminate the possibility of anyone ever again producing a nuclear weapon. To do that will be surprisingly easy. It will require just four simple steps: first, that we abolish nuclear energy plants; second, that we destroy by nuclear fission, or otherwise make inaccessible, all the world's existing plutonium; third, that we make it illegal to enrich uranium-235; and fourth, that we make it illegal to even mine uranium ore.

Probably the most important of the four steps is to abolish nuclear power plants. That step is necessary because nuclear power plants cause large amounts of fuel for nuclear weapons to be created. In fact, that fuel is created at both ends of the production process for nuclear power. On the input side, nuclear

---

*Uranium-233 can also be used, but this does not occur naturally. It must be made by nuclear reactions from the element thorium, and those nuclear reactions must use uranium-235 or plutonium as fuel. So you are still dependent on uranium-235 or plutonium.

power plants must acquire enriched uranium-235, because that is their energy source. And on the output side, they produce, as their major waste product, plutonium. Since, therefore, large amounts of both of these substances, enriched uranium and plutonium, are constantly passing through the plant, "small" amounts are routinely "lost." That is just unavoidable. But those small amounts are plenty to produce many nuclear bombs. No matter how hard the F.O.N. tried to regulate nuclear power plants, "small" amounts of plutonium and enriched uranium-235 would constantly be lost, and hence a terrorist, or a member nation's national government, could easily divert those small amounts to produce bombs. From the point of view of preventing the production of nuclear weapons, the only effective regulation of nuclear power plants is to abolish them altogether.

The second step in this four step plan is the most innovative. It is that we destroy by nuclear fission all the world's plutonium. There are two reasons for doing that: first, it destroys the supply of this potential fuel for bombs, and second, it is the only way of getting around the intractable problem of storing plutonium waste. Plutonium is highly radioactive and is among the most toxic substances in the world. Moreover, it has a half-life of *24,000 years!*, which means we have to store it for about a million years before it might be safe. Fortunately, though, there is one way to destroy this plutonium: nuclear fission, the same process that consumes the plutonium in an atomic bomb. Although fission of plutonium will not completely eliminate the radioactive waste problem (fission converts plutonium into a mixture of other elements, some of which are not radioactive, and some of which, like cesium-137, are) it does greatly alleviate it. Though we would still have radioactive waste, there would be less of it, and, since the products all have half-lives of 30 years or less, we would have to store the waste for "only" two or three centuries, instead of for a million years.

But that was a digression. For the purpose of this discussion, which is about trying to eliminate the risk of nuclear war, the primary reason to destroy all the world's plutonium is to eliminate the danger that it could be used as a fuel for weapons. The most complete way to eliminate the possibility that plutonium could be used as a fuel for weapons is, of course, just to destroy it all. And with only a few tons of this man-made element in existence, it is still technically possible to do that. (The alternative way to make plutonium unavailable as a weapons fuel would be to bury it in a permanent storage facility. But since no storage site has yet been found that would be safe for a million years, and since none is likely to be found as long as we live on a planet with continents that drift, I think destroying the plutonium would be a better option.)

The third point on this list is to ban the enrichment of uranium-235. This doesn't need any explanation. Obviously if we are going to ban the possession of nuclear weapons and the production of nuclear power, uranium-235 has no use and its enrichment should be illegal.

The fourth step of the plan is to make even the mining of uranium ore illegal. If we are going to try to stop all efforts to produce nuclear bombs, the best place to stop them is right at the beginning, at the mining of uranium ore. Although it will probably be fairly easy to detect any efforts to enrich uranium-235, it will be even easier if there is no uranium mining and if it is illegal to even possess uranium. (Although uranium does have some nonnuclear uses, they are few and unimportant, and we will be none the poorer without them.)

To execute this plan of eliminating all nuclear weapons, it is not essential that every single nuclear-armed nation be a member of the F.O.N. All we need is to have almost every nuclear power be a member. Then, through the peaceful means of economic boycotts and embargoes, the F.O.N. should be able to coerce the few nonmember nuclear powers to destroy their nuclear weapons and nuclear reactors.

Once that happy state is reached, with the entire world devoid of nuclear weapons and devoid of the facilities that would be needed to quickly produce them, the F.O.N. should extend its bans on the enrichment of uranium-235, the possession of plutonium, and the mining of uranium ore not only to member nations but to nonmember nations as well. At that point, the F.O.N. will comprise at least half the nations on earth and will be far more militarily powerful than any other society. Having peacefully achieved the banishment of nuclear weapons, it will have the military strength to see that that banishment is maintained. It should do so. It should state that any action by a nonmember nation that could lead to the production of nuclear weapons, from the construction of a nuclear power plant to even just the mining of uranium ore, will be considered to be an act of war against the F.O.N. and will be met with military force.

Finally, I should say that although the F.O.N. will have the ability to totally banish nuclear weapons from the earth, it may not choose to do that. It may choose to continue to hold a small supply of nuclear weapons as a defense against the possibility that a member nation or a nonmember nation or a terrorist group could, despite the safeguards discussed here, somehow produce a nuclear device and then threaten the F.O.N. Whether the F.O.N.'s possession of nuclear weapons would make any difference in that situation, I don't know, but in any case some will argue that the F.O.N. should continue to hold a few nuclear weapons, and that view may prevail. Moreover, the F.O.N. might choose to operate a small nuclear reactor in order to produce radioisotopes for scientific investigation and medicine, and in order to conduct research on nuclear physics. So my point in this chapter isn't to say that the F.O.N. necessarily should completely destroy all nuclear weapons and all capability to produce them. My point is only that it will have the ability to do that and that it certainly should and will at least come close to achieving that goal, although it may choose to stop slightly short of fully achieving it.

Conclusion

As soon as the Federation of Nations contains almost all the nuclear powers in the world, which should happen within a few decades of its formation, it will have the ability to destroy every nuclear weapon in existence and make it almost impossible for anyone to ever produce another one. It will come as close to the goal of entirely eliminating the possibility of nuclear war as we will ever come without somehow unlearning our knowledge of nuclear weapons. And that, although I have deferred it to almost the end of this book, is one of the strongest arguments for forming this Federation of Nations. If the current world situation of independent nations, with several of them possessing nuclear weapons, continues indefinitely, nuclear war *will* eventually happen. There can be no serious debate about that. And "eventually," I believe, means within one thousand years at the very longest and almost certainly within two or three centuries. Our only possible salvation from that fate will be world government. In the past we have tried to hide from that fact because we believed that world government was impossible, and because we believed that world government would mean surrendering our affairs to evil men appointed by the tyrants in Russia, China, and South Africa. But in this book, I have explained the error of those beliefs. World government is not impossible, but rather inevitable. It will grow organically from the gradual confluence, one by one, of nations doing what they have always done, which is to attempt to increase their power. And world government in the F.O.N. will not mean surrendering our affairs to tyrants appointed by dictators, but will rather mean the spread and defense of democracy and human rights. Recognizing that good news, then, we can finally face the truth that our only salvation from inevitable nuclear war must be international government, must be the Federation of Nations.

Summary of Chapter 15

- Once the F.O.N. includes as member nations almost all the world's nuclear powers, it will have the ability to destroy every nuclear weapon in existence and make it almost impossible for anyone to ever produce another one.

- To do that will require just four simple steps: 1. Close down all nuclear power plants. 2. Make the world's existing plutonium unavailable as a fuel for nuclear weapons, either by destroying it through nuclear fission or by burying it in an inaccessible permanent storage site. 3. Ban the enrichment of the fissionable isotope uranium-235 and maintain active monitoring to make sure that ban is not violated. 4. In order to make it even more difficult to obtain uranium-235, ban even the mining of uranium ore.

- The fact that the F.O.N. will be able to eliminate the possibility of nuclear war, or come as close to that goal as we will ever come without unlearning our knowledge of nuclear explosions, is one of the strongest arguments for forming the Federation of Nations. If the current world situation of independent nations continues indefinitely, nuclear war *will* eventually happen. Our only possible salvation from that fate is some form of international government. Our only possible salvation is the Federation of Nations.

Chapter 16

Two Truths

Always tell the truth. This will amaze your friends and confound your enemies.

That is the approach I have tried to take in this book. Specifically, I have told two difficult, but I believe obvious, truths that so far almost no one seems to have had the courage to confront. The first difficult but obvious truth is that to achieve peace we must fuse our national militaries—we must surrender our militaries to the control of a democratically run supranational organization. There is no other way about it. If you oppose that step, you oppose peace. The second difficult but obvious truth is that the cause, in part or in whole, of virtually every problem in the world is overpopulation. To cure almost any problem at all, we must reduce our population. There is no other way about it. Moreover, since reducing the population will come about only through the sum of our individual actions, it is simply a moral duty for each of us to limit ourselves to having two or fewer children. That is, I suppose, a difficult truth, at least for some people, but it is a truth nonetheless, and a truth we can no longer afford to ignore.

Chapter 17

The Third Era

I bring you good news. We living today have been given everything we need to usher in a new era in human history. We living today can create a world in which war no longer exists.

I have described in this book *exactly* how that can be done. It can be done without demanding any unrealistically ethical behavior, without demanding that nations, groups, and individuals give up pursuing their self-interests, and without even demanding that all the nations of the world, or even a majority of the nations of the world, agree to this plan. All that is necessary for this plan is that a small group of nations pursue an increase in their own power—something that nations are very good at doing. The best way in today's world for any group of nations to increase both the power of the group and the power of each nation individually is to fuse their militaries. So it is inevitable that some small group of nations will soon choose to take that step. Once the first pioneers have taken that rational step, the selection for power, which has controlled the evolution of our societies for the past 10,000 years, will take care of the rest. Once those first pioneers have formed the Federation of Nations, the other nations of the world will see that the F.O.N. members have increased their power, and so, wishing to increase their own power or simply fearing the growing power of the F.O.N., the other nations of the world will one by one choose to join the F.O.N. also. In that way, as dictated by the selection for power, the F.O.N. will grow and grow until it encompasses all or nearly all the nations on earth.

By this process, permanent world peace will come about. And curiously enough, it will not be goodwill and the renunciation of violence that will bring it about, but the pursuit of national interest and the selection for power.

Incredible as it may seem, though, the ending of war is not the greatest thing this process will achieve. The greatest achievement of this process, rather, will be the ending of the selection for power. Although it will be the selection for power that will direct this process and will ultimately end war, in doing so it will also destroy itself. The reason is that the selection for power operates by selecting between separate and autonomous competing societies. After this process is complete, though, with the nations of the world having all fused their militaries, there will no longer be separate and autonomous competing societies. As far as the selection for power is concerned, there will only be one society and there will no longer be anything to select amongst.

It is not possible to overstate the importance of ending the selection for power. Ever since we left the hunter-gatherer state, the selection for power has been the one most important factor that has controlled the evolution of our societies and cultures. The way it has done that is by limiting our choices whenever we chose where our societies should go. To understand this, it is necessary to understand the general history of human culture, which is why I discussed that subject in Chapter 2.

Our species is about 100,000 years old. For the first 90,000 years of our history, virtually nothing changed. During that time, all human societies were hunter-gatherer societies; all were composed of nomadic bands of about 40 people as the fundamental unit of society; all used fire for cooking and warmth;

and all used stone tools. And one other thing—all lived in peace. What we would think of as war just did not exist.

But about 10,000 years ago things began to change. During the 90,000 years of our hunter-gatherer history, population slowly grew. At first this was not a problem because vast amounts of land remained uninhabited. So as population grew, humans simply expanded their range. But at about 10,000 years ago we reached the ends of the earth. There was no longer any uninhabited land. Now, for the first time, as population grew, adjacent societies were truly in conflict with each other for limited resources.

To respond to this crisis, societies had two options. First, they could fight their neighbors and try to drive them away so as to secure the limited resources for themselves. And second, they could take up agriculture. Agriculture had several disadvantages relative to hunting and gathering. It required more work. It yielded a less varied and poorer quality diet. And it was riskier—that is, since crops sometimes fail, an agricultural society runs a much greater risk of starving than does a hunter-gatherer society. Agriculture offered only one advantage over hunting and gathering: It could support more people on less land. That is why, wherever archaeologists have looked, agriculture and war seem to have always arrived in a particular place at the same time.

These comments about agriculture run so counter to everything most of us have been taught that they require some explanation here. We've all been taught that agriculture developed, not out of necessity, as I have described here, but rather by the eager adoption of someone's brilliant new discovery that plants come from seeds and that by planting seeds you can later harvest a crop. Really, it shouldn't take much thought to realize that that story, though it is the story we have all been taught in school, is ridiculous. Hunter-gatherer societies discovered how to purify, by an elaborate distillation process, the poison from the skin of a rare species of frog to make poison for their arrows. They discovered how to purify medicines from particular tissues of rare species of plants. They closely observe the habits of all the animals and plants around them. Yet we are supposed to believe that for 90,000 years they somehow failed to notice that new plants come from seeds?! It's ridiculous.

Rather, as anthropologists now realize, the principles of

agriculture are known to all existing hunter-gatherers and were undoubtedly known to all prehistoric hunter-gatherers from the dawn of time. They simply chose not to put those principles to use. And they chose not to for very good reasons. Hunting and gathering requires less work and provides a more nutritious and reliable food supply than agriculture. Agriculture has just one advantage over hunting and gathering: It can support more people on less land.

To repeat, about 10,000 years ago we ran out of land. As a consequence, three things arrived on the scene: war, agriculture, and the selection for power. War arrived because it was the only way societies could increase the amount of land they controlled. Agriculture arrived because it was the only way societies could make do *without* increasing the amount of land they controlled. And the selection for power arrived, basically, because war had arrived.

War means, of course, that one society attempts to exert power over another. When that happens, as Andrew Schmookler's parable of the tribes explains, the other society basically has just two options: it can be defeated or it can defend itself. With either option, the ways of power spread. If the attacked society is defeated, then the more aggressive and more powerful society expands its range into the range of the defeated society and thus spreads its ways of power. And even if the attacked society successfully defends itself, the ways of power spread, because in the course of defending itself, the attacked society will naturally do all it can to maximize its power. It will, for instance, tend to improve its weapons, to glorify militarism in its culture, and to increase its population. Whatever happens, whether the attacked society is defeated or successfully defends itself, the ways of power spread.

What this means is that for the past 10,000 years, when we have chosen what directions to take our societies, our options have been limited. We could only choose certain directions. Specifically, we could only choose directions that would increase our society's power.

Needless to say, the directions for cultural evolution that increased societal power were not always those that improved human well-being. As a consequence, the selection for power brought to modern societies a few problems that were not present in our ancestral hunter-gatherer societies. Among these problems have been slavery, inequality of wealth, starvation, the 100-hour work-week (or, for that matter, the 40-hour work-week), pollution, and nuclear war.

The selection for power, however, is about to end. And with it will end all of the cancers that it has inflicted upon our societies. As of a few decades from now, for the first time in 10,000 years, we will be free to guide our societies in *any* direction we choose, instead of in just those directions that increase societal power.

When that day comes, I can guarantee you that some amazing things will happen. All of a sudden, life will steadily improve. All of a sudden, we will discover that we are not as hopeless a species as we have been led to believe for all these centuries. All of a sudden, all of our "work-saving" technology may actually start saving us work.

I say that these wonderful things will happen and that life will steadily improve because I know what human beings are capable of. I know that in the long run we hit what we aim at. For the past 10,000 years we have aimed at increasing the power of our societies, and we have succeeded beyond reckoning. The difference in power between a hunter-gatherer band of 40 people and the United States is like the difference in size between an amoeba and a whale.

In this new era that is about to begin, though, we will no longer have any reason to aim at increasing the power of our societies. We can instead aim at increasing the satisfaction of our lives. When we take aim at that new goal, I see no reason we will not succeed every bit as spectacularly as we succeeded in reaching our last goal.

The Three Eras

Millenia from now, I believe that historians and anthropologists will look back on the course of human history and say that it is clearly divisible into three distinct eras. The first, lasting from the dawn of our species until about 10,000 years ago, was the hunter-gatherer era. As I have described at length in this book, contrary to what is popularly believed, the hunter-gatherer era, according to all anthropological evidence, was a very happy time indeed. In fact, in many ways I believe that the biblical Garden of Eden can be considered to be a metaphor for the hunter-gatherer era. In hunter-gatherer times war did not exist, starvation did not exist, and inequality of wealth did not exist. Life was very easy. To gain the necessities of life, people had to work remarkably little, probably less than 20 hours a week (though of course they didn't know what a week was). In short, we were living the life that evolution had equipped us to live. And as with any biologically evolved species, we were very well equipped for that life. Just as a wolf is happiest in the forest, living the life it has evolved to live, rather than in a zoo, so we should expect that we too were happiest when we were hunter-gatherers, living the life we were evolved to live.

The second era of human history has been the era of the selection for power. In this second era, which began about 10,000 years ago, population pressures forced societies to abandon the hunter-gatherer lifestyle and to take up war and agriculture. The characteristic feature of this era is the competition between different autonomous societies for limited land and resources. This competition between societies imposed a natural selection upon the system, much like the natural selection that drives biological evolution, and this natural selection that was imposed upon the system was a selection for power. Since societies were competing with each other, meaning they were attempting to exert power over each other, the societies that could successfully exert power survived and those that could not perished. In that way, the selection for power has very successfully winnowed out any cultural traits that hurt societal power and has nurtured and cultivated any cultural traits that aid societal power. Thus, our societies are magnificently evolved for exercising power. They are so powerful they can actually extinguish our species. Unfortunately, though, our societies are not so magnificently evolved for purposes other than exercising power. For instance, they are not so magnificently evolved for satisfying human needs.

An important defining feature of this second era of human history, the era of war and the selection for power, is the rapid cultural change during this time. During the first era of human history, the hunter-gatherer era, virtually nothing ever changed. Throughout that entire era, people lived in nomadic groups of about 40, got their food by hunting and gathering, and used fire and stone tools. There are really no general differences between the societies of ten-thousand years ago and those of a hundred-thousand years ago. But in the brief time of the era of the selection for power, everything has changed. A space alien comparing the culture of New York City with the culture of a hunter-gatherer band would have a hard time grasping that both groups of beings represent the same species.

That brings us to the third era of human history, which is the era that I believe we are about to enter. That is the era of world order. In this third era, a world order will control the world's military forces and prevent nations from waging war on each other. By ending war, this world order will have put an end to the selection for power. There will no longer be a selection for power because a selection for power arises from competition between autonomous societies, and under a world order like the Federation of Nations there will effectively no longer be autonomous societies. There will be just one world society.

I should clarify, though, what I mean by one world society. I do not mean that the nations of the world will have one common culture, much less one religion and one set of values. On the contrary, the nations will almost certainly become even more distinct and divergent in their cultures than they are now. Nor do I mean that nations will surrender sovereignty over the large majority of their affairs. I do not even mean that the nations will cease to compete with one another (although I do think that the intensity of international competition will greatly dissipate). All I mean is that the different nations and societies of the world will no longer be completely autonomous because some matters of government will be under joint control. Most important, the military will be under joint control. Thus, while nations may still compete, that competition will be of an entirely different sort than has existed for the last 10,000 years. It will be more like a boxing match than a fight to the death. In fact, it will probably be more like a tennis match than a fight to the death.

Why I Wrote This Book

This transition into the third, and possibly last, era of human history is almost inevitable. The selection for power at the moment is still controlling the evolution of our societies, and the direction it is taking us, as plain as day, is toward the fusing of the national militaries of, at first, a group of nations, and then, in all probability, of all the nations of the world. So in a sense, I didn't need to write this book. Permanent world peace is probably coming whether we want it or not. But I wrote this book anyway. In part I did that simply as an outlet for my joy. When you and your ancestors have lived for 10,000 years in the dark, with only a few stars for illumination, and you suddenly see the top edge of the sun rising on the horizon, you want to yell about it and wake people up.

The primary reason, though, that I wrote this book is that the transition to this third era is only *almost* inevitable. We could still screw it up. To get there, we will have to realize that it is possible, and we will have to think in advance about how it can best be brought about. Those are the purposes of this book: to point out that this entirely new era of human history is possible, and to point out what will be necessary to bring it about—the primary necessary step being to fuse our national militaries.

A Warning

The message in this book is one of transcendent, perhaps unprecedented, joy. We are about to enter the era that all mankind has always dreamed of but generally believed could never happen: the era of permanent world peace. The period of this transition will be an exciting and glorious time to be alive. But it will also be a very difficult and perilous time to be alive.

It will be a difficult and perilous time to be alive because, along with being blessed with the chance to usher in permanent world peace, we have also been cursed with the worst overpopulation and environmental destruction in the earth's history. In the next few decades we can, and I expect will, create a new world order. But in the next few decades we will also have to suffer the consequences of our overpopulation. Those consequences will be the same ones we see today—starvation, poverty, and environmental degradation—only much worse. The starvation we will see, like the starvation we are seeing in 1992 and 1993 in Somalia, will make the recent famines in Ethiopia and Sudan seem truly minor. Poverty and homelessness too, both in the Third World and in the industrialized world, will inevitably worsen as our obscene overpopulation becomes even more obscene. Likewise, the environmental degradation that we are witnessing today—the soil erosion, the desertification, the pollution, and the deforestation—will be even worse in the years to come.

Tragically, while we are ushering in the third era of human history and taking our first steps into the promised land, we will also be enduring the worst starvation and some of the worst suffering of all time.

This suffering, however, will finally stop. It will stop because population will finally decline. In part, population will decline because starvation and the rising death rate will cause it to. But primarily it will decline because, having learned the hard way the lessons of overpopulation, and having formed the F.O.N., so that nations no longer need to maintain large populations to maintain their security, we will at long last choose to get serious about birth control and reduce our birth rates. We will at long last choose to reduce our population to a sustainable level at which starvation will no longer exist and at which all can have a decent middle-class existence without inevitably depleting the environment.

To conclude this section, then, I will warn you that although we are entering a new and glorious era, we are not out of the woods yet. In the next few decades we will see some of the worst human suffering and the worst environmental degradation ever seen. It may be difficult to believe that this is the dawn of a glorious new era and not the dawn of Armageddon, but I want to reassure you that it is the former. After a few decades, the population will decline, the starvation will end, the earth's wounds will heal, and our species will live out its time on this planet in a new era of prosperity, a new era of living in harmony with nature and with an understanding of man's place in nature, and a new era in which war and starvation will never again ravage our species.

Conclusion

We have endured many horrors in the twentieth century. We endured a world war that everyone who lived through it assumed was the war to end all wars. Surely, they thought, no nightmare like this could ever happen again. Then that nightmare did happen again and we endured a second world war, at least as horrible as the first. Between the wars, much of the world suffered through the worst economic depression of all time. In this century we have also seen the worst and most wanton environmental degradation of all time. We have witnessed several mass starvations in Africa and elsewhere and will witness much worse in the years and decades to come. We have lived with nuclear weapons pointed at our temples, threatening to destroy us all at any moment. And, of course, we have witnessed and perpetrated a reckless and insane explosion of our population that has packed us all on top of each other, frayed our nerves, depleted our resources, impoverished most of the world, and destroyed our environment.

Many who have witnessed these horrors have believed that, quite literally, this must be the end of the world. As it turns out, they are in a sense correct. These horrors do signal the end of a world. They signal the end of the world that has lasted for the past 10,000 years—the world of war and the selection for power. That world is truly ending and an entirely new world is about to begin.

This new world is a world in which war will no longer exist. It is a world in which the selection for power will be dead. In this new world, when we choose in which directions to move our societies, we will at last be free, for the first time in 10,000 years, to worry only about how to improve people's lives, not about how to compete with other societies. As a consequence, we will undoubtedly choose to work less, we will undoubtedly choose to make our technology and our social institutions smaller and more personal, we will undoubtedly choose to create greater social equality, and we will undoubtedly choose to live in harmony with nature and with an understanding of our place in nature. But most important, in this new world, we will undoubtedly choose to limit our populations—for, by removing the need for nations to compete for power, we will have removed the need for them to maintain large populations, and having learned the lessons of the ecological catastrophes and starvations we are now suffering and are about to suffer, we will at last understand the need for population control. Thus, having reduced our populations, our destruction of the earth will stop, there will be more resources for each of us, all will be able to live in prosperity, and starvation will never again exist.

But, incredible as it seems, even that glowing description probably does not do justice to what this new world we are about to enter will be like. We have lived for so long with war, starvation, widespread poverty, and environmental destruction, that I don't think it is entirely possible for us to imagine what the world will be like when those things no longer exist. But that world is coming, and our descendants will forever thank us for having brought it about.

So, again, I bring you good news. Yes, we have seen many horrors in the past several decades. But it is darkest before the dawn. And the cock crows.

Afterword

Today's International Organizations

Do any of today's international organizations show any promise of developing into something resembling the Federation of Nations or have any relevance for the formation of the Federation of Nations? Only one—the European Community.

The United Nations is so fatally flawed and has so little resemblance to the F.O.N. that there is no chance it could somehow evolve into the F.O.N. Everything about its design is contradictory to the principles that will have to be followed in any meaningful international government. First, its representatives are appointed by governments. As I have indicated here, that cannot be the case in the F.O.N. Representatives must be democratically elected by the people. Second, its "laws," to the extent that it has any such things, apply to governments rather than individuals. Again, that cannot be the case in the F.O.N. As was explained in Chapter 6, there is no practical way to enforce laws over governments. Laws must apply to individuals. Third, its system of apportioning representation is misguided. Representation shouldn't be, as in the U.N.'s General Assembly, one nation/one vote, and it cannot be, as in the Security Council, arbitrarily given only to a few nations. There has to be some coherent basis for distributing representation between the nations, such as, as I have proposed here, land area or wealth. Fourth, the U.N.'s "judgements" are nonbinding. Obviously that cannot be the case in any meaningful government. And fifth, the U.N. controls no military. Government operates, ultimately, by the threat of physical force. There can be no government without a police or military.

Perhaps the most important reason the U.N. could not evolve into the F.O.N., though, is that the U.N. is dedicated to having every, or almost every, nation in the world as a member. That forces it to go for the lowest common denominator. It forces it, in essence, to be meaningless. Whenever everyone agrees on something, you can guarantee that that something is meaningless. When something is important, people are going to disagree about it. Any meaningful international organization, therefore, such as the F.O.N., must initially form with only a few member nations and then gradually grow. It cannot attempt to satisfy, all at once, the desires of every nation in the world.

Much has been made of the U.N.'s "renewed importance" since the Persian Gulf War. But that is absurd. The U.N. had almost nothing to do with expelling Saddam Hussein's army from Kuwait. Yes, the armies fought under the U.N. banner, but each nation fought for its own self-interested reasons, and the nations would have fought together whether or not the U.N. existed.

The next type of international organization to mention is military treaty organizations, in particular the North Atlantic Treaty Organization or NATO. These come a bit closer to the idea of the F.O.N. in that they focus on the military, which must be the first thing we focus on in the F.O.N. But in the final analysis, NATO and all similar treaty organizations are of almost no significance. They merely codify that each nation intends to help any other in time of war. When war finally comes, however, each nation will decide for itself whether war is in its self-interest. At that time, as history shows, the nations are as likely as not to renege on their treaty commitments. Military treaty organizations are unimportant because the nations still individually control their own militaries. The key to the Federation of Nations and to any meaningful international government is that the nations must surrender their militaries to the control of the international government.

The last international organization to discuss is the European Community or E.C. In many ways the design of the E.C. is exactly the opposite of what the design of the Federation of Nations has to be. Almost everything about it is wrong. One of the primary things wrong about it is its dedication to free trade as its guiding principle. The primary purpose of the E.C. is to break down trade barriers—to deny member nations the right to assess import taxes and to regulate the goods that are imported into their nation. Now, there are a lot of things nations should not have the right to do. They should not have the right to attack their neighbors, to violate human rights, to exterminate species, or to recklessly pollute the air and water of neighboring nations. But one thing nations *should* have the right to do is to regulate their economies—in other words, to protect certain domestic industries, to assess import taxes, and to regulate what goods may be sold within their borders.

The issue here, as I indicated in Chapter 8, is not whether breaking down its trade barriers is in general a wise policy for a nation to take, or whether breaking down international trade barriers increases total economic activity. The issue is whether nations should have the right to economic self-determination. It may be unwise for a nation to assess import taxes, but it is absurd to claim that a nation should not have the right to make that mistake. Certainly it is absurd to make the prohibition of import taxes the guiding principle of international government.

On other matters also the E.C. is seriously flawed. While it tries to deny nations an important right they should have—the right to regulate their economies—it permits them a number of rights they should not have—the rights to attack other nations, violate human rights, and pollute the environment of neighboring nations. It permits those things because its member nations still retain individual control of their national militaries and because the E.C.'s "laws" apply to nations rather than individuals—and are nonbinding even on the nations.

The theory behind the E.C., the theory that breaking down trade barriers must be the cornerstone of international government, is the predominant theory of international government today. But it is the most bizarre theory imaginable. Its proponents say to national governments, in essence, "O.K., you can jail without charge; you can slaughter your citizens; you can violate whatever human rights you want. Those are all internal matters for you and your people to settle. We won't intervene. And O.K., you can spew toxins into rivers that flow into neighboring nations; you can pollute the air of neighboring nations; you can cut down forests, destroy international ecological treasures, and even take actions that alter the global climate. That's all between you and your God. And O.K., you can even invade neighboring nations. We don't want to intervene in those kinds of 'disputes.' But taxing the sale of our products?! Now that's going too far!"

Despite my jaded view of the European Community, though, I do see a glimmer of hope for it (a very faint glimmer). The E.C. shows signs of moving in the direction of accepting and adopting almost all the principles that are advocated in this book as being necessary for the Federation of Nations. Specifically, although the steps are very, very small and the movement is almost imperceptible, there are slight hints that the E.C. is moving in the direction of adopting a unified military, of developing "laws" that no longer need to have quotation marks around them, that is, laws with actual sanctions, and of no longer being completely controlled by the national governments.

Potentially, the most important trend, although at this point the actions are only symbolic, is that Germany and France have proposed forming a "European Corps," which theoretically could someday become a united European military. However, what France and Germany have proposed so far is light years away from the type of true unified international military that I have proposed in this book. All that has been proposed so far is that the French contribute one division and the Germans two brigades to this European Corps. The overwhelming majority of the two nations' militaries would remain as separate national militaries. And even the paltry manpower they would contribute to the unified corps would remain separated as French or German divisions or brigades, rather than being intermingled and integrated. Furthermore, the troops would remain under the command of their respective national governments rather than under the command of the E.C. government. But still, if we want to be optimistic about it, we can say that at least this is a step in the right direction. At least there is some discussion of a unified international military.

The next area where some signs of improvement can be seen is in the design of the E.C.'s governmental bodies and their relationships with the national governments. Currently, essentially all E.C. power rests with persons who are either appointed by the national governments or are officials of the national governments. Executive power rests with the European Commission, which consists of 17 commissioners appointed by their national governments. Legislative power rests with the Council of Ministers, which is just the foreign ministers or other cabinet ministers of the member nations.* And judicial power rests with the European Court of Justice, which consists of 11 judges appointed by the member nations' national governments. Again, all of these officials are either appointed by the national governments or are actually officials of the national governments. The E.C. is thus completely controlled by the national governments. It has no independent existence. As was discussed in Chapter 5, that is a serious flaw in the design of an international organization that is supposed to have some power over those national governments. For effective relations with the national governments, all officials of the Federation of Nations must derive their power directly from the people, not from the national governments.

The good news is that there is one body in the E.C. where the officials are directly elected by the people—the European Parliament. Until now, however, the European Parliament has had almost no power. It has been only a sort of advisory legislative body, with the Council of Ministers being the real legislative body. But there is a movement to grant the Parliament a bit more power, and that would be a step in the right direction

---

*Most of the time it is the foreign ministers who vote in the Council of Ministers. But when an issue under a particular field such as agriculture of the environment is under consideration, it is the national ministers of agriculture or the environment (or whatever the field may be) who vote.

if the E.C. is ever to evolve into something resembling the Federation of Nations.

Finally, the most crucial flaw of the E.C., other than its not controlling a military, is that it has no enforcement powers. It relies solely on embarrassing national governments into compliance with its "laws." This is beginning to change, though, as there is now a movement to allow the E.C. to fine member nations for noncompliance. Ultimately, however, as Chapter 6 indicated, that is not enough of a change. Ultimately, an international government, like any other level of government, must apply its laws to individuals, not to other governments. It must have the power to jail individuals.

In conclusion, the European Community is very far from becoming the Federation of Nations. It has many major flaws in its design. But it is moving in the general direction of adopting almost all of the principles of the Federation of Nations that I have advocated here, and thus, there is a glimmer of hope that the E.C. could evolve into the F.O.N. Overall, however, I would consider it much more likely that the Federation of Nations will be formed from scratch by some other group of nations, possibly including some E.C. members.

Appendix A

The Proposed Constitution of the Federation of Nations

We the people of the Federation of Nations, in order to create peace between the nations, ensure justice and domestic tranquility within the nations, protect the natural environment, and create a stable and sustainable world in which to ensure the blessings of liberty for ourselves and our posterity, do ordain and establish this constitution for the Federation of Nations.

Article I

The Legislature

Section 1.

1. All legislative powers herein granted shall be vested in a legislature of the Federation of Nations, which shall consist of a Senate and a House of Representatives. [pp. 169-170]

Section 2.

1. The House of Representatives shall be composed of representatives chosen every second year by the people of the member nations in direct popular elections. [pp. 54-58, 61, 170]

2. The number of representatives shall be divided between the member nations in direct proportion to the revenues received from each nation from the general sales tax of the Federation of Nations (Article 1, Section 6, Provision 12) over the previous ten year period. Every ten years the revenues received from each member nation from the general sales tax shall be recalculated and the number of representatives shall be reapportioned between the nations. (For nations that were not members for the full ten years, their tax contributions shall be extrapolated to a ten year period for the purpose of determining their number of representatives.) [pp. 130-131, 150-151, 160-161]

3. When redistricting occurs every ten years, the legislature may by law change the total number of senators and representatives. However, each legislative house must always have at least three times as many members as the number of member nations and at least one member from every member nation.

4. Within each member nation, each representative shall be elected from a separate district, and the districts shall be drawn within the nation so that each district holds an approximately equal number of persons. Therefore, every ten years, the Federation of Nations shall count the persons living in its member nations and in the different districts of its member nations, and when it reapportions the representatives between the member nations shall also re-draw the representatives' districts within each member nation.

5. If vacancies happen by resignation or otherwise, a new representative shall be chosen by the senator or senators whose districts coincide with the House of Representatives district of the seat vacated, and the person so chosen shall fulfill the remainder of the representative's term of office.

Section 3.

1. The Senate of the Federation of Nations shall be composed of senators chosen for eight year terms of office by the people of

the member nations in direct popular elections. [pp. 54-58, 61, 170]

2. Senators may be elected to the Senate only once in their lives. [p. 170]

3. Immediately after they are assembled in consequence of the first election, the senators from all of the Federation of Nations and from each nation shall be divided as equally as may be possible into four classes. The seats of the senators from the first class shall be vacated at the expiration of the second year, the second class at the fourth year, the third class at the sixth year, and the fourth class at the eighth year, so that one quarter may be chosen every second year. [p. 170]

4. Senate seats shall be allotted to the different member nations in proportion to their arable land area—arable land being defined as dry land that receives a minimum of 250 millimeters [10 inches] of precipitation in an average year and that has an average daily temperature during the warmest month of at least 11°C [52°F]. [pp. 130-131, 150-151]

5. Within each member nation, each senator shall be elected from a separate district, and the districts shall be drawn within the nation so that each district has an approximately equal arable land area. The Senate seats shall be reapportioned between the member nations and the districts re-drawn every 50 years, if necessary, in response to changing weather data, or earlier if there is a change in the nation's borders or a change ordered by law in the total number of senators in the Federation of Nations.

6. If vacancies happen by resignation or otherwise, a new senator shall be appointed by the representative or representatives whose districts coincide with the senate district of the seat vacated, until a special election can be held to choose a person to fill out the original term.

7. No person shall be a senator or representative who shall not have attained the age of 28 years, been for at least seven years a citizen of the nation from which he shall serve, and reside at the time of his election in the district from which he shall be elected.

8. The senators from each nation shall have the responsibility for re-drawing, when necessary, the districts in their nation both for Senate seats and for House of Representatives seats. However, the redistricting plans they propose must also be approved by a

majority vote of all senators not from the nation concerned. [p.310]

9. When a new nation joins the Federation of Nations, the full Senate shall be responsible for determining the number of senators and representatives to represent that nation, based on the nation's arable land area and an estimate of the expected Federation of Nations tax revenues from the nation, and shall be responsible for drawing the legislative districts for that nation.

Section 4.

1. The times, places, and manner of holding elections for senators and representatives shall be prescribed by the legislature by law. But unless a different date is prescribed by law, the elections shall be held on the first Thursday in November in even-numbered years.

2. The terms of office for senators and representatives shall begin on January 3 of the year following their election.

3. The legislature shall assemble at least once every year, and such meeting shall begin on January 3, unless a different date is appointed by law.

4. Each house shall be the judge of the elections, returns, and qualifications of its own members, and a majority of each shall constitute a quorum to do business; but a smaller number may be authorized to compel the attendance of absent members, in such manner and under such penalties as each house may provide.

5. The legislature shall be the judge of the fairness and results of Federation of Nations referendums.

6. Each house shall be responsible for establishing its own procedures and rules needed for orderly operations. These may include restricting the right to debate and to introduce proposed legislation to only some representatives and senators, but at least one representative and one senator from each nation must have the right to debate and to introduce legislation. All representatives and senators shall have equal and full power to vote. [p. 310-311]

7. Each house may punish its members for disorderly behavior, and, with the concurrence of two-thirds, expel a member.

8. Each house shall keep a journal of its proceedings. The votes of the members on any question shall, at the desire of one-

fifth of the members present, be recorded in the journal. The journal shall be regularly published, excepting such parts as may, in the judgement of four-fifths of the members present, require secrecy. However, for any action or item of business to be kept secret, the vote of every member on the motion to authorize secrecy must be recorded and published, and a general description of what the action or item was and why the specifics of it must be kept secret must also be published.

9. Neither house, during the session of the Legislature, shall, without the consent of the other, adjourn for more than three days, nor shall it move its meeting to any other place than that in which the two houses shall be sitting.

10. The senators and representatives shall receive a compensation for their services to be ascertained by law, and to be paid out of the treasury of the Federation of Nations, but the compensation for each senator shall be neither increased nor decreased during his continuance in office.

11. Senators and representatives shall in all cases, except treason, felony, and breach of the peace, be privileged from arrest during their attendance at the session of their respective houses, and in going to and returning from the same; and for any speech or debate in either house, they shall not be questioned in any other place.

12. No senator or representative shall, during the time for which he was elected, be appointed to any civil office under the authority of the Federation of Nations that shall have been created or the emoluments whereof shall have been increased during such time; and no person holding any office under the Federation of Nations shall be a member of either house during his continuance in office.

Section 5.

1. Every bill that shall have passed the House of Representatives and the Senate shall, before it becomes law, be presented to the president of the Federation of Nations; if he approve, he shall sign it, but if not, he shall return it, with his objections, to that house in which it shall have originated, who shall enter the objections at large on their journal, and proceed to reconsider it. If after such reconsideration, three-fifths of that house shall agree to pass the bill, it shall be sent, together with

the objections, to the other house, by which it shall likewise be reconsidered, and if approved by three-fifths of that house, it shall become a law. But in all such cases the votes of both houses shall be determined by yeas and nays, and the names of the persons voting for and against the bill shall be entered on the journal of each house respectively. If any bill shall not be returned by the president within ten days after it shall have been presented to him, the same shall be a law, in like manner as if he had signed it, unless the legislature, by their adjournment prevent its return, in which case it shall become a law during the next session of the legislature if not then returned within ten days. [p. 311]

2. Every order, resolution, or vote to which the concurrence of the Senate and House of Representatives may be necessary, except on a question of adjournment, shall be presented to the president of the Federation of Nations; and before the same shall take effect shall be approved by him, or being disapproved by him, shall be repassed by three-fifths of the Senate and House of Representatives, according to the rules prescribed in the case of a bill.

3. In all cases listed in this constitution in which legislative power is granted to senators and representatives from a particular nation, independent of the other Federation of Nations senators and representatives, the bill, order, or resolution must be passed by a majority of all senators from that particular nation and a majority of all representatives from that particular nation, not just a majority of those present. After having been passed by the senators and representatives from that particular nation, these bills, resolutions, and orders shall become law immediately and shall not be subject to presidential veto. [pp. 67-69, 75-77, 82-83, 97-98. The provisions referred to are Art. I, Sec. 6, Provs. 1 and 16, and Art. II, Sec. 4, Prov. 5]

Section 6.

1. The Federation of Nations legislature shall have the power to raise and support military forces. To do that, the full legislature shall first determine the number of enlisted military personnel needed. After that number is determined, a quota shall be assigned to each member nation in direct proportion to its population. The senators and representatives from each nation

shall then be solely responsible for raising their nation's quota of soldiers and for raising revenue from their own nation in order to pay for those soldiers. To raise revenue to pay for their nation's soldiers, they may assess any type of uniform taxes they wish, but those taxes must apply only to their own nation. If, as determined in Federation of Nations courts, the senators and representatives from a particular nation are being derelict in their duty by raising more than 10% over or fewer than 10% under their nation's quota of soldiers, or by failing to deliver promised payments to those soldiers, the power to raise soldiers from that nation and raise revenue from that nation to pay for those soldiers shall pass to the president of the Federation of Nations. He shall carry out those powers for up to three years, or may relinquish them earlier at his discretion. [pp. 97-98, 119-121]

2. The compensation for military officers shall be uniform for officers from all member nations and shall be determined by the full Federation of Nations legislature.

3. No military appropriation shall be for a term longer than two years.

4. The legislature shall have the power to purchase land in member nations for the use of the Federation of Nations military or Federation of Nations government and shall have the power to specify by law the price to be paid for such land, although the price must be a fair compensation. The legislation authorizing such purchase, in addition to requiring approval by majorities in both houses of the legislature, shall also require approval by a majority of the legislators from the nation concerned in both houses of the legislature, unless the legislation is approved by two-thirds of all legislators present in both houses of the legislature. But in no cases whatsoever may the Federation of Nations purchase for this purpose in a member nation an area of land equivalent to more than 5% of that nation's arable land area.

5. The legislature shall have the power to constitute tribunals inferior to the Supreme Court.

6. The legislature shall have the sole power to declare war. [pp. 170-171, 177, 206]

7. The legislature shall have the power to make rules concerning the exercise of war and military force.

8. The legislature shall have the power to make rules for the government and the military forces.

9. The legislature shall have the power to make laws limiting the numerical manpower of national guard and police forces in all member nations. Such laws shall be consistent in all member nations, limiting the national guard and police forces to a certain percentage of the nation's population. Likewise, the legislature may limit the types and numbers of weapons available to national guard and police forces. [pp. 44-49, 53, 311]

10. The legislature shall have the power to ban or regulate the manufacture, sale, and/or possession of firearms and weapons but must allow and may not regulate or restrict the manufacture, sale, and possession of at least some types of firearms. The Federation of Nations may, though, ban or regulate the possession of any type of weapon by persons convicted of felony violations of Federation of Nations, national, or local laws. This provision restricts only the Federation of Nations and not national or local governments. [pp. 203-204, 242, 244]

11. The legislature shall have the power to exercise exclusive legislation in all cases whatsoever over such district as may, by voluntary cession of particular nations and by the acceptance of the legislature become the seat of government of the Federation of Nations, and over all land purchased in the member nations for the use of the Federation of Nations military or government.

12. The legislature shall have the power to assess a flat percentage sales tax, which shall apply uniformly to all sales of all final goods and services in all member nations. [pp. 99-103, 111, 164-165, 167]

13. The legislature shall have the power to borrow money on the credit of the Federation of Nations.

14. The legislature shall have the power to pay the debts of the Federation of Nations and purchase goods and services for the Federation of Nations. No national or local government in the Federation of Nations may tax, prohibit, or regulate the sale of any good or service to the Federation of Nations government. [pp. 99, 100, 311]

15. The Federation of Nations is forbidden to spend or loan funds for projects designed solely to economically aid or promote the economic development of a part or the whole of the Federation. [pp. 92-94, 110]

16. The Federation of Nations is forbidden to regulate trade among or within member nations or between member and

nonmember nations, except for the powers of enforcing boycotts and embargoes granted in Provisions 18 and 19, and except for the powers specifically granted by other provisions of this constitution, such as Provisions 10, 26, 27, and 28 of this section. [pp. 92-96, 110, 279-280]

17. The Federation of Nations is prohibited from coining or printing money. [pp. 103-105, 111]

18. The Legislature shall have the power to enact embargoes and boycotts against nonmember nations. [pp. 78-82, 84, 86]

19. The legislature shall also have the power to enact embargoes and boycotts against particular member nations. However, any embargo or boycott against a member nation must be approved by majorities of the senators and representatives from that particular nation. [pp. 82-83]

20. If the economic burden of an embargo or boycott would be unevenly distributed between member nations, the legislation ordering the boycott or embargo may direct that compensatory payments be made from the Federation of Nations treasury to those nations that would otherwise be disproportionately burdened. [pp. 81-82]

21. A majority of the Federation of Nations senators or representatives of any member nation may file a lawsuit in Federation of Nations courts that legislation for an economic boycott or embargo unfairly burdens their nation relative to other Federation of Nations member nations without adequate compensation (except of course for the case of a member nation being disciplined by an embargo or boycott enacted under Provision 19). If the court finds this to be true, it shall declare the legislation null and void. [pp. 81-82]

22. The legislature shall have the power to enact laws regulating pollution of the air, water, land, and outer space. All such laws shall apply uniformly to all member nations. [pp. 144-146, 151]

23. The legislature shall have the power to enact laws protecting or creating natural areas within the territory of Federation of Nations member nations. Such areas shall not exceed an area equivalent to 15% of the arable land area (as defined in Article 1, Section 3, Provision 4) of the nation containing them. Such areas may be separate from or coincident with areas already protected by national or local governments.

These areas may be given any degree of protection the Federation of Nations wishes, but the Federation of Nations must purchase the land from its owners at fair value or give fair monetary compensation to the owners for the restrictions on the land's use. [pp. 144-145, 146-148, 151]

24. In enacting laws protecting natural areas, the Federation of Nations may only increase or keep constant the legal protections on the land already enacted by national or local governments; and after creation of Federation of Nations-protected natural areas, the national and local governments shall retain the power to enact laws giving still more stringent protection to the areas. [p. 148]

25. If a member nation later withdraws from the Federation of Nations, it must buy back at fair value any Federation of Nations-owned areas within its borders (except such district as shall contain the seat of government of the Federation of Nations, which shall be permanently ceded to the Federation of Nations), or, if it wishes and the Federation of Nations legislature agrees, it may permanently cede those areas to the Federation of Nations.

26. The legislature shall have the power to ban or restrict the killing or harming of particular wild or endangered species of life and to ban or restrict the trade of products derived from such species. [pp.144-145, 148-149, 151]

27. The legislature shall have the power to regulate the use of the oceans and the oceans' natural resources by the member nations and their citizens outside of the member nations' territorial waters, which extend 10 kilometers from their shores, and likewise shall have the power to regulate the use of Antarctica and outer space by member nations and their citizens. [p. 149]

28. The legislature shall have the power to regulate the use of rivers that flow through more than one member nation, of aquifers that reside under more than one member nation, and of lakes and rivers that form the borders of member nations and are thus shared by more than one member nation. [p. 312]

29. The legislature shall have the power, by a majority vote in both houses, to remove from office any official of the government or military forces of the Federation of Nations, including the president, vice president, judges, and legislators. [p. 312]

30. Any person convicted of violating a felony statute of

Federation of Nations, national, or local laws may, at the Federation of Nations president's discretion or as specified by Federation of Nations law, be removed from, and permanently barred from holding, office in the Federation of Nations government or military forces, or in the national or local governments of member nations, or in national guard or police forces of member nations. Felony statutes for the purposes of this provision and other provisions of this constitution shall be defined by the legislature, but may be any statutes of Federation of Nations, national, or local governments. [pp. 63-65, 71, 188-190]

31. In order to prevent Federation of Nations elections and referendums from being decided by the amount of money available to the different candidates and sides, the legislature may enact reasonable restrictions on the amount of money spent in Federation of Nations political campaigns, may fund political campaigns from the Federation of Nations treasury, and may tax spending by candidates or on behalf of candidates or referendum positions in Federation of Nations political campaigns. [pp. 312-313]

32. The legislature shall have the power to make all laws that shall be necessary and proper for carrying into execution this constitution and the foregoing powers and all other powers vested by this constitution in the government of the Federation of Nations or in any department or officer thereof. [p. 63]

Section 7.

1. No money shall be drawn from the treasury but in consequence of appropriations made by law, and no payments shall be made to nations, organizations, or individuals that are not in exchange for goods or services rendered, except for compensatory payments to nations authorized under Article 1, Section 6, Provision 20, and except for payments made as a result of the Federation of Nations consenting to be sued for any violations of its laws or Constitution by its government or military forces. A regular statement and account of the receipts and expenditures of all public money shall be published from time to time. [pp. 92-93, 110]

2. No Federation of Nations senator, representative, president, vice president, judge, or other high-ranking official that may be

specified by law shall accept any individual gift of value greater than 1% of the official's annual compensation nor accept any gifts in any one year of cumulative value greater than 10% of the official's annual compensation, excluding gifts from the official's spouse, children, or parents.

Article II
The Executive

Section 1.

1. The executive power shall be vested in a president of the Federation of Nations. He shall hold his office for a term of six years and be permanently barred from reelection. [pp. 171-173, 206]

2. The president, along with his vice president, shall be chosen as follows: Those eligible to be selected as president or vice president shall be only those former senators who have finished their terms of office sometime during the previous six years. From these former senators, the current senators shall select two to be candidates for the presidency. Each senator shall vote for one person for president, and the two highest vote-getters shall be presented to the House of Representatives as candidates for the presidency. This selection of candidates shall be made by the last Friday in September of the odd-numbered year prior to the year in which the new presidential term shall begin, unless a different date is specified by law. After the selection of presidential candidates, each candidate shall choose from among the other former senators who were eligible for the presidency a candidate for the position of vice president. The presidential candidate and his vice presidential candidate, however, shall not both be citizens of the same nation. Then, on the Friday seven weeks after the selection of presidential candidates, unless a different date is specified by law, the House of Representatives shall by recorded vote choose between the two pairs of candidates the new president and vice president. On January 3 of the next year the new president and vice president shall begin their six year terms of office. [pp. 173-176, 206]

3. The president and vice president shall, at stated times, receive for their services a compensation, which shall neither be increased nor decreased during the period of their service in

office, and they shall not receive within that period any other emolument from the Federation of Nations or any national or local government.

4. Before entering on the execution of his office, the president shall take the following oath or affirmation:

"I do solemnly swear (or affirm) that I will faithfully execute the office of president of the Federation of Nations, and will to the best of my ability preserve, protect, and defend the constitution of the Federation of Nations."

Section 2.

1. In case of the removal of the president from office or his death or resignation, the vice president shall become president (except in the case of replacement of the president under Article II, Section 4, Provision 6). In the case of the removal, death, resignation, or disability of both the president and vice president, the legislature shall specify by law who shall become president.

2. If, at the time fixed for the beginning of the term of president, the president-elect shall have died, the vice president-elect shall become president.

3. Whenever there is a vacancy in the office of the vice president, the president shall nominate and, with the consent of majorities in both houses of the legislature, appoint a vice president from among the former senators who shall have left office in the previous six years.

4. Whenever the president transmits to the officers of the Senate and House of Representatives his written declaration that he is unable to discharge the powers and duties of his office, and until he transmits to them a written declaration to the contrary, such powers and duties shall be discharged by the vice president as acting president.

5. Whenever the vice president and a majority of either the principal officers of the executive departments or of such other body as the legislature may by law provide, transmit to the officers of the Senate and House of Representatives their written declaration that the president is unable to discharge the powers and duties of his office, the vice president shall immediately assume the powers and duties of the office of acting president.

6. Thereafter, when the president transmits to the officers of the Senate and House of Representatives his written declaration

that no inability exists, he shall resume the powers and duties of the office unless the vice president and a majority of either the principal officers of the executive departments or of such other body as the legislature may by law provide transmit within four days their written declaration that the president is unable to discharge the powers and duties of his office. Thereupon the legislature shall decide the issue, assembling within 48 hours for the purpose if not in session. If the legislature within 21 days determines by two-thirds vote of both houses that the president is unable to discharge the powers and duties of his office, the vice president shall continue to discharge the same as acting president; otherwise, the president shall resume the powers and duties of his office.

Section 3.

1. The president and his officers shall take care that all the laws of the Federation of Nations be faithfully executed and shall have the power to prosecute accused violations of the laws. But 10% of the senators or 10% of the representatives may also initiate prosecutions of any current or former Federation of Nations government or military officials for crimes believed to have occurred when the officials were in office. Prosecutions initiated in this way by the senators or representatives may be funded by private contributions or, if authorized by law, by funds from the treasury. [pp. 171, 189-190, 207]

2. The president shall receive ambassadors and other public ministers and shall have the power to negotiate treaties with nonmember nations, which shall become law when ratified by majorities in both houses of the legislature. [pp. 171-172]

3. The president is authorized, in so far as it is permitted by laws that the legislature may enact, to gather information about the capabilities and actions of nonmember nations. [p. 176]

4. The president shall have the power to nominate and, with the consent of majorities in both houses of the legislature, appoint ambassadors, other public ministers and consuls, and all other officers of the Federation of Nations whose appointments are not herein otherwise provided for, and which shall be established by law. But the legislature may by law vest the appointment of such inferior officers as they think proper in the president alone, in the courts of law, or in the heads of departments.

5. The president shall have the power to fill up all vacancies that may happen during the recess of the legislature by granting commissions that shall expire at the end of the next legislative session.

6. The president shall, from time to time, give to the legislature information on the state of the Federation and recommend to their consideration such measures as he shall judge necessary and expedient. He may, on extraordinary occasions, convene both houses of the legislature, or either of them, and in case of disagreement between them with respect to the time of adjournment, he may adjourn them at such time as he shall think proper.

7. The president shall be commander-in-chief of the military forces of the Federation of Nations. [pp.171-172, 176-177, 206]

Section 4.

1. Any use of the military forces of the Federation of Nations outside of the territory of the member nations must be authorized in advance by either a declaration of war from the legislature or, if and only if secrecy is necessary, by a vote of the Federation of Nations Security Committee. [pp. 170-171, 176-187, 206]

2. The Federation of Nations Security Committee shall consist of the president, seven senators, and seven representatives. The senators and representatives on the Security Committee shall be chosen by the members of their respective houses but shall be chosen in such a way as to represent the distribution of political views in their houses. Any secret actions, military or otherwise, against a nonmember nation must be approved in advance in recorded vote by eight of the fifteen Security Committee members. The deliberations and any actions not approved by the Security Committee may be kept secret at the Security Committee's discretion. However, when any action is approved by the Security Committee, the precise action approved along with the vote by which it was approved, including the names of the members voting for and against, must, in all cases whatsoever, be publicly revealed within one year after the vote authorizing the action. After an action is authorized by the Security Committee, it shall be a crime for any member of the Committee to reveal that action before it can be carried out, unless the one year period after the vote authorizing the action

has expired, at which time the action and vote authorizing it must be revealed, whether or not it has been carried out. [pp. 176-187, 206, 313-314]

3. The legislature may order the minutes of Security Committee meetings to be publicly revealed or revealed in secret to the legislature or particular legislative officers by a majority vote in both houses of the legislature.

4. Except in pursuance of a legally declared war against a nonmember nation, and except for use of the military in law enforcement under Provision 8, and except for military actions authorized under Provision 5, use of the Federation of Nations military in a member nation for anything other than routine training shall require the approval in a recorded vote in both legislative houses of a majority of the legislators from that particular nation and a majority of all legislators present in that house. Provisions enacted in this manner may be vetoed by the president, whose veto can then be overridden by a three-fifths vote of all the legislators present in each legislative house and, again, a simple majority of the legislators in each legislative house from the nation concerned. [pp. 67-69, 71]

5. Alternatively, a military action in a member nation may be dictated simply by a three-quarters vote in both legislative houses of all legislators from that particular member nation, regardless of voting by legislators from other nations. Provisions enacted in this manner may not be vetoed by the president and must be faithfully executed by the president and the military with all reasonable force available to them. [pp. 68-69, 75-77]

6. If, 48 hours or more following a vote dictating military action in a member nation under Provision 5, three-quarters of the senators from the nation concerned and three-quarters of the representatives from the nation concerned believe that that directive has not been fully carried out under the requirements of Provision 5 by the president, his executive branch officers, and the military forces, those legislators shall receive an immediate hearing before the Federation of Nations Supreme Court, at which hearing the Court shall expeditiously decide whether the requirements of Provision 5 have been fully carried out by the executive branch and the military forces. If the Court finds that they have not been fully carried out, the group of Legislators petitioning the Court shall have the right at that time to replace

any and every official in the executive branch and the military who they feel bears responsibility for the failure to carry out the requirements of Provision 5, including, if they wish, the president. The executive branch and military officials appointed in this manner shall hold office for one year, after which time the positions shall again be subject to normal selection procedures. [pp. 76-77]

7. In time of attack against a member nation or of other emergency that will not allow delay, the president may order military forces into combat without one of the authorizations from the legislature or Security Committee described in this constitution. But in those cases he must, within 48 hours after ordering the forces into action, receive a temporary authorization from seven of the 14 other Security Committee members, which authorization shall expire in 30 days unless a permanent authorization from the legislature by one of the procedures described in this constitution is given. If the Security Committee authorization is not given within 48 hours, the president must withdraw the military forces from combat as soon as is practicable.

8. The president and his executive branch officers may use any force available to them, including the Federation of Nations military, for the limited purpose of apprehending specific persons, named in advance in legally obtained warrants, for questioning or arrest in connection with accused Federation of Nations crimes or in connection with extradition orders issued by a Federation of Nations court. [pp. 69-70]

Article III
The Judiciary

Section 1.

1. The judicial power of the Federation of Nations shall be vested in one Supreme Court and in such inferior courts as the legislature may from time to time establish. The judges, both of the Supreme and inferior courts, shall hold their offices during good behavior for twenty years, and shall, at stated times, receive for their services a compensation which shall not be diminished during their terms in office. Judges who complete their full twenty-year terms of office shall continue to receive an

undiminished compensation for the rest of their lives unless convicted of violating a felony statute. [pp. 198-199, 314]

2. The Supreme Court shall consist of a panel of eleven judges. If there are eleven or more member nations in the Federation of Nations, no two Supreme Court judges may be citizens of the same nation. If there are fewer than eleven member nations, the number of Supreme Court judges shall be divided between the nations as evenly as possible (except that those judges already on the Supreme Court shall not be required to leave office merely to create a judgeship for a newly joined member nation). [p. 198]

3. Judges, both of the Supreme Court and inferior courts, shall be nominated by the president, with the nominations then requiring ratification by majorities of each of four different groups of legislators: the senators from the nominee's nation, the senators not from the nominee's nation, the representatives from the nominee's nation, and the representatives not from the nominee's nation. However, if the president's nomination for a particular judgeship is rejected by the legislature, the power of nomination for that judgeship shall pass to the senate or the officers of the senate that the full senate may designate. The senate's nominee shall then again require approval by the same four groups of legislators. [pp. 199-200]

Section 2.

1. The judicial power of the Federation of Nations shall extend to all cases, in law and equity, arising under this constitution, under the laws of the Federation of Nations, and under treaties made by the Federation of Nations; to all cases affecting ambassadors, public ministers, and consuls of nonmember nations in member nations or in Federation of Nations territory; to all cases of admiralty and maritime jurisdiction involving the Federation of Nations, Federation of Nations member nations, or citizens of Federation of Nations member nations; to controversies to which the Federation of Nations shall be a party; to controversies between two or more member nations; to controversies between a member nation and citizens of a different member nation; to controversies between citizens of different member nations; and to controversies between a member nation or citizens thereof and a nonmember

APPENDIX A: THE PROPOSED CONSTITUTION OF THE FEDERATION OF NATIONS

nation or citizens thereof. [pp. 200-201]

2. The legislature may direct by appropriate legislation those cases in which the Supreme Court shall have original jurisdiction. In all other cases, the Supreme Court shall have appellate jurisdiction. In civil suits in which the Supreme Court shall have original jurisdiction, but not in any criminal trials, the right to a trial by jury may be denied.

3. This constitution and the laws of the Federation of Nations that shall be made in pursuance thereof, and all treaties made by the Federation of Nations, shall be the supreme law of the land in every member nation; and the national and local legal systems in every member nation shall be bound thereby, anything in the constitution or laws of the member nation notwithstanding. [p. 201-202]

4. The Federation of Nations judiciary shall have appellate jurisdiction over the legal systems of member nations in claims arising under this constitution, under the laws of the Federation of Nations, and under treaties made by the Federation of Nations. The rulings of the courts of the Federation of Nations in such cases shall be binding upon the legal systems of national and local governments of member nations. [pp. 201-202]

5. The Federation of Nations judiciary shall have the right and the duty to review whether the laws in cases that come before it are consistent with this constitution. Any laws found to be inconsistent with this constitution, whether laws of the Federation of Nations or of national or local governments in member nations, shall be declared null and void. [p. 202]

6. The president, all other executive branch officials, and all Federation of Nations citizens must faithfully execute all Federation of Nations court decisions, whether or not they agree with them. [pp. 202-203]

7. Any member nation may request of the Federation of Nations executive branch the extradition of individuals in other member nations who are accused of violating the first nation's laws. The executive branch may then arrest those individuals and bring them before Federation of Nations courts for extradition hearings. Alternatively, a member nation may go directly to a Federation of Nations court to request the extradition of an individual from another member nation. If the court grants the extradition request, that request must then be faithfully carried

out by the Federation of Nations executive and by the appropriate officials in local and national governments. [p. 162, 164-167, 201]

8. Although the Federation of Nations military may have its own judicial and legal system, all military personnel are fully accountable at all times to the Federation of Nations constitution, laws, and civilian courts, and convictions or legal actions under any military legal system may be appealed to Federation of Nations civilian courts. Moreover, it shall not be considered a violation of Article IV, Section 3, Provision 2 of this constitution for a person to be tried in civilian courts for a criminal offense after having answered for the same offense to the military judicial system, even if he was convicted and punished for the offense under the military judicial system. [pp. 204-205]

9. Judges and juries in Federation of Nations courts may acquit persons who violate laws for sincerely held and objectively valid moral reasons. [pp. 314-315, see also 216-219]

Section 3.

1. Treason against the Federation of Nations shall consist only in levying war against it, or in adhering to its enemies and giving them aid, or in unconstitutionally attempting to overthrow the Federation of Nations government. [pp. 315-316]

Article IV
The Bill of Rights

Section 1.

1. The Federation of Nations shall neither make nor enforce any law respecting an establishment of religion. Neither shall the Federation of Nations or any national or local government within the Federation of Nations make or enforce any law prohibiting the free exercise of religion; or abridging the freedom of speech, or of the press; or the right of the people peaceably to assemble, and to petition the Federation of Nations or any other level of government for a redress of grievances. [pp. 59-61, 63]

Section 2.

The provisions in this section are to be observed by the Federation of Nations government, by all national and local governments in the Federation of Nations, and by all individuals in the Federation of Nations. [pp. 63-65, 71, 192-195]

1. No person may be detained or arrested without being immediately told the reason, and no person may be jailed for more than 24 hours without being charged with a crime and informed of the accusations against him. [pp. 63, 193-194]

2. No person may be deprived of life, liberty, or property without due process of law. [pp. 63, 193, 194]

3. No person may be denied equal protection and equal treatment under the law. [pp. 193, 194]

4. In all criminal prosecutions, the accused shall enjoy the right to a speedy and public trial, to be informed of the nature and cause of the accusations against him, to have compulsory process for obtaining witnesses in his favor, and to have the assistance of counsel for his defense throughout the legal process. [pp. 193-194]

5. Excessive bail shall not be required, nor excessive fines imposed, nor cruel and unusual punishment inflicted. [pp. 63, 193, 195]

6. No person may be held to answer for a crime without reasonable basis for the charge, nor may any person be detained or jailed unless for reasonable cause. [pp. 63, 193]

7. No *ex post facto* laws may be either made or enforced. [pp. 38, 193]

8. Neither slavery nor involuntary servitude, except as punishment for a crime whereof the party shall have been duly convicted, shall exist in any member nation or any territory of the Federation of Nations. [pp. 119-120, 193, 194]

Section 3.

The provisions in this section are to be observed by the Federation of Nations government but are not required of national and local governments. [pp. 195-198]

1. The right of the people to be secure in their persons, houses, papers, and effects, against unreasonable searches and seizures, shall not be violated, and no warrants shall issue but upon probable cause, supported by oath or affirmation, and particularly describing the place to be searched and the persons or things to be seized. Any evidence gathered by Federation of Nations officials or by anyone else in violation of this provision

shall not be allowed in Federation of Nations courts. [pp. 195, 196]

2. No person shall be subject for the same offense to be twice put in jeopardy of life or liberty. [pp. 195, 196]

3. In all criminal prosecutions, the accused shall enjoy the right to trial by an impartial jury of the nation and district wherein the crime shall have been committed. For crimes that did not occur within any member nation, the legislature shall have the power to determine where the trial shall take place. [pp. 195, 196-197]

4. No person shall be held to answer for a felony crime unless on indictment of a grand jury, except in cases arising in the military forces when in actual combat. [pp.195, 316]

5. All civil and criminal trials shall begin within 100 days of when the suit or criminal charges were filed, unless it is ruled that the defense needs more time to prepare its case. The Federation of Nations legislature is also empowered to enact time limits for the filing and deciding of appeals. [pp.195-197]

6. No person shall be compelled in any criminal case to be a witness against himself or to offer evidence against himself, either in the courtroom or at any other stage of the justice process. [pp. 196, 316-317]

7. In all civil suits in which the value at controversy shall be a large amount of money, the right of either party to insist on trial by jury shall be preserved, except in cases in which the Supreme Court shall have original jurisdiction. No fact or award tried by any Federation of Nations jury shall be otherwise reexamined in any Federation of Nations court than for an error in the original trial with respect to the law or constitution. [pp. 196, 317]

8. The burden of proof in a criminal trial shall be with the prosecution, and no person shall be convicted of a criminal offense unless he has been proven guilty beyond reasonable doubt. [pp. 196-198]

9. The Federation of Nations may not take private or governmental property without just compensation. [p. 196]

10. No soldier shall in time of peace be quartered in any home without the consent of the owner and tenant, nor in time of war but in a manner prescribed by law. [pp. 196, 198]

Section 4.

1. Member nations shall have the right to control their immigration but not their emigration. [p. 134]

2. Having children is a basic right of all human beings, so neither the Federation of Nations nor any lower level of government may restrict the right of all individuals to father or mother one child each. However, population control is and always shall be a requirement of humankind, so national and local governments are not forbidden from taking any other measures necessary to limit their birth rates. The Federation of Nations itself, however, while permitted to enact voluntary population control measures, is forbidden to enact legislation restricting the right of people to have children. [pp. 132-134]

Section 5.

1. The enumeration in this constitution of certain rights shall not be construed to deny or disparage others retained by the people. [pp. 317-318]

Article V
Other Provisions

Section 1.

1. Any willful violation or willful attempted violation of this constitution by a Federation of Nations senator, representative, judge, military officer, president, vice president, or top executive branch official in the exercise of his office is a crime. Conviction of that crime shall carry a penalty of immediate removal from office, even if an appeal of the verdict is planned (the official shall be reinstated in office if the verdict of guilty is reversed on appeal), and permanent disqualification from holding Federation of Nations office and shall carry a mandatory sentence of at least ten years in prison with no possibility of parole or early release. [pp. 187-188, 203, 318]

2. All individuals in the Federation of Nations are fully responsible for their actions and for defending this constitution. In keeping with that principle, whether or not a person may have

been following orders is irrelevant to his legal responsibility for his actions and shall not be recognized as a defense or a mitigating factor in Federation of Nations courts. Also in keeping with that principle, no soldier or other person in the Federation of Nations may be punished for refusing to carry out an unconstitutional or illegal order. If a person is punished, he may seek redress in Federation of Nations courts from those who punished him. [pp. 216-219, 243, 244, 314-315]

Section 2.

1. For purposes of resolving the ambiguity in meaning that will inevitably arise from translating the laws and constitution of the Federation of Nations into many languages, the version of those laws and the constitution in English is to be considered the definitive version. [pp. 318-319]

Section 3.

1. The Federation of Nations shall recognize as citizens of a particular member nation all persons that are recognized by that nation as its citizens and in addition all persons born within the current borders of that nation who do not claim citizenship in any other nation. [p. 320]

2. All Federation of Nations-recognized citizens of a member nation who have attained the age of 18 years shall be entitled to vote in that nation's Federation of Nations elections and referendums, except any persons convicted of violation of a Federation of Nations felony statute or convicted of violating any national or local statutes of member nations that the Federation of Nations may by law recognize as felony statutes for this purpose. However, persons who hold citizenship in two or more member nations may only vote in one nation's Federation of Nations elections.

3. The right of these eligible persons to vote in Federation of Nations elections and referendums shall not be denied or abridged in any way. In particular, no poll taxes may be assessed and no literacy tests required.

Section 4.

1. Any nation is welcome and encouraged to join the

Federation of Nations. To do so, a nation must hold a national referendum at which all persons living in that nation who would be recognized by this constitution as citizens of the nation and eligible Federation of Nations voters shall be eligible to vote and shall be asked to answer Yes or No to the following question:

"Do you wish for (your nation) to join the Federation of Nations, and if (your nation) does join the Federation of Nations, do you personally agree to abide by the laws and constitution of the Federation of Nations?"

If this referendum is passed by a majority of those voting, the nation shall become a member of the Federation of Nations as soon as its membership is accepted by majority vote in both houses of the Federation of Nations legislature. [pp. 50-52, 56-58, 320-321]

2. When the Federation of Nations is first formed, it shall take effect two years following the date of the referendums in the founding nations. In that interim two year period, elections for Federation of Nations senators and representatives shall be held, the legislature shall then be assembled, laws may be passed to take effect on the date that the Federation of Nations officially takes effect, a president shall be selected from among the senators, and judges and other officials may be appointed.

3. To withdraw from the Federation of Nations, a member nation need only hold a referendum at which 55% of the persons voting answer Yes to the following question:

"Do you wish for (your nation) to withdraw from the Federation of Nations?" [pp. 50-53, 56-58]

4. The nation's withdrawal from the Federation of Nations shall then take effect exactly five years following the date of the referendum on withdrawing, unless the vote to withdraw is rescinded by a majority vote in another referendum within that time. Only a maximum of two referendums on rescinding the vote to withdraw may be held in that five year period. [p. 51]

5. To hold a referendum on withdrawing from the Federation of Nations, a nation must present a petition holding the signatures of 5% or more of its eligible Federation of Nations voters. Referendums on withdrawing from the Federation of Nations may be held no more often than once in a ten year period, and after a nation joins the Federation of Nations, no referendum on rescinding that vote may be held and no

referendum on withdrawing may be held in that nation until it has been a member for ten years.

6. If this constitution is ever amended to make it more difficult for nations to withdraw from the Federation of Nations, the latter part of Provision 5 of this section of the constitution shall be temporarily waived to grant any member nation five years to hold a referendum on withdrawing from the Federation of Nations under the terms of the constitution prior to the amendments, and if that referendum is passed, the nation shall then be allowed to withdraw from the Federation of Nations under the schedule and terms of the constitution prior to the amendments.

Section 5. [pp. 321-324]

1. The Federation of Nations shall recognize the division of a member nation into more than one nation (all of which shall remain members) if both of the following conditions are met:

(a) The division is approved in recorded vote by majorities of both the senators and representatives of the nation concerned.

(b) Within two years before or after the vote by the nation's Federation of Nations legislators authorizing the division, the division is approved by popular referendum in at least one of the two territories involved if the nation is to be divided into two, or in all but one of the territories involved if the nation is to be divided into more than two. [p. 322]

2. The Federation of Nations shall recognize the transfer of territory from one member nation to another only when the transfer is approved in a recorded vote by majorities of both the senators and the representatives from both of the nations concerned and is further approved, within a two year period before or after said vote, by majorities in popular referendums in both nations concerned, as well as by a majority in the territory concerned, unless the population of that territory is less than 2,000.

3. The Federation of Nations shall recognize the transfer of territory between a member and nonmember nation only when all three of the following conditions are met:

(a) The transfer is approved in a recorded vote by majorities of the senators and representatives of the member nation concerned.

(b) Within two years before or after the above vote by the legislators from the member nation concerned, the transfer is approved by a majority in a popular referendum in the member nation concerned, and a majority in the same or separate popular referendum in the territory concerned, unless the population of that territory is less than 2,000.

(c) Within two years before or after the vote by the legislators from the member nation concerned, the transfer is approved by majorities of all representatives and all senators of the Federation of Nations and by the president, or, following presidential veto, is approved by 60% of the senators and 60% of the representatives.

Section 6.

1. The powers not delegated to the Federation of Nations by this constitution nor prohibited by it to the nations and the people are reserved to the individual nations or to the people.

Section 7.

1. Amendments to this constitution shall take effect only when ratified within a ten year period by majority votes in general referendums in three-quarters of all Federation of Nations member nations, collectively comprising at least three-quarters of the arable land area or three-quarters of the population of the Federation of Nations. If it wishes, the legislature may propose amendments and require that referendums be called on them in every member nation, but approval by the legislature shall not be required for enacting amendments. [p. 205]

Appendix B

Additional Commentary on Provisions of the Constitution

Art. I, Sec. 3, Prov. 8.

Since senators will be barred from running for reelection, they can be impartial in re-drawing Senate districts and can clearly be more impartial than representatives could in re-drawing House of Representatives districts. However, since senators may plan on running for the House of Representatives after they leave the Senate, I specify that approval also be required by the senators not from the nation concerned.

Art. I, Sec. 4, Prov. 6.

The F.O.N. legislature is likely to be enormous. To have reasonable representation of local interests, we will probably need an average of about 10 representatives and 10 senators from each nation. That means a worldwide F.O.N. would have close to 2,000 legislators in each legislative house. To have workable procedures, then, the legislative houses are likely to have to restrict the right to debate and the right to introduce legislation to only some of the legislators.

Art. I, Sec. 5, Prov. 1.

The modification here from the U.S. Constitution is that overriding a presidential veto requires only a 60% majority in both houses of the legislature rather than a two-thirds majority. I make that revision because the veto has given the president in the United States too much power over legislative affairs. President Bush, for instance, only had one veto overridden in his four year term.

In weighing the balance of power between the legislative branch and executive branch, we should err on the side of giving the legislative branch more power. There is far less danger of tyranny from the legislature than from the executive. The legislature will be composed of many different political factions fighting against each other and checking each other's power. The executive, though, is unified, being controlled by a single person. If it decides to abuse our rights it can move forcefully in a single direction and abuse them efficiently. Furthermore, the executive has a much greater tendency than the legislative to take actions in secret.

Art. I, Sec. 6, Prov. 9.

As was discussed in Chapter 4, in order for the F.O.N. to keep the peace between member nations, the F.O.N. must have a vastly larger and more powerful military force than any of the nations. This means that the F.O.N. must have the power to restrict the manpower and weapon power available to the national paramilitary forces—the police and national guards.

Art. I, Sec. 6, Prov. 14.

Since the F.O.N. will not have the power to regulate trade, we need a constitutional safeguard to insure that it is not taken advantage of by a member nation or prevented from buying the goods it needs for the common military defense. That is the purpose of the second part of this provision.

Art. I, Sec. 6, Prov. 28.

When a body of water is shared by two or more nations, it seems clear that an international government should have authority to regulate disputes over that body of water.

Art. I, Sec. 6, Prov. 29.

This power is stronger than the power of impeachment in the U.S. Constitution. In the U.S., removal of these high government officials requires impeachment by the House of Representatives and conviction by the Senate on a charge of committing "high crimes and misdemeanors." I think that is too high a standard. An official shouldn't have to be convicted of committing a crime before he can be removed from office. There are other legitimate reasons for removing someone from office. An official may be suspected, but not proven, to have committed a crime. In that case, he should be removed. Our top officials should be above suspicion. Another person who might be legitimately be removed from office is someone who has suffered an accident or illness that has left him physically or mentally unable to perform his job. And I think in some cases, political reasons should be a basis for removing officials. Let us say that some person is appointed by the president to the post of Minister of the Environment and is confirmed by the legislature because he says he is a strong environmentalist. Then let us say that he takes office and begins selling all the F.O.N. lands he can sell and refusing to enforce legal protections on the land he can't sell. The legislature should be able to remove this official. They shouldn't have to prove that he is taking bribes. They should just be able to say, "This is not what we want out of a minister of the environment."

Art. I, Sec. 6, Prov. 31.

The U.S. political system has become (well, actually I suppose it always was) hopelessly corrupted by money. Candidates for the Senate and House of Representatives routinely spend more than a million dollars on their campaigns. The only way any candidate can hope to be elected is to have access to huge amounts of money. A candidate must, therefore, either be very wealthy himself or he must appeal to the interests of wealthy individuals or wealthy political action groups. Any candidate who does not meet one of those conditions, which would include almost any candidate promoting real reform, will not be able to raise sufficient money to conduct a viable campaign and will have almost no chance of being elected.

One result of this system is that incumbents are almost always reelected. The rate of turnover in the U.S. House of Representatives is actually lower than the rate of turnover in the British House of Lords, where members have to die to leave office, and lower than it was in the Soviet Politburo. The reason for this is that incumbents have enormous advantages in raising money. The longer a congressman stays in office, the more power he accumulates. In order to buy access to that power, contributors shower incumbent congressmen, particularly senior incumbent congressmen, with money. As a result, incumbents can usually greatly outspend any people who are foolish enough to run against them.

This disgraceful system is not democracy, and I do not wish it to happen to the F.O.N. To see that it doesn't, I have included provision 31 in my proposed constitution.

This provision is necessary because the powers it describes are not granted anywhere else in this constitution, and in order to prevent F.O.N. elections from being decided by money, at least one of those powers is going to have to be exercised.

Some might worry that this provision could be used by those in office to enact restrictions on spending that effectively prevent anyone from challenging them. But the first part of the clause, "In order to prevent F.O.N. elections ... from being decided by the amount of money available to the different candidates," clearly indicates that any such laws would be unconstitutional, and I assume the courts would strike them down.

Art. II, Sec. 4, Prov. 2.

A key point of this provision not discussed in the text is that the senators and representatives on the Security Committee "shall be chosen in such a way as to represent the distribution of political views in their houses." This is designed to insure that there are members of opposition parties on the Security Committee. If the president and all the legislators on the Security Committee were all members of the same party and they authorized a secret action that turned out to be a disaster (as most secret actions turn out to be), it would be very tempting for them all to just agree to keep it secret, in violation of this constitution. But if there are members of opposition parties on the Security Committee, they could be trusted to insist that those actions be revealed.

Art. III, Sec. 1, Prov. 1.

The one modification here from the comparable provision in the U.S. Constitution is that judges be appointed for 20 year terms rather than for life. I had two reasons for making that change. One is that judges in the U.S. sometimes abuse their lifetime appointments by hanging on well into old age, after failing health and diminished capacity for work should have induced them to retire. The other is that presidents sometimes abuse the lifetime appointment by appointing to judgeships very young ideologues who share their ideological views. Allowing judges to be appointed for life creates an artificial incentive for the president or other person doing the appointing to appoint very young persons, because by appointing young persons he can have a more lasting effect on the judiciary. But in appointing extremely young judges, presidents usually pass up more experienced and better qualified candidates. By making the term of office for judges 20 years, we will remove this artificial incentive to appoint young and underqualified candidates, and we will get better judges.

Art. III, Sec. 2, Prov. 9 and Art. V, Sec. 1, Prov. 2.

Note that Art. V, Sec. 1, Prov. 2 says only that "no person may be punished for refusing to carry out an unconstitutional or illegal order," not an immoral order. This might appear to contradict my urging in Chapter 12 that people should obey their consciences first, the F.O.N. constitution second, and the F.O.N.'s laws third, but it does not. That statement was an urging of what people ought to do on moral grounds. It was not necessarily a description of what a government can legally afford to recognize as a justification for behavior. We cannot, of course, in legal terms, grant a blanket authority for people to do whatever they want as long as they believe it is moral. That would lead to anarchy. This is not to say, however, that judges or juries should never acquit persons who break laws for moral reasons, only that they should not be constitutionally required to acquit them. The judges and jurors have to use their discretion. They have to decide, as Art. III, Sect. 2, Prov. 9 says, whether the person sincerely holds the moral principles he claims to hold and whether those moral principles are valid.

Even then, though, judges and juries cannot be required to acquit people. That is why Art. III, Sec. 2, Prov. 9 says only that they "may" acquit them. There are too many objectively valid moral principles out there for us to be required to acquit every lawbreaker who might be following one of them. For instance, some abortion opponents believe that it is their moral duty to physically block pregnant women from going into abortion clinics. Clearly, those breaking the law in this case "sincerely hold" their moral principles, and those principles are, at least in some measure, "objectively valid"—that is, they are not totally unreasonable. But if we as a society decide to permit abortion, then we cannot allow this type of behavior to go forever unchecked. We might be able to acquit the first few individuals taking this action—perhaps demanding a promise that they not do it again—but if they continually go back and block women again, or if the number of protestors becomes so great that it is impossible for women to get an abortion, then something has to be done.

It is important that courts have the right to acquit people who break laws for moral reasons. But we cannot acquit all such people or we will fall into anarchy.

This is only as it must be. When we violate an immoral law we should expect to be punished for it and we should be willing to be punished for it. It is only by accepting the punishment that we show how deep our moral commitment is and how wrong we believe the law to be. The primary purpose in breaking an immoral law is to get the law changed, and the best way to impress on people the need for that change is to accept an unjust punishment. Basically, we should not break any law, moral or immoral, unless we are willing to accept punishment for it.

Art. III, Sec. 3, Prov. 1.

A common ploy of tyrannical governments is to indiscriminately accuse their opponents of treason. Disagreement with government policies or personal opposition to particular leaders is defined as treason. To prevent that abuse, it is appropriate to constitutionally define treason.

Art. IV, Sec. 3, Prov. 4

A grand jury is a jury assembled, not to determine the guilt or innocence of a person in a criminal trial, but to determine before a person is even charged with a crime whether there is enough evidence to charge him. In other words, the burden of proof before a grand jury is not to prove guilt beyond a reasonable doubt but just to prove that there is a reasonable basis for pressing charges and holding a trial.

This provision, then, is inserted into the constitution to insure that before a person is charged with a serious crime, which will inevitably mean great inconvenience and suffering in his life, regardless of the ultimate verdict, there is a reasonable basis for the charge.

Art. IV, Sec. 3, Prov. 6.

No provision of the U.S. Constitution has been as widely criticized as this one, since it enables the one person who might know most about a crime to avoid having to tell what he knows, and since to some it appears to be useful only to the guilty. But in fact it is a shield for the innocent as well as the guilty and is a very important right.

U.S. Supreme Court Justice Stephen J. Field explained the right this way in 1894:

> It is not every one who can safely venture on the witness stand though entirely innocent of the charge against him. Excessive timidity, nervousness when facing others and attempting to explain transactions of a suspicious character, and offences charged against him, will often confuse and embarrass him to such a degree as to increase rather than remove prejudices against him. It is not every one, however honest, who would, therefore, willingly place himself on the witness stand.

This right, like the right against unreasonable searches and seizures, comes under so much criticism only because we in the U.S. have never had to live without its protection. If we had, as the people of 17th century England did before this right was enacted into English law, we would more easily appreciate it.

The right against self-incrimination is central to our Anglo-American tradition of a presumption of innocence. Without it, the innocent can be held in police stations indefinitely and questioned over and over and over again until they "voluntarily" confess to the crime they are accused of. When this right is absent, authorities have the power to compel confessions and are almost invited to use physical and psychological torture to compel them. When this right is absent, it can be made a crime for the defendant not to help the prosecution, in essence a crime to defend himself.

Art. IV, Sec. 3, Prov. 7.

The U.S. Constitution says only that "no fact tried by a jury shall be otherwise reexamined ...," rather than "no fact or award," as I have written here. The result is that *over* 50% of the awards granted by juries in civil suits are altered by appeals courts. It's gotten to the point where there's no reason to try civil suits in lower courts at all. We might as well just try the cases in the appeals courts to begin with. In my opinion this situation constitutes a violation of the right to trial by jury, because in effect, the cases are no longer tried by juries; they are tried by appeals court judges.

If there was a serious error with respect to the law or constitution in the original trial, then obviously an appeals court should be able to order a new trial or overturn the verdict entirely. But appeals courts should not have the power to just retry an entire case and alter a jury's award for no other reason than that they disagree with it.

Art. IV, Sec. 5, Prov. 1.

This provision is included, first, to allow for rights that may seem so obvious that we neglect to include them when we draw up a constitution, and second, to allow for the gradual recognition in a society of more rights than are in universal acceptance when the society's constitution is drawn up. An example of how this provision could be used comes from the case of Griswold vs. Connecticut, which came before the U.S. Supreme Court in 1965. In that case, the Court ruled unconstitutional a Connecticut law banning the use of contraceptives by married couples. The court invoked a right to privacy, which is not specifically mentioned in the Constitution but could be construed to be one of the "other" rights "retained by the people."

Art. V, Sec. 1, Prov. 1.

The word "willful" is included in this provision to allow room for reasonable debate about what exactly the constitution means. That is, I don't want to see half of the legislature thrown in jail for 10 years every time a law they pass is declared unconstitutional.

Most times that legislators pass laws which are later ruled unconstitutional, and most times that executive branch officials take actions which are later ruled unconstitutional, they believe they are acting consistently with the constitution. Most of the time, they can offer a reasonable, if mistaken, interpretation of the constitution under which their actions would be allowed. Under those circumstances, then, the officials would not be "willfully" violating the constitution and should not be imprisoned.

But when an official knows, or should know, that his actions are clearly in violation of the constitution, and yet he persists in carrying them out, it is time to put him in his place and time to end his continuance in office.

Art. V, Sec. 1, Prov. 2.

See discussion of Art. III, Sec. 2, Prov. 9.

Art. V, Sec. 2, Prov. 1.

I want to emphasize here that I am not proposing English be designated the "official" language of the F.O.N., only what might be called the "central" language. Obviously the F.O.N. will include peoples speaking many, many different languages. I am not stupid enough to ask that we impose one language on all of them. The representatives, senators, and judges will speak as many different languages as are included within the F.O.N., and that is fine. In general, we do not need to give any language favored status over another.

But to settle differences in meaning that will inevitably arise from translating the F.O.N.'s laws and constitution into dozens of different languages, it will be almost essential to give one language special status and to declare the version of the laws and constitution in that language to be the definitive version. Without one definitive version of the law, we will have perhaps over 100 or more equally valid translations and will have no way to decide, when those translations differ in meaning, which holds the correct meaning. Having one definitive version, though, gives a standard that can be referred to to resolve those differences of translation. Moreover, having one central language will promote consistency of the different translations because it will insure that all translations come directly from the central language rather than being derived perhaps by translating a translation of a translation of a translation.

Now, what language will be the central one? The obvious most likely choice, as I have proposed here, would be English, which is already essentially the accepted international language of science and, to a lesser extent, of business. That suits me fine, since English happens to be my native tongue and I have little or no ability with foreign languages. So I'm obviously biased. But English does have a few points in its favor as a central language. At least it only has 26 written characters. I certainly hope, for that reason, that no oriental language is chosen as the central one. And although the spelling and pronunciation of English are both chaotic nightmares, the grammar is incredibly simple. Grammatically, English is almost the simplest language in existence. In fact, it is actually simpler in its grammar than Esperanto, an artificial language that was supposedly designed to be as simple as possible. Nouns in English have the same form whether used as subjects or objects, and verbs, except for the addition of an s when the subject is the third person singular, have the same form regardless of the subject (I run, you run, we run, and they run, but he runs). Moreover, the word order of English sentences is almost always the same—subject, verb, object. In fact, word order generally defines the grammatical relationship between the words. So, although I am biased, I think English is not without its virtues as a central language.

Art. V, Sec. 3, Prov. 1.

This provision is just designed to insure that the F.O.N. does not recognize any racist or otherwise unjust denials of citizenship to particular persons in a member nation.

Art. V, Sec. 4, Prov. 1.

Note that approval by the F.O.N. legislature is required here before a nation can join the F.O.N. Thus, the F.O.N. will have the power to reject a nation's application for membership. There are three reasons for that. The first is that it allows the F.O.N. a graceful way out if a national government tries to block its nation from joining after a national referendum on joining passes. In that situation we would have a populace that has expressed its desire to join the F.O.N. but a national government that has declared its intention to block that. This puts the F.O.N. in a difficult situation. It could stand up for principle and say, "The people have expressed their desire to join. We will honor that wish and take military action if we must to integrate the nation into the F.O.N." Or it could decide that discretion is the better part of valor and declare that for the moment it will not consider that nation to be a member of the F.O.N. Both options are valid ones and the F.O.N. should have both options available to it. Thus, the F.O.N. legislature should have the right in this situation to cast a vote accepting the nation's membership and directing the F.O.N. military to take all necessary steps to bring that membership about. Likewise, the F.O.N. legislature should also have the right in this situation to back down gracefully. It should have the right to cast a vote rejecting the nation's membership and permitting, for the moment, that nation's government to have its way.

I should point out, however, that this situation is likely to be very rare. In order for a referendum on joining the F.O.N. to be held, the nation's government will have to allow it to be held. Presumably, then, that government will be agreeing to abide by the results. So the only time this problem should arise is when a new national government comes to power immediately after a nation holds its referendum on joining the F.O.N.

The discussion above assumed that the F.O.N. would want any nation to be a member. But there are two valid reasons why the F.O.N. might not want a particular nation to be a member, and it will need the right to reject a nation's membership for those reasons also. The first is that the nation's need for defense might present too great a burden for the F.O.N.'s military forces—the obvious example of this being Israel, surrounded as it is by enemies constantly threatening to attack it. When the F.O.N. is newly formed and consists of only a few members, it might feel that the burden of defending Israel, or some other nation similarly situated, would be too great a burden for it to take on.

The second and more important reason that the F.O.N. might wish to reject a nation's membership is that it might object to what the nation claims as its borders. If a nation were holding conquered territories (although in one sense or another every nation is holding conquered territories) or were holding territories against the will of the people in those territories, the F.O.N. might want to make the relinquishing of those territories a condition of the nation's joining. The obvious example here again would be Israel. Israel currently holds two territories conquered in the 1967 Seven Days war—the Golan Heights and the West Bank of the Jordan River—and those territories have been perennial sources of conflict. The F.O.N., therefore, might object to admitting Israel while it holds those territories, since once Israel joins, the F.O.N. would have thrust upon it partial responsibility for the impossible task of keeping the peace in those territories.

In the case of Israel, incidentally, allowing the F.O.N. to reject Israeli membership could go a long way toward creating peace in the Middle East. That is because a desire to join the F.O.N. might induce Israel to relinquish the occupied territories. Currently Israel feels unable to relinquish those territories because it believes they are strategically necessary for its defense. But a powerful Federation of Nations could guarantee Israeli security even without the occupied territories, and could thereby allow Israel to relinquish those territories and thus take an enormous step towards settling its disputes with its Arab neighbors and bringing peace to the region.

Art. V, Sec. 5.

Changes of borders are a difficult issue. In fact, the desire to avoid controversy over border changes is a primary reason, as explained in the commentary on Art. V, Sec. 4, Prov. 1, that I have advocated that the F.O.N. have the right to block a nation's joining the F.O.N. If a nation has obvious border problems, either in terms of territories wishing to secede from the nation or in terms of border disputes with its neighbors, it is best if it resolves those issues before it joins the F.O.N. Then, when a nation joins the F.O.N., its borders should be considered to have been approved by the F.O.N., and thereafter it should be quite difficult to change those borders. Thus, Provision 2 of this section specifies that the transfer of territory from one member nation to another shall require the consent of both nations concerned—as shown by approval by the legislators of both nations and by popular referendums in both nations.

Note that in this case the constitution does not specify that approval be needed also from the full F.O.N. legislature. That is because the transfer of territory between two member nations does not involve the gain or loss of territory for the full F.O.N. Thus, it is really only a concern of the two nations involved. In Provision 3, though, concerning transfer of territory between a member and nonmember nation, I specify that approval shall also be required from the full F.O.N. legislature, because in that case we are dealing with the gain or loss of territory for the F.O.N., and that concerns all members.

The only point that may need explanation in Provision 1 is that approval is required here by referendum in only one of the two territories involved when a nation is being divided in two (or in all but one if a nation is being divided into more than two). The logic behind that is that if the people of a small territory wish to secede from a nation and the legislators from that nation are willing to permit them to, there is no reason the people of the dominant territory should be able to block the secession. It is difficult enough to get the elected representatives of the dominant territory to permit a secession; there is no reason to also require the direct approval of the people of that territory.

Collectively, the provisions of this section give a nation's F.O.N. legislators absolute veto power over any changes in their nation's borders—any transfer of territory to or from their nation or any recognition of independence for a territory within their nation. You may be objecting, though, that this could be a problem sometimes. A territory that currently belongs to one nation may have been conquered from and legitimately belong to another nation. Or the people of a small territory may legitimately want and deserve independence from a larger nation. Yet in these cases, under the provisions of this constitution, we still must wait for the representatives of the nation concerned to recognize these legitimate demands for a change in their borders. There is nothing we can do to force the change upon them.

I have chosen that route, although it has its drawbacks, because I believe that allowing the F.O.N. to force a border change upon a member nation without the consent of the nation itself is just too dramatic an infringement on national sovereignty to ever be accepted. There is no chance that a provision that permitted such an action would be allowed into the F.O.N.'s ultimate constitution.

But before we get too upset about our inability to forcefully correct the situation of a territory being held unjustly in a member nation, we should remember what other powers the F.O.N. will have to minimize injustice. It will be able to guarantee a bill of rights through the force of law, and it will be able to remove from national or local government office any officials who violate those rights. Thus, the situation of the people in a territory that is being held unjustly in a member nation will not be all that desperate. They will have basic rights. There will be no grave injustices inflicted on them. It will simply be a matter of their preferring to have self-rule or to be affiliated with another country and not getting their wish.

Finally, it should be pointed out that although the provisions in this section allow the F.O.N. a degree of supervision over a nation's dividing, there is no reason a nation could not *de facto* divide without official recognition by the F.O.N. The F.O.N. has, under this constitution, almost no formal relations with national governments. Although it can ban convicted felons from holding positions in national governments and can declare any national laws that violate the F.O.N.'s bill of rights to be invalid, for the most part it has no relations with the national governments and doesn't even have to recognize, in cases of dispute, which of perhaps several groups claiming to be a nation's government is the legitimate government. So there is no reason a nation could not in fact divide and have two separate governments governing two separate territories as distinct nations without the F.O.N.'s authorization.

Bibliography

Agee, Phillip. 1975. *Inside the Company: C.I.A. Diary.* New York: Bantam Books.

Ahlstrom, Richard P. 1991. "The European Community Faces 1992." *Current History,* Novemeber, pp. 374-378.

Alderman, Ellen, and Caroline Kennedy. 1991. *In Our Defense: The Bill of Rights in Action.* New York: William Morrow.

Berry, Wendell. 1977. *The Unsettling of America: Culture and Agriculture.* San Francisco: Sierra Club Books.

Bertsch, Gary K., Robert P. Clark, and David M. Wood. 1986. *Comparing Political Systems: Power and Policy in Three Worlds.* Third edition. New York: John Wiley and Sons.

Birdsall, George A. 1944. *A Proposed World Government.* Washington: The Shaw Press.

Blum, William. 1986. *The C.I.A.: A Forgotten History.* London: Zed Books.

Branch, Taylor. 1988. *Parting the Waters: America in the King Years, 1954-63.* New York: Simon and Schuster.

Brewer, William C. 1940. *Permanent Peace.* Philadelphia: Dorrance and Co.

Brown, Lester R., et al. Annual 1984-1993. *State of the World.* New York: W.W. Norton.

Brown, Lester R., and Edward C. Wolf. 1984. "Soil Erosion: Quiet Crisis." Worldwatch Paper 60. Washington: Woldwatch Institute.

Catton, Bruce. 1960. *The Civil War.* Boston: Houghton Mifflin.

Claude, Inis L., Jr. 1964. *Swords Into Plowshares: The Problems and Progress of International Organization.* Third edition. New York: Random House.

Cohen, Mark Nathan. 1977. *The Food Crisis in Prehistory: Overpopulation and the Crisis of Agriculture.* New Haven, Connecticut: Yale University Press.

Commoner, Barry. 1990. *Making Peace With the Planet.* New York: Pantheon Books.

Coon, Carleton S. 1971. *The Hunting Peoples.* New York: Nick Lyons Books.

Cousins, Norman. 1945. *Modern Man is Obsolete.* New York: Viking Press.

Cousins, Norman. 1987. *The Pathology of Power.* New York: W.W. Norton.

Culbertson, Ely. 1943. *Total Peace: What Makes Wars and How to Organize Peace.* Garden City, N.Y.: Doubleday, Doran, and Co.

Daltrop, Anne. 1982. *Politics and the European Community.* London: Longman Group.

Daly, Herman E., and John B. Cobb, Jr. 1989. *For the Common Good: Redirecting the Economy Toward Community, the Environment, and a Sustainable Future.* Boston: Beacon Press.

Darwin, Charles. 1859. *The Origin of Species.* London: Penguin Books (1985).

Dawkins, Richard. 1987. *The Blind Watchmaker.* New York: W.W. Norton.

Debo, Angie. 1970. *A History of the Indians of the United States.* Norman, Oklahoma: University of Oklahoma Press.

Diamant, Rudolph M.E. 1982. *Atomic Energy.* Ann Arbor, Michigan: Ann Arbor Science Publishers.

Diamond, Stanley, ed. 1964. *Primitive Views of the World.* New York: Columbia University Press.

Dunnigan, James F. 1988. *How to Make War: A Comprehensive Guide to Modern Warfare.* New York: William Morrow.

Dupuy, Trevor N. 1984. *The Evolution of Weapons and Warfare.* New York: Da Capo Press.

Durant, Will. 1951. *The Story of Philosophy: the Lives and Opinions of the Greater Philosophers,* Second edition. New York: Simon and Schuster.

Dyson, Freeman. 1984. *Weapons and Hope.* New York: Harper and Row.

Easterlin, Richard A. 1980. *Birth and Fortune.* New York: Basic Books.

Eaton, Howard O. 1944. *Federation: The Coming Structure of World Government.* Norman, Oklahoma: University of Oklahoma Press.

Ehle, John. 1988. *The Trail of Tears: The Rise and Fall of the Cherokee Nation.* New York: Doubleday.

Ehrlich, Paul R. 1968. *The Population Bomb.* New York: Ballantine.

Ehrlich, Paul R., and Anne H. Ehrlich. 1990. *The Population Explosion.* New York: Simon and Schuster.

Farb, Peter. 1968. *Man's Rise to Civilization: The Cultural Ascent of the Indians of North America.* New York: Bantam Books.

Fischer, Louis. 1954. *Gandhi: His Life and Message for the World.* New York: New American Library.

French, Hilary F. 1991. "The E.C.: Environmental Proving Ground." *World Watch,* November/December, pp. 26-35.

Freuchen, Peter. 1961. *Book of the Eskimos.* New York: Fawcett Premier.

Ganoe, William A. 1943. *The History of the United States Army.* New York: D. Appleton-Century Co.

Gato, John T. 1992. *Dumbing Us Down.* Philadelphia: New Society Publishers.

Goldstein, Walter. 1992. "E.C.: Euro-Stalling." *Foreign Policy,* Winter 1991-92, pp. 129-147.

Grant, Lindsey. 1992. *Elephants in the Volkswagen: Facing the Tough Questions About Our Overcrowded Country.* New York: W.H. Freeman and Co.

Hague, Rod, and Martin Harrop. 1987. *Comparative Government and Politics: An Introduction.* Second edition. Atlantic Highlands, New Jersey: Humanities Press International.

Hamilton, Alexander, James Madison, and John Jay. 1788. *The Federalist Papers.* New York: New American Library (1961).

Harris, Marvin. 1977. *Cannibals and Kings: The Origins of Cultures.* New York: Random House.

Harris, Marvin. 1989. *Our Kind.* New York: Harper-Collins.

Hart, B.H. Liddell. 1967. *Strategy.* Second edition. New York: Penguin.

Hartley, Shirley Foster. 1972. *Population Quantity vs. Quality: A Sociological Examination of the Causes and Consequences of the Population Explosion.* Englewood Cliffs, N.J.: Prentice-Hall.

Hughan, Jessie Wallace. 1923. *A Study of International Government.* New York: Thomas Y. Crowell, Co.

Hunt, Stanley E. 1980. *Fission, Fusion, and the Energy Crisis.* Oxford, U.K.: Pergammon Press.

Immerman, Richard H. 1982. *The C.I.A. in Guatemala: The Foreign Policy of Intervention.* Austin, Texas: University of Texas Press.

Jacobson, Jodi L. 1987. "Planning the Global Family." Worldwatch Paper 80. Washington: Worldwatch Institute.

Kant, Immanuel. 1795. *Perpetual Peace. In Perpetual Peace and Other Essays.* Indianapolis, Indiana: Hackett Publishing Co. (1983).

Konner, Melvin. 1982. *The Tangled Wing: Biological Constrainsts on the Human Spirit.* New York: Harper and Row.

Krugman, Paul A. 1991. "Myths and Realities of U.S. Competitiveness." *Science* Vol. 254, pp. 811-815.

Lee, Richard. 1969. "!Kung Bushman Subsistence: An Input- Output Analysis." In *Environment and Cultural Behavior,* A.P. Vayda, ed., pp. 47-79. Garden City, N.Y.: Natural History Press.

Lee, Richard. 1979. *The !Kung San: Men and Women in a Foraging Society.* Cambridge, England: Cambridge University Press.

Leopold, Aldo. 1949. *A Sand County Almanac.* New York: Oxford University Press.

Lesser, Alexander. 1968. *In War: the Anthropology of Armed Conflict and Aggression,* Morton Fried, Marvin Harris, and Robert Murphy, eds., pp. 92-96. Garden City, N.Y.: Natural History Press.

Lovins, Amory B. 1977. *Soft Energy Paths: Toward a Durable Peace.* San Francisco: Friends of the Earth International.

Locke, John. 1690. *Two Treatises on Government.* Ruttland, Vermont: Charles E. Tuttle Co. (1990).

Lukacs, John. 1993. "The End of the Twentieth Century." *Harper's,* January, pp. 39-58.

Luttwak, Edward N. 1985. *The Pentagon and the Art of War.* New York: Simon and Schuster.

Mahler, Gregory S. 1992. *Comparative Politics: An Institutional and Cross-National Approach.* Englewood Cliffs, New Jersey: Prentice-Hall.

Mann, Charles C. 1993. "How Many is Too Many?" *The Atlantic,* February, pp. 47-67.

Marchetti, Victor, and John D. Marks. 1974. *The C.I.A. and the Cult of Intelligence.* New York: Alfred A. Knopf.

Mason, Jim and Peter Singer. 1990. *Animal Factories.* Second edition. New York: Harmony Books.

McNeill, William H. 1982. *The Pursuit of Power.* Chicago: University of Chicago Press.

McPherson, James. 1988. *Battle Cry of Freedom: The Civil War Era.* New York: Oxford University Press.

Meadows, Donella H., Dennis L. Meadows, Jorgen Randers, William W. Behrens III. 1972. *The Limits to Growth.* New York: New American Library.

Meadows, Donella H., Dennis L. Meadows, and Jorgen Randers. 1992. *Beyond the Limits: Confronting Global Collapse, Envisioning a Sustainable Future.* Post Mills, Vermont: Chelsea Green Publishing.

Menninger, Karl A. 1973. *Whatever Became of Sin?* New York: Hawthorn Books.

Millett, Allan R., and Peter Maslowski. 1984. *For the Common Defense: a Military History of the United States of America.* New York: The Free Press.

Morgenthau, Hans J. and Kenneth W. Thompson. 1985. *Politics Among Nations: The Struggle for Power and Peace.* Sixth edition. New York: Alfred A. Knopf.

Morland, Howard. 1979. "The H-Bomb Secret." *Progressive*, November, pp. 14-23.

Moyers, Bill. 1988. *The Secret Government: The Constitution in Crisis.* Cabin John, Maryland: Seven Locks Press.

Musicant, Ivan. 1990. *Banana Wars: A History of United States Military Intervention in Latin America from the Spanish- American War to the Invasion of Panama.* New York: Macmillan.

Nash, Roderick. 1989. *The Rights of Nature: A History of Environmental Ethics.* Madison, Wisconsin: University of Wisconsin Press.

Neibuhr, Reinhold. 1949. *The Illusion of World Government.* Whitestone, N.Y.: The Graphics Group.

Newfang, Oscar. 1942. *World Government.* New York: Barnes and Noble.

Newman, J.H., ed. 1912. *Ohio State Library Digest of State Constitutions.* Columbus, Ohio: F.H. Heer Printing Co.

Nugent, Neill. 1991. *The Government and Politics of the European Community.* Second edition. Durham, North Carolina: Duke University Press.

Padover, Saul K. and Jacob W. Landynski. 1983. *The Living U.S. Constitution.* New York: New American Library.

Paepke, C. Owen. 1993. *The Evolution of Progress: The End of Economic Growth and the Beginning of Human Transformation.* New York: Random House.

Patterson, Francine, and Eugene Linden. 1981. *The Education of Koko.* New York: Holt, Rinehart, and Winston.

Pianka, Eric R. 1983. *Evolutionary Ecology.* Third edition. New York: Harper and Row.

Pojman, Louis P. 1990. *Ethics: Discovering Right and Wrong.* Belmont, Calif.: Wadsworth.

1987. *Population Growth and Economic Development: Issues and Evidence.* Madison, Wisconsin: University of Wisconsin Press.

Powledge, Fred. 1991. *Free at Last?: The Civil Rights Movement and the People Who Made It.* New York: Harper- Collins.

Rachels, James. 1990. *Created from Animals: The Moral Implications of Darwinism.* New York: Oxford University Press.

Regan, Tom. 1983. *The Case for Animal Rights.* Berkeley, California: University of California Press.

Roosevelt, Kermit. 1979. *Countercoup: The Struggle for Control of Iran.* New York: McGraw-Hill.

Rosseau, Jean-Jacques. 1762. *The Social Contract.* In *The Social Contract and Discourses.* London: J.M. Dent and Sons (1973).

Russell, Bertrand. 1941. *A History of Western Philosophy.* New York: Simon and Schuster.

Samuelson, Paul A. 1980. *Economics.* Eleventh edition. New York: McGraw-Hill.

Sarid, Yossi. 1989. "Night of the Broken Clubs." *Harper's,* September, pp. 31-32.

Schell, Jonathon. 1984. *The Abolition.* New York: Avon Books.

Schmookler, Andrew Bard. 1984. *The Parable of the Tribes: The Problem of Power in Social Evolution.* Berkeley, California: University of California Press.

Schmookler, Andrew Bard. 1988. *Out of Weakness: Healing the Wounds that Drive Us to War.* New York: Bantam.

Schmookler, Andrew Bard. 1989. *Sowings and Reapings: The Cycling of Good and Evil in the Human System.* Indianapolis, Indiana: Knowledge Systems.

Schumacher, E.F. 1973. *Small Is Beautiful: Economics as if People Mattered.* New York: Harper and Row.

Service, Elman R. 1966. *The Hunters.* Englewood Cliffs, N.J.: Prentice-Hall.

Simon, Julian. 1981. *The Ultimate Resource.* Princeton, N.J.: Princeton University Press.

Singer, Peter. 1975. *Animal Liberation.* New York: Avon Books.

Slater, Philip. 1991. *A Dream Deferred: America's Discontent and the Search for a New Democratic Ideal.* Boston: Beacon Press.

Stockwell, John. 1978. *In Search of Enemies: A C.I.A. Story.* New York: W.W. Norton.

Stone, Christopher D. 1972. *Should Trees Have Standing: Toward Legal Rights for Natural Objects.* Palo Alto, Calif.: Tioga Publishing.

Streit, Clarence. 1939. *Union Now.* New York: Harper and Brothers Publishing.

Taylor, Paul W. 1986. *Respect for Nature: A Theory of Environmental Ethics.* Princeton, N.J.: Princeton University Press.

Thoreau, Henry David. 1854. *Walden. In Works of Henry David Thoreau.* New York: Avenel Books (1981).

Thoreau, Henry David. 1849. *Civil Disobedience. In Works of Henry David Thoreau.* New York: Avenel Books (1981).

Thurow, Lester C. 1980. *The Zero Sum Society: Distribution and the Possibilities for Economic Change.* New York: Penguin Books.

Treverton, Gregory F. 1987. *Covert Action.* New York: Basic Books.

Turnbull, Colin M. 1962. *The Forest People.* New York: Simon and Schuster.
Vitousek, Peter M., Paul R. Ehrlich, Anne H. Ehrlich, and Pamela A. Matson. 1986. "Human Appropriation of the Products of Photosynthesis." *BioScience* Vol. 36, pp. 368-373.
Wattenberg, Ben. 1987. *The Birth Dearth.* New York: Pharos Books.
White, Leslie. 1959. *The Evolution of Culture: the Development of Civilization to the Fall of Rome.* New York: Grove Press.
Williams, Juan. 1987. *Eyes on the Prize: America's Civil Rights Years, 1954-1965.* New York: Penguin.
Wolf, Edward C. 1986. "Beyond the Green Revolution: New Approaches for Third World Agriculture." Worldwatch Paper 73. Washington: Worldwatch Institute.
Wonnacott, Paul and Ronald Wonnacott. 1982. *An Introduction to Macroeconomics.* Second edition. New York: McGraw-Hill.
Yergin, Daniel. 1977. "The Terrifying Prospect." *Atlantic,* April, pp. 46-65.
Young, Louise B. ed. 1968. *Population in Perspective.* New York: Oxford University Press.

Acknowledgements

I would like to thank Paula Harding of West Fork Press for her help in bringing this book to market. Most of all, though, I want to thank my editor, Horst Löblich. The dedication he has shown to this project has been unbelievable. No writer ever had a better editor or a more supportive friend.

Index

adjournment of legislature, 287-288, 297
advertising, 221
age, minimal for senators and representatives, 285
Afghanistan, 27, 32, 78
aggression, military, 77, 80-81
Agrarian Reform Law, 181
agricultural-industrial societies, 6
agriculture, 6, 8, 11, 13-14, 92, 106-107, 116, 123-124, 143, 154, 268-269, 271, 281
aircraft carrier, 28-29
Allende, Salvador, 183-184
amendments to constitution, 205, 308-309
anarchy, 37, 39, 42, 83, 92, 128, 150, 314-315
Andamann islanders, 125
Anglo-Iranian Oil Co., 180
Angola, 184-185
animal rights, 40, 135-140
animals, domestic, 137, 139
animals, wild, 139-140, 155
Antarctica, 149, 154, 292
anti-aircraft missiles, 27, 203
appellate jurisdiction of F.O.N. courts, 201, 207, 301
Arab-Israeli 1973 War, 27
arable land, 130, 143, 147-148, 150, 161, 169, 205, 232, 285-286, 289, 291, 309
Arbenz, Jacobo, 181-182
Argentina, 32, 56, 246
Armas, Castillo, 181-182
arms race, 25-26, 33, 247
Articles of Confederation, 44
Arunta, 125

Australia, 99, 247

automobiles, 123

bail, 63, 193-194, 303
bills, 170, 288
birth control, 133-134, 147, 151, 234, 236-238, 274
  ethics, 234-238, 240, 262-263, 240, 262-263
Bolivia, 81
Bond, James, 179
border changes, 308, 309, 321-324
borrowing money, 290
boycotts and embargoes, 40, 78, 80-82, 84, 86, 94, 96, 163, 165, 252-253, 260, 290-291
Brazil, 146
bribery, 293-294
Brown vs. Board of Education, 46
burden of proof, 76, 196-197, 304, 316
bureaucracy, 105, 108, 111
Bush, George, 214, 224, 252, 311
Bushmen, see !Kung San

C.I.A., see Central Intelligence Agency
Canada, 99, 247
capitalism, 87, 89, 95, 133, 220, 249
cartels, 96
Castro, Fidel, 183, 185
Central Intelligence Agency, 180-184, 324, 326-327, 329
character, national, 19, 22-23, 32
checks and balances, 168-169
Cherokee Indians, 188, 202, 325
Chile, 56, 183-185, 246
chimpanzees, 135-136
China, 55, 117, 133, 156, 248, 257, 262

chlorofluorocarbons, 144
citizenship, 306, 320
civil lawsuits, 196, 201, 304, 317, 318
Civil War, U.S., 18, 30, 47-48, 202
civil wars, 49, 62-65, 71-72, 117, 156, 189, 252
civilization, 8, 13-14
class, 8, 16
coercion, 7-8, 78, 80-82, 84, 86, 88, 132, 252
colonialism, 21
commander-in-chief of the military, 172, 217
Common Sense, 158
Commonwealth of Independent States, 18, 247-248, 257
communication, 20
communism, 180-182, 185, 251-252
competition, 16, 21-23, 25-27, 31-33, 36, 92, 116, 119, 124, 128-129, 133, 150, 211-212, 229, 253, 271-272
condors, 139
Confederate States, 48
constitution, 1, 37, 43-44, 51, 55, 58-59, 63-65, 68-69, 75-77, 81, 86, 90, 97, 105, 110, 120, 131, 134, 147-148, 160-161, 169, 173-174, 177, 180, 183-184, 187-192, 195-196, 199-205, 207, 216-217, 219, 242-243, 246-247, 249-251, 283-324
  carrying out the, 63, 293
  United States, 1, 37, 43-44, 58-59, 169, 189
  violating, 187-188, 203, 206-207, 305, 318
cooperation, 73-74, 79-80
corporations, 39, 113, 145, 165, 181, 221

cost of defense and government, 3, 28-29, 39, 73, 80-81, 101, 105-111, 125, 128, 143, 158-159, 164, 210, 232-233, 235, 248, 253
coups, 180, 183-184, 241-244, 246
courts, 46, 64, 79, 197, 231
  F.O.N., 64-65, 69, 76, 82, 90, 96, 105, 120, 145, 187, 194-205, 207, 219, 231, 239, 243, 247, 289, 291, 296, 298-306, 313, 315-318
covert actions, 176-187
  history of, 179-187
criminals, 65, 162, 166, 172, 188, 191, 203
crop breeding, 153
crop diseases, 9
cultural evolution, 6-7, 11-13, 35-36, 209, 269
currency exchange, 121, 131

Darwin, Charles, 5
death of president, 295
debt, foreign, 88, 116
defense, 12, 17, 27-28, 33, 38-39, 89, 97, 101, 106-109, 130, 164, 193-194, 196, 219, 239, 243, 248, 253, 261-262, 303-305, 311, 320-321, 324, 327
  advantage over the offense, 27-29
deficit
  budget, 103-105
  trade, 115
democracy, 16, 23-25, 40, 54-61, 89, 164, 170, 175, 178, 182, 185-186, 197-199, 202, 206, 210-211, 213-216, 246-252, 256, 262, 313
deterrence, 75
diplomacy, 19, 23, 171-172, 234

333

disputes, 45, 201, 280, 312, 321-322
districts
  House of Representatives, 284-285
  Senate, 285-286
diversity, 34, 59, 210, 213, 239, 242
dolphins, 136-137
double jeopardy, 195-196
drought, 9, 124

economic development, 88-89, 92-95, 110, 290
economic regulation, 87, 91-92, 103-104, 164-165, 279
economy, 15-16, 19, 23, 25, 34, 73, 78-79, 87, 92-94, 100, 103-104, 110, 118, 130-131, 155-156, 159, 210-211, 247
ecosystems, 140-142
education, 7, 16, 24-26, 46, 78, 106-107, 231, 328
Eisenhower, Dwight, 46, 181-182, 224
elections and referendums, judging, 286
elections for senators and representatives, 54-58, 61, 286
elephants, 135, 326
Eleventh Commandment, 144, 151
embargoes, 40, 78-82, 84, 86, 94, 96, 163, 165, 253, 260, 290-291
endangered species, 123, 128, 148-149, 151, 164, 223, 292
energy, 107, 116, 172, 233, 257-259, 325-327
enforcing laws, 69-70, 151, 171, 296, 299
English language, 306, 318-319
environmental protection, 9-10, 40, 93, 107, 116, 122, 125, 127-129, 131, 133, 135, 137, 139, 141, 143-145, 147, 149, 151, 153, 155, 157, 159, 161, 163, 168, 223, 226, 237, 250, 253, 274-275, 279, 281, 283, 312
environmental ethics, 134-144
Eskimos, 125
ethics, 134-135, 140-142, 144, 148, 208, 211, 213, 215, 217, 219, 221-240
Ethiopia, 158, 273
Europe, 7, 9, 16, 56, 95, 154, 248, 251-252
European Commission, or Common Market, 281
European Community, 94, 96, 277, 279-280, 282, 324-325, 328
European Corps, 280
European Court of Justice, 281
European Council of Ministers, 281
European Parliament, 281
evolution
  biological, 5-6, 34-35, 135, 139-140, 142
  cultural or societal, 3, 6-7, 11-17, 23, 34-36, 42, 72, 208-209, 267, 269, 271-272
evolution of weapons, 27-29
ex post facto laws, 38, 193, 303
expenses of F.O.N., 96, 99, 105-108, 111
exploitation of poor nations by rich nations, 89-90
extinction, 25, 127, 146-147, 149, 151
extradition of criminals, 69, 162, 299, 301

fame, 10
famine, 7-10, 124

334

farming, 15, 123-124, 139, 210, 213, 231-232, 235
Federalist Papers, 1, 3, 44
felonies, 64-65, 188, 195, 198, 204, 287, 290, 292-293, 299, 304, 306
fertilizers, 124, 153, 210
feudalism, 15-16
fines, 66, 193, 303
food, 6-9, 18, 34, 91, 94-95, 116, 124, 137-138, 152-155, 213, 232, 269, 271
Ford, Gerald, 184
France, 16, 117, 257, 280
free speech, 38, 54-55, 57, 59, 61, 63, 214, 216, 248, 252, 302
free trade, 38, 95, 114-115, 117, 279
freedom, 12, 139-140, 187, 192, 198, 207, 211, 230, 253
　of religion, 59-61, 63, 192, 302
　of the press, 59-61, 63, 192, 214, 302

Gandhi, Mohandas, 245
Garden of Eden, 271
Genesis, 140
geography, 18, 20-21, 32-33
Germany, 49, 117, 126-127, 155, 159, 280
goals
　of F.O.N., 74, 80, 84, 86, 162-167
　of supranational organization, 37-42
Goodall, Jane, 137
gorillas, 135-136, 139
Grand Canyon, 146
grand jury, 195, 304, 316
Great Britain, 16, 32, 180, 214, 257
grief, 137-138
gross national consumption, 99-102, 108-109, 111, 130, 160

gross national product, 15, 99, 111, 160
growth of F.O.N., 34, 54-58, 61, 249-253, 255, 267
Guatemala, 64, 89-90, 181-183, 185, 326
gun control, 203-204, 242, 244

Hamilton, Alexander, 1, 44, 326
Harding, Paula, 331
Hawwarra, 217-218
health care, 40, 91, 165
height, human, 9-10
Hitler, Adolph, 16, 18, 127, 210, 216
homelessness, 125, 127-128, 224, 231-233, 235-237, 253, 273
House of Representatives, F.O.N., 130-131, 160, 169-170, 175, 283-285, 287-288, 294-295, 310, 312-313
housing, 101, 107, 125, 232-233, 235
hunger, 138, 231-232
hunter-gatherer societies, 6-11, 13-15, 267-272
Hussein, Saddam, 278

immigration and emigration, 114-115, 134, 151, 304
impeachment, 312
individual importance, 219-222, 240
individual responsibility, 208, 216-239, 243-244
individuals, application of law to, 65-67, 71
Indonesia, 182-183
industrial capacity, 18-19, 21-22, 25-26, 32-34, 73, 85
industrialization, 22, 89
inequality, social, 8, 270-271
inevitability of F.O.N., 35-36, 249-250, 255, 262, 266,

335

272-273
intelligence, mental, 138
intelligence or espionage, 20, 176
Iran, 21, 79, 81, 180-181, 184-186, 229
Iraq, 20, 117
irrigation, 154
Israel, 20, 26-27, 50, 155, 214, 217-219, 247, 257, 321
Italy, 49, 180

Jackson, Andrew, 187, 202-203
jail, 57, 66, 165, 171, 194, 197, 214, 217, 280, 282, 318
Japan, 16, 34, 94, 100, 117, 126, 155, 159, 161, 229, 247
Jay, John, 1, 44
Jesus, 141, 225
joining the F.O.N., 33-34, 50-52, 54-56, 61-62, 67, 74-75, 78, 82-86, 88-91, 93, 100, 109-110, 132, 216, 246-249, 251-252, 257, 267, 306-307, 320-321
joy, 138, 273
judges, 99, 105, 187, 197-200, 281, 292, 299-300, 302, 307, 314-315, 317-318
   appointment of, 199, 200, 300
judicial review, 202, 301
jury, 190, 195-197, 214, 216, 301, 304, 317

Kennedy, John, 183, 224
Keynes, John Maynard, 112
kidnapping, 63, 183, 194
Koko, 136-137
!Kung San, 8, 125
Kuwait, 20, 117, 247, 278

labor, 7, 18, 22, 91, 113-114, 116, 159, 165, 195
land, 16, 18, 20, 28, 33, 99, 102,
   115-116, 123-126, 130-131, 139-140, 143-148, 150, 152-154, 161, 164-165, 169, 181, 187, 201-202, 205, 210, 213, 232-233, 235, 238, 250, 268-269, 271, 274, 278, 285-286, 289-292, 301, 309, 312
   buying, 289, 292
   protection, 146-148, 151, 291-292
   zoning, 165
language, 48, 135-137, 173, 213
   central, 306, 318-320
lead in gasoline, 230-231
League of Nations, 43-45, 47, 201
Lee, Richard, 8
legal counsel, right to, 193-194, 303
legislature, F.O.N., 51, 63, 65, 68, 99, 110, 119, 121, 129-131, 145, 147-150, 160, 169, 176-177, 188, 195-196, 198, 200, 203, 205-206, 283-284, 286-293, 295-300, 304, 307, 309-312, 318, 320, 322
literacy tests, 306
loans, 93-94, 175
Löblich, Horst, 331
Locke, John, 169
loneliness, 10

Madison, James, 1, 44
Malaysia, 81
Marshall, John, 202
Mbuti, 125
Mein Kampf, 127
member nations, 33-34, 39-40, 43-56, 58-59, 61-62, 64-65, 67-68, 70-75, 77-89, 91, 93-94, 96-98, 100-104, 110-111, 120, 129, 131-132, 134, 145-147, 149-150, 162-164, 169-170, 179, 189, 194-195,

198, 200-202, 205, 213,
247-248, 260, 263, 278-279,
281-282, 284-285, 289-293,
297, 299-301, 304, 306, 309,
311, 322
Menninger, Karl, 224
Mexico, 88, 113-114, 158
militarism, 269
military, 7, 18-19, 24-28, 31-34,
39, 44-49, 54, 55, 61, 73,
80-81, 85, 89-90, 101, 108-
109, 111, 157, 163-167, 171,
180, 182-183, 186, 210-213,
215, 246-248, 251-255, 272,
278, 280-281
   appropriation, 289
   courts, 204-205, 302
   draft, 27, 81, 98, 119-121, 210
   F.O.N., 44-49, 51, 54-55, 61-
62, 67-71, 73-78, 85-86, 89-
90, 96-98, 101, 106, 108-
111, 119-121, 163-167, 171-
172, 174, 176-178, 188,
190-191, 195, 201, 206,
241-244, 251-255, 260-261,
272, 288-290, 292-293, 296-
299, 301-302, 304-305, 311,
320-321, 327-328
   preparedness, 18, 24-32
   use in a member nation, 67-
71, 75-77
   strategy, 26
   treaty organizations, 34, 278-
279
mining, 21, 143, 184, 258, 260-
261, 263
Mission indians, 125
missionaries, 13
modesty, 142
money
   effect on elections, 293, 312-
313
   printing of, 103-105, 111, 165,
291

monkeys, 135, 137-138
morale, national, 19, 23-26, 32,
97
Morgenthau, Hans, 17-18
Mossadeq, Mohammed, 180, 185
Mother Teresa, 236
murder, 38, 42, 63, 84, 117, 126,
182, 184-185, 194, 226, 236

Napoleon, 18
national governments, 44, 56-58,
61-63, 66, 71, 82, 93, 102-
105, 107-108, 113, 242, 252,
279-281, 301
   relations with F.O.N., 56-59,
323
national guard, 46, 48, 65, 69, 71,
189, 242, 290, 293
national militaries, 48, 53, 73, 78,
253, 255-256, 264, 273,
279-280
national security, 72, 74, 77, 85-
88, 132, 181, 246, 249, 253
NATO, *see* North Atlantic Treaty
Organization
natural resources, 18, 21-22, 32-
34, 45, 73, 75, 80, 85, 124-
127, 143-144, 146, 149, 153,
155, 160, 180, 212-213, 232,
268, 271, 275, 292
natural selection, 5-6, 13, 17, 35,
271
Nazis, 7
New York, 127, 272
Nicaragua, 177, 181, 184-185
Nixon, Richard, 183, 189
nomadism, 6, 13-14, 126, 267,
271
nonbinding judgements, 45, 278-
279
nonmember nations, 39-40, 56-
57, 61, 68, 74-75, 77, 80-81,
83, 85-86, 89, 94, 96, 149,
163, 170, 172, 176-178, 187,

200, 206, 260-261, 290-291, 296-298, 300, 308, 322
Noriega, Manuel, 79
Norplant, 133
North Atlantic Treaty Organization, 34, 278
nuclear energy, 257-259, 261, 263
nuclear war, 40, 256-257, 259, 261-263, 270
nuclear weapons, 14, 16-17, 25-28, 31-32, 77, 128, 203, 209-210, 257-261, 263, 275
nuclear winter, 25-26

ocelots, 139
officers, military, pay of, 289
Official Secrets Act, 214-215
orangutans, 136
orders, disobeying of illegal, unconstitutional, or immoral, 216-219, 243-244, 305-306, 314-316
otters, 135
overpopulation, 4, 45, 88, 92, 118, 122, 124-129, 131, 133-135, 137, 139, 141, 143, 145, 147, 149-151, 153, 155, 157, 159, 161, 163, 215, 231-233, 235, 237, 240, 264, 273-274
ozone, 145, 223

P.L.O., *see* Palestinian Liberation Organization
Paine, Thomas, 158
Pakistan, 56, 257
Palestinian Liberation Organization, 214
Panama, 79
Parable of the Tribes, 5-7, 12-13
parable of the tribes, 34, 128-129, 208, 254, 269
pardons, 190
Patterson, Penny, 136-137

peace, 2-3, 12-13, 19, 39, 44, 46-50, 52-54, 60-62, 68, 70-73, 88, 106, 117, 145, 162-163, 168, 195-196, 201, 215-217, 238-239, 249-250, 252-255, 264, 267-268, 273, 283, 287, 304, 311, 321
Perry, Commodore Matthew, 15-16
Persian Gulf War, 20, 117, 252, 278
pesticides, 124, 154, 210, 223-224
police, 39, 46, 48, 64-65, 69, 71, 180, 189, 194, 196, 231, 242, 247, 278, 290, 293, 311, 317
Politics Among Nations, 17
poll taxes, 306
pollution, 39-40, 89, 123-124, 128, 140, 144-146, 149, 151, 164, 223, 235-236, 270, 274, 291
poor nations, 88-91, 100-101, 114, 119, 121
population, 4, 19, 22, 26, 32-34, 40, 73, 80, 85-86, 89-90, 94, 97, 99, 102, 110, 114, 116, 122-134, 139, 150-161, 168, 196, 203, 205, 207, 209, 212, 232-239, 253, 264, 268-269, 271, 274-275, 288, 290, 305, 308-309
  control, 131-132, 134, 151, 237-238, 275, 305
Portugal, 184
poverty, 91-92, 124, 127-128, 156, 215, 233, 235, 237, 253, 273, 276
power, 3, 36, 39, 40, 44-45, 47, 49, 55-56, 72-75, 77-81, 83-86, 89-90, 187, 215, 226, 239, 275
  national or societal, 12-27,

31-36, 39, 47, 49, 56, 72-74, 77-81, 83-89, 128-129, 132, 150, 163, 187, 208-213, 215, 220-222, 226, 229, 234, 239-240, 246-250, 252-255, 262, 266-267, 269-272, 275
   personal, 43, 191, 251
prairie chickens, 139
president
   F.O.N., 65, 67-69, 75-76, 99, 171-178, 188-192, 199-200, 206-207, 287-289, 292-301, 305, 307, 309, 311-314
   selecting, 173-176
   term of office, 173
   national, 56-57, 69, 172, 181-183
   U.S., 46, 173, 177, 185, 187-188, 190, 199, 202-203, 214, 224
presumption of innocence, 196-197, 317
primitive societies, 10, 13-15
propaganda, 23, 178, 181
property, 39, 63, 98, 193, 196, 303-304
prosecution of F.O.N. officials, 188-190, 296
protectionism, 93
Pygmies, *see* Mbuti

quality of government and diplomacy, 19, 23-25, 32-33
quartering soldiers, 196, 198

racism, 124, 128, 223, 230, 235
racoons, 135
Reagan, Ronald, 173, 184-185
rebellion, 2, 63-65, 67, 71, 183, 189, 242
referendums on joining and leaving the F.O.N., 51, 53, 56-57, 251, 286, 293, 306-308, 320

religion, 45, 59-61, 63, 152, 157, 192, 224, 272, 302
removing criminals from office 63-65, 71, 188-190, 292-293
removing F.O.N. officials from office, 63, 76-77, 188-190, 292-293, 299, 312
representation, distribution of between the F.O.N. nations, 128-132, 278
representatives, F.O.N., 54-57, 61, 67-71, 74-76, 80, 82-83, 96-98, 102-103, 105, 110, 119-121, 130-131, 160, 164, 169-171, 175, 190-192, 199-200, 206-207, 214, 216, 277, 283-289, 291, 294-298, 300, 307-310, 312-313, 318, 322-323
responsibilities of F.O.N., 43-44, 49, 53, 58, 106, 135, 144
Ricardo, David, 112
rich nations, 88-91, 100-101, 119, 121
right to bear arms, 203-204
rights,
   bill of, 39-40, 59-61, 63, 65, 163, 192-198, 207, 302-305, 323
   civil, 46-47, 133, 230
   human, 3, 23, 39-40, 59-61, 63-65, 71-72, 133, 163-165, 168, 189, 191, 216, 246-248, 250, 262, 279-280
Rossi, Vincent, 144
Russia, 18, 25, 33, 248-249, 257, 262

salaries for senators and representatives, 287
Schmookler, Andrew Bard, 6, 12-13, 125, 269
Schneider, Rene, 183
schools, 220-221

science, 25-26, 107, 142, 152, 210, 319
secession of a territory from a member nation, 308, 322-324
secrecy
 in government or legislature, 186, 214-215, 286-287, 297-298, 311, 313-314
 in military actions, 176-187, 206, 297-298, 313-314
Security Committee, 177-178, 191, 206, 297, 299, 313-314
selection for power, 12-15, 17, 23, 33, 35-36, 55, 61, 132, 134, 208-213, 215, 220, 222, 226, 239, 249-250, 252, 254-255, 267, 269-272, 275
self-determination, national, 65, 67, 72
self-incrimination, right against, 195-196, 304, 317
self-interest, 2-3, 88, 132, 216, 245-246, 249, 253, 255, 266, 278
self-sacrifice, 138, 224-230, 233-234, 240
Semang, 125
Senate
 F.O.N., 169-170, 199-200
 U.S., 199-200
senators
 F.O.N., 76, 82, 169-170, 174-175, 188, 190, 192, 199, 206-207, 216, 284-289, 291, 293-298, 300, 305, 307-310, 313
 U.S., 199-200
separation of powers, 169, 206
Shah of Iran, 21, 180-181
sharing, 85, 139
sign language, 136
sin, 223-227, 229-231, 233, 236, 240

slavery, 119-120, 193, 230, 270, 303
Smith, Adam, 112
socialism, 87
societal
 absorption/transformation, 12
 destruction, 12
 imitation, 12
 withdrawal, 12
soil, 123-124, 140-141, 153-154, 230-231, 235, 274
soldiers, recruiting and paying, 96-98, 110, 119-121
Somalia, 273
South Africa, 8, 55-56, 79, 184, 257, 262
South Korea, 56, 156
sovereignty, national, 32, 38-39, 42, 84, 86, 110, 178, 272, 323
Soviet Union, 16-17, 25, 27, 32, 56, 78, 182-184, 220, 246, 248-249, 252
space, outer, 149
specialization, economic, 157
sports, 27
Sri Lanka, 156
Stalin, Joseph, 210
starvation, 8, 10, 124, 127-128, 155, 224, 232, 235-237, 253, 270-271, 273-276
Steel, Danielle, 158
stress, 10, 244
submarines, 28-29
Sudan, 273
Sukarno, Achmed, 182
supranational government, 33, 35, 37-38, 43
supranational military, 34, 38
supranational organization, 33-34, 36-41, 49, 264
supremacy of F.O.N. laws and constitution over national laws and constitutions,

201-202, 301
Supreme Court
    F.O.N., 76, 187, 196, 198, 289, 298-301, 304, 316-317
    U.S., 46, 202

tanks, 18, 28, 182
tariffs, 92, 94-95, 110, 112, 116-117, 279-280
taxes, 66, 98-103, 105, 108-111, 119, 131-132, 164-167, 253, 279, 289-290
technology, 12, 15, 18, 21, 25-27, 34, 152-153, 155, 209-211, 213, 232, 239, 270, 275
territory, transfer between member nations, 308-309, 322-324
theft, 63, 187, 194
Third World, 75, 89-93, 97, 114, 116, 121, 131, 155-156, 169, 232, 246-247, 249, 273
Thoreau, Henry David, 59, 225, 234
three eras, 270-272
tin, 81-82
Tito, Marshal, 50
Todas, 125
tolerance, 210, 213-214
tooth loss, 10
torture, 63-64, 182, 195, 317
trade, 15, 40, 42, 79, 92, 94-96, 100, 104, 112-118, 148, 164, 279, 290, 292, 311
traffic jams, 10, 123, 127
Trail of Tears, 202, 325
transportation, 20, 107, 123-124
treason, 188, 243, 287, 302, 315-316
treaties, 16, 171-172, 200-202, 296, 300-301
tyranny, 169, 177, 192, 194, 203, 206, 311

uncertainty, 31
United Fruit Co., 181
United Nations, 43-45, 47, 66, 201, 277-278
    General Assembly, 278
    Security Council, 278
United States, 1, 6, 15-18, 21, 24-25, 27-29, 32, 34, 37-38, 43-44, 46-49, 58-59, 74, 78-79, 81, 88-93, 95, 97, 106-109, 113-114, 116-117, 127, 130, 132, 143, 146, 154, 157, 169, 173, 177, 179-185, 187, 189-190, 197, 199-200, 202, 209, 214, 220-221, 224, 230, 232-233, 235, 246-249, 257, 270, 311-314, 316-317
Uruguay, 156
uranium, 18, 257-261, 263
    enrichment, 258, 260, 263
    mining, 260-261, 263

Van Buren, Martin, 202
veto, presidential, 67-69, 287-288, 298, 309, 311, 322
veto power over military actions in their nation, by F.O.N. legislators, 67-68, 71, 74, 298
Vietnam, 27, 32, 177, 188
violating laws for moral reasons, 217, 302, 314-315

wages, 114-115, 118, 159
Wallace, Alfred, 5
war, declaration of, 170-171, 177, 289, 297
water use, 292
Watergate, 189
wealth redistribution
    between citizens, 87, 91, 110
    between nations, 87, 88, 100, 110

weapons, 14, 16-18, 20, 25-32,
    34, 73, 77, 96, 99, 105, 126,
    128, 182-183, 203-204, 209-
    210, 244, 247, 257-261, 263,
    269, 275, 290
welfare state, 91, 110
Western Shoshone, 125
White, Leslie, 10
wilderness, 122, 127-128, 143-
    144, 146, 148, 235
withdrawal from the F.O.N., 50,
    52, 56-58, 307-308
wolves, 271
work ethic, 209, 239
work load, 7, 210-213
World Bank, 93
World Court, 184
World War I, 26, 30
World War II, 16, 19, 25-26, 30,
    32, 117, 126, 153, 159, 179,
    188, 216, 219, 230

xenophobia, 211
Yahgan, 125
Yugoslavia, 49-50

To order this book, call **1-800-517-7377**.
MasterCard and Visa accepted.

Or send check or money order for $17.95 per copy paperback,
$24.95 per copy hardcover, plus $3.00 shipping and handling for
the first copy, $1.50 for each additional copy, to:

West Fork Press
2564 State Route 132W
Dixon, KY 42409

Quantity discounts are available